Antebellum Women

American Controversies Series
Series Editor: Douglas R. Egerton, Le Moyne College

Students love debate. They love contention, which they see all about them in modern society. Yet too many monographs or biographies erase the controversies that existed in earlier decades. Slavery and institutionalized sexism, for example, strike modern readers as being so clearly wrong that they cannot understand why rational Americans endorsed slavery or thought it foolish to enfranchise women. How could a politician as brilliant as Thomas Jefferson believe that forced assimilation was the best policy for Native Americans? Why did Americans allow Hitler to become so powerful before confronting him? Why were many of the so-called Greatest Generation indifferent to social justice at home? How did the Vietnam War become such a political and cultural powder keg? Hindsight is often the enemy of understanding, and what strikes us as obvious was often anything but simple to earlier generations.

This series deals with major controversies in American history. The events depicted in this series were either controversial at the time (such as militant abolitionism) or have sparked modern historiographical controversies. (Did slave conspiracies actually exist, for example? Why did witch trials in Salem spiral out of control in 1692?) Each volume in the series begins with an extensive essay that explains the topic, discusses the relevant historiography, and summarizes the various points of view (contemporaneous as well as modern). The second half of the volume is devoted to documents, but each is annotated and preceded by a brief introduction. By contextualizing each document, this series pulls back the curtain, so to speak, on the process of writing history, even as the essays, letters, laws, and newspaper accounts that follow allow important American actors to speak in their own voices. Most of all, by examining both sides in these debates, and by providing documents that see each issue from different angles, the American Controversies Series will bring history alive—and enliven history classrooms.

Volumes Published

Slavery and Sectional Strife in the Early American Republic, 1776–1821
Gary J. Kornblith

Antebellum Women: Private, Public, Partisan
Carol Lasser and Stacey Robertson

Antebellum Women

Private, Public, Partisan

Carol Lasser and Stacey Robertson

ROWMAN & LITTLEFIELD PUBLISHERS, INC.
Lanham • Boulder • New York • Toronto • Plymouth, UK

Published by Rowman & Littlefield Publishers, Inc.
A wholly owned subsidary of The Rowman & Littlefield Publishing Group, Inc.
4501 Forbes Boulevard, Suite 200, Lanham, Maryland 20706
http://www.rowmanlittlefield.com

Estover Road, Plymouth PL6 7PY, United Kingdom

British Library Cataloguing in Publication Information Available

Library of Congress Cataloging-in-Publication Data

Lasser, Carol.
Antebellum women : public, private, partisan / Carol Lasser and Stacey Robertson.
    p. cm. — (American controversies series)
Includes bibliographical references and index.
ISBN 978-0-7425-5196-1 (cloth : alk. paper) — ISBN 978-1-4422-0560-4 (electronic)
1. Women—United States—Social conditions—19th century. 2. Women—United
States—Social conditions—18th century. 3. Women—Political activity—United
States—History—19th century. 4. Women—Political activity—United States—
History—18th century. I. Robertson, Stacey M. II. Title.
HQ1418.L37 2010
305.40973'09034—dc22   2010012724

∞ ™ The paper used in this publication meets the minimum requirements of
American National Standard for Information Sciences—Permanence of Paper
for Printed Library Materials, ANSI/NISO Z39.48-1992.

Printed in the United States of America

To all our boys:
Max, Simon, Russell, Gary, Isaac, Evan, and Tom

Contents

Preface

This book is possible because of the richness of U.S. women's history. When we first conceived the idea several years ago we understood that our project would involve synthesizing the voluminous scholarly work of the past few decades. This was no easy task. Talented and creative historians have transformed the field by challenging old assumptions, developing fresh areas of research, and incorporating new theoretical approaches. They have slowly dismantled the "separate spheres" narrative that deeply influenced early works in women's history. Despite the vibrancy and excitement of the field today, however, we believe that it needed a sustained, compelling revision to replace the older synthesis. *Antebellum Women* brings together the outpouring of gender history on the early republic and offers a new construction that we believe reflects the innovations in this recent scholarship. It engages with the categories of race, ethnicity, socioeconomic status, gender, sexuality, and religion, and it tells the multiple meaningful stories of diverse women's lives. It makes accessible the evolving story of women and gender in the early republic.

The first section of *Antebellum Women* lays out our new narrative. It divides the period between the Revolution and the Civil War into three overlapping stages and argues that even as gender deeply impacted and constricted women's lives, their daily experiences never excluded their "public" engagements. We define the "public" not as a physical space inhabited primarily by men, but as a shifting set of notions about civic identity and activity. Women did not passively watch as their public identities came into focus. They actively participated in influencing how these changes transpired. The first stage, which occurred in the early decades after the Revolution, is characterized by *deferential domesticity*. Though primarily defined by their multiple domestic roles, women across the United States also gained increased access to literacy, education, and group work in the form of charitable organizations. These activities remained tied to the home even as they offered women an expanded notion of their place in the nation. In the second stage, beginning in the 1820s, women served as *companionate co-laborers*. Emboldened by education and community participation, women enlarged their civic identity to include paid labor and reform work. Acting as moral arbiters in a complex, changing world, they used their public voices with increased boldness and confidence. By the 1840s, with the rise of morally driven third parties, women became *passionate partisans*. This third stage was characterized by a continuing emphasis on moral issues as motivating partisan activity, but it also included women's direct involvement in politics as inspired by economic, cultural, and religious issues. Women began to see their civic role as a key element of their overall identity, which might yet incorporate, even if it no longer necessarily foregrounded, domestic concerns.

The second section of *Antebellum Women* limns the contours of women's increasingly public lives in the early republic through the voices and activities of individual women and groups. We chose thirty original documents that speak to the diversity and complexity of women's experiences and reflect the themes of our narrative. We include famous women such as Harriet Beecher Stowe, Sojourner Truth, and Lydia Maria Child, as well as lesser known local activists like Peoria, Illinois, resident Mary Brown Davis and Oberlin College student Mary Sheldon. Readers will find a diary entry, excerpts from novels, public petitions and appeals, group constitutions, poetry, and a song. These documents are designed to allow readers to reflect on the larger arguments of the book and to gain a sense of the lived experiences of antebellum women.

This book would not have been possible without our series editor Doug Egerton. Patient, thoughtful, and supportive, Doug never wavered in his belief that we would produce an important new narrative for our field. Elisa Weeks steered us into the publication process, and Melissa McNitt saw us through. We are grateful as well to Jim O'Brien who has honored us by inviting us into the company of the distinguished authors whose works he has indexed. We would like to thank our smart, fun, talented colleagues in the field of the early republic, especially our friends in the Society of Historians for the Early American Republic, and our new friends in BrANCH, the British American Nineteenth-Century History group, to whom Elizabeth Clapp generously introduced us.

Stacey is very grateful for the sociable, inspiring environment of the History Department at Bradley University, the unwavering support of Dean Claire Etaugh and her entire office, Courtney Wiersema's transcripting brilliance, and all of the generous, wonderful family and friends both in Peoria and elsewhere. She sends her love and profound thanks to her sons, Evan and Isaac, and her partner Tom Thurston, who never questioned her passion for dusty archives and long hours in front of the computer screen. She is also eternally indebted to her coauthor for modeling scholarly integrity and collegiality, opening her home and heart, and conceiving the idea for this project and asking her to participate!

Carol returns the thanks to her coauthor with a shout-out for an engaged and engaging scholar whose boundless energy and ebullient intellect continue to amaze her. She also thanks her sons Max, Russell, and Simon, who have grown up asking questions about gender and history, and of course Gary Kornblith, who knows when to work—and when not to work. She is grateful to her endlessly supportive and intellectually engaging Oberlin colleagues, and to the many wonderful Oberlin students who inspired this work by reacting to ideas and documents, and by caring about the lives of women in the early republic. A special note of appreciation goes out to Brady Higa and Wanda Morris, who did outstanding transcription work. Finally, Carol thanks her parents, and regrets that her mother did not live to see the appearance of this volume. Carol thinks she would have liked it.

Introduction

Writing about revolutionary France from London in 1792, Mary Wollstonecraft addressed her *Vindication of the Rights of Woman* to a proponent of national education in the tumultuous country. The egalitarian energies of the new government promised large-scale transformations, and, for Wollstonecraft, the female sex urgently needed reform: "They dress; they paint, and nickname God's creatures. . . . Can they govern a family, or take care of the poor babes whom they bring into the world?" she asked, pointedly identifying flaws that led to women's domestic failures. Wollstonecraft admitted women's present inferiority but argued that this was the result of early training that had left most women "only fit for a seraglio." "It is time," Wollstonecraft proclaimed, "to effect a revolution in female manners—time to restore to them their lost dignity—and make them, as a part of the human species, labour by reforming themselves to reform the world."[1] Rescued from subjugation, educated women would contribute to the common good—of themselves, their families, society, and the nation. For Wollstonecraft, public and private virtue intertwined—in both men and women. They had both the right and the responsibility to learn the wise exercise of liberty at home, to provide a foundation for a virtuous, moral society.

Although Wollstonecraft wrote her *Vindication of the Rights of Woman* about and for the "old world"—France and her own native Britain—she reached a transatlantic audience that, in the closing years of the eighteenth century, recognized the interconnections of "public" and "private." Historians exploring the gendered experiences of women in the early republic have

*Mary Wollstonecraft.
Although largely ignored
in the early years of
the American republic,
Wollstonecraft's* Vindication
of the Rights of Woman
*called for the reform of
female education as a part
of the elevation of the status
of women. Photograph of a
stipple engraving by James
Heath, ca. 1797, after a
painting by John Opie.
(Source: Library of Congress)*

also employed the categories of "public" and "private," yet, following the lead of 1960s scholars, have most frequently established them as distinct, mutually exclusive categories, as "separate spheres," not the interconnecting and interactive orientations of multifaceted women. Recent work has revealed the limitations to understanding the history of women when the rhetoric of domesticity is taken too literally to imply a distinctive place or position inhabited. New studies instead suggest that antebellum American women were everywhere: in parades, in charitable associations, in literary circles, and even in political parties. Moreover, recognizing the variations of class, race, and regional experience of the population now suggests new ways to understand the lives of women in the West, enslaved women, free women of color, employed women, single women, and immigrant women.

This volume suggests an alternate framework that will help integrate the vast new historiography into understandings that move beyond "separate spheres." It asks the question: How did diverse women in America understand, explain, and act upon their varied constraints, positions, responsibilities, and worldviews in changing American society between the end of the Revolution and the beginning of the Civil War? To answer, it posits the evolution of different forms of women's engagement in civic and political activities—disentangling three particular phases of women's "publicness" in the period between ratification of the American Constitution and the coming of the Civil War, each in relation—not in opposition—to women's personal situations.

In phase 1, after the achievement of American independence and the subsequent conservative "counterrevolution" in gender roles, women participated in social debates and organizations in the guise of deferential domestic partners. Yet, while oriented toward the household, women still generally retained what we are calling "publicness," that is, a public presence defined in their interactions with the developing economy and the growing markets of this era, and in the expansion of literacy and educational opportunities.

In phase 2, the transformations wrought by the Second Great Awakening, and concomitant changes in Jacksonian politics, created possibilities for some women to engage in public action within reform movements. These women—generally white and more often northern than southern—worked as auxiliaries to men, sometimes within the same organizations, and sometimes in autonomous associations; they took for themselves an identity that we have called companionate co-laborers, based largely on claims to the sensitivity of women to moral matters and their importance in shaping public opinion. For them, then, "publicness" played out in benevolent and charitable organizations, in social organizations. Meanwhile, a few particularly outspoken women slowly began to construct an argument for "co-equality" that reached beyond voluntary associations to suggest gendered claims on their rights as Americans.

In phase 3, the inflamed politics and controversial rights struggles of the 1840s and 1850s began to erode the Second Party System, that is, the rivalry between the Whig and Democratic parties in American politics. Empowered and restrained by gender definitions, some women joined the controversy as passionate partisans. They entered the political fray claiming their rights as citizens to stake positions in electoral contests and in party matters; many sought significant engagement at the polls but did not demand the vote for themselves. Yet, conservative critics rejected the idea that any women should claim a political presence and, in reaction, created some of the most elaborate explanations for separate spheres, invoking a past that had never been, a mythical age in which women had no public presence.

Writing a history of women in the American republic before the Civil War that recognizes and transcends the rhetoric of separate spheres allows us to better comprehend different phases of the contest over gender in the antebellum period. In the period following the Revolution, male and female writers constructed a rationale for the separation of women from a variety of public roles, and particularly explicitly political—and even more pointedly partisan—activities. But while women were pushed from participation in some types of public identities they had enjoyed during the Revolution, they continued to engage in activities beyond their households. Women from different classes and regions continued to conduct commercial exchanges, whether involving goods or labor, often in the name of domestic financial security. In the expanding market economy, women were not excluded from participation in a larger world; rather, in an unstable compromise, certain activities were defined as domestically linked. Thus, poor women of all races used various economic strategies on behalf of household survival, while white women from the emergent middle class took their places in churches and voluntary societies, before the law, and in the classroom. Clearly, however, wherever they appeared, they were not equals. Instead, women found themselves ranked as inferiors, as subordinates to men, and frequently acquiescing to their status as deferential domestics.

Major alterations came as the great religious revivals of the early republic moved unprecedented numbers of women into religious congregations at the same time that religious disestablishment—especially in New England—changed the powers and responsibilities of the clergy. Women found new roles as partners in moral suasion, articulating their moral missions first within, and then on behalf of, the churches. Armed with principled positions, women "went public" to claim gendered work as partners in the project of constructing the American nation, demonstrating what Mary Kelley has called "gendered republicanism."[2] Free, northern women in particular created intricate networks of philanthropy and developed modes of participation in a wide range of reform campaigns, from public schooling to temperance and antiprostitution work and to concerns over the forced relocation of Native Americans, as well as the physical and spiritual condition of enslaved people. "The daughters of free men" claimed their responsibility to secure a national future by ensuring its moral foundations. Free women of color also sought to establish their respectability and then use it as a foundation to claim liberty and freedom for the enslaved of their race. Despite the opposition of conservative clergy and southern patriarchs, women's roles as moral agents were firmly established, and women from a vast range of diverse communities put their understanding into action, not only within their own households, but in the larger world as well. Bolstered by their status as wives and mothers, they worked in public, in concert with men who wanted to (literally) re-form the world. But they rarely claimed autonomy; instead, most women worked with men as companionate co-laborers. Even the tentative claims to their status as citizens acknowledged gendered difference and defended their presence on the basis of their distinctiveness.

When the moral rhetoric of the 1830s and 1840s became political rhetoric in the 1840s and 1850s, women followed this politicization of moral culture. Antislavery evangelicals turned to politics and mobilized women followed them. In particular, the abolitionists debated within their own ranks over the propriety of political engagement in struggles that seemed to some to involve "higher laws" determined by religious and humanitarian principles. In the end, some women found new places as passionate partisans, dissolving the ethical distance at which their gendered roles had kept them from political participation. North and South, women formulated positions, especially with respect to the politics of slavery. Their stances resonated with partisan leaders. Meanwhile, some political parties articulated their positions as moral choices, and they sought to transform public opinion in the electoral realm, turning for assistance to those who had claimed the high ground. Whigs, in particular, invited women to campaign for "family values," and women accepted the invitation. Fearful male opponents looked on with horror, charging that women's embrace of partisanship—of party politics—meant the loss of their selfless, calming influence, their salutary ability to soothe and tamp down the combustible party battles of the antebellum years. Thus, women, as a whole, no longer served in their distinctive role as moral consciences beyond the combustible world of politics. As passionate partisans, women played a critical role in the collapse of the Second Party System.

This volume, then, revises our understanding of antebellum women. It suggests a way to rethink the relationship of "public" and "private" as categories. It views "publicness" not as an alternative to domesticity but rather as part of the lived experiences of men and women. In the extended text of Section I that follows, and in the documents presented in Section II, this book outlines important stages in the transitions of women's diverse understandings of their public roles in relation, not in opposition, to their familial and household roles. In different classes, races, and regions, American women experienced differently the changes in the social, economic, and political context of the United States between the end of the American Revolution and the beginnings of the Civil War. They also made lives within a world where gender shaped fundamental rhetoric about distinctive spheres, reflecting the debates of antebellum culture wars and their call to return to a tradition that had not existed.

Notes

1. All quotes in this paragraph are from: Mary Wollstonecraft, *Vindication of the Rights of Woman* (originally published 1792: Project Gutenberg, 2002), www .gutenberg.org/dirs/etext02/vorow10.txt, Introduction and Chapter 3.

2. Mary Kelley, *Learning to Stand and Speak: Women, Education, and Public Life in America's Republic* (Chapel Hill: University of North Carolina Press, 2006), 245.

Antebellum Women

Phase 1: Deferential Domestics

Despite the political revolt that declared the equality of all men, and a constitution that established the new government in the name of "we the people," historians question whether women as a gender benefited from the new order. Although the American Revolution overthrew the rule of the British monarchy, the American Founding Fathers did not explicitly address the relationship of the new nation's female inhabitants to the political structures of the emergent United States. During the War for Independence, both patriot and loyalist women took on extraordinary duties that suggested the possibilities for new public roles for women. Yet some historians argue that the Treaty of Paris of 1783 that marked the establishment of peace after the American Revolution also heralded what has been called a "domestic counterrevolution," a movement to limit the freedoms that women had enjoyed when they shouldered the responsibilities of wartime. Did the years after independence see women's status under law circumscribed? Were women restrained from general participation in civil society? Did women lose autonomy? What happened within the households of American women?

This phase looks closely at the diverse experiences and representations of variously situated American women in the period after the American Revolution. While recognizing some of the countervailing factors and arguments, it suggests that, on the whole, women's power in society and in the household declined as the new nation developed during the first decades of the nineteenth century. "Women," as a gender, remained subordinate before the law in the early years of the American republic; writers and political theorists idealized women as obligated to submission within hierarchically structured households that reclaimed their prerevolutionary patriarchal legitimacy. Phase 1 also looks at how the law "constructed" dependence. On a parallel but different trajectory, increasing restrictions on white female sexuality reinforced the subordination of women, with implications for household size as well as social relations among Euro-Americans. At the same time, changes in women's labor in various parts of the nation, and in different classes, in response to the growth of the market economy in the early American republic, bolstered distinctions among women on the basis of class, color, and region.

Political Thought and the Law

Many historians now argue that the impact of the American Revolution on the political perception of women was something of a paradox. On the one hand, leaders of the new nation celebrated modern notions of liberty and human rights, of public virtue upheld by private sacrifice. Moreover, the Revolution undermined older ideas about the legitimacy of hierarchy, proclaiming, in the words of Thomas Jefferson, "all men are created equal." In this context, American revolutionaries paid tribute to the brave women who managed domestic economies on the home front while men mustered into militias and armies; they celebrated women's courage and sacrifice, and honored women who took up arms, gathered intelligence, or carried messages. Yet, on the other hand, once the war was over, neither the new states nor the federal government made efforts to change women's relationship within the household or to the government outside it. Suggestions that women might gain liberty and independence clashed with the ideology of patriarchy that had once served to buttress allegiance to the British monarchy as a system of rule; but older, patriarchal structures of authority remained largely intact within Euro-American households even after the political revolution eroded earlier hierarchies. In fact, as the newly established states eliminated property qualifications for enfranchisement, they clarified the exclusion of women from the electorate, even as they extended the vote to ever-increasing numbers of white men in the half-century following independence. Thus, gender, in conjunction with race, increasingly defined the grounds for exclusion from political participation; the so-called evolution of democracy from the Revolution into the Jacksonian Era empowered free, white men, while it held negative consequences for women of all races and people of color of both sexes.[1]

Gender was a political category. Various aspects of state and federal laws subordinated women as women; poor women, Native American women, enslaved women, and free women of color felt the impact of gender-defined subordination in different ways. Native American women lost their standing as their tribes increasingly embraced Euro-American expectations for male leadership in treaty talks that accompanied displacement and loss of traditional lands. Northern African American women stood to benefit as gradual emancipation came to people of color throughout the mid-Atlantic states and New England, yet racially based ideologies of inferiority remained, shaping the lives of women of color in ways that denied their humanity as well as their capacities for cultural advancement. The achievement of Phillis Wheatley, the African American poet of Boston, was a remarkable event, a triumph that challenged the inferiority of both categories. Yet, generally, white women joined their male counterparts to reinforce gendered and racialized hierarchies. That is, white women rarely questioned the subordination or enslavement of women of color.[2]

Why did the democratic fervor of the American War for Independence destabilize the popularity of patriarchy as a political theory but fail to revolutionize its impact on household relations? In their rebellion against the king of England, American patriots popularized notions of government based on contract among equals. Monarchy, they believed, had connected the king and his subjects in the familylike relations of duty and obedience of father and children. Revolutionary Americans had argued that the virtue of the King and Parliament had been despoiled by selfish conniving. Thus, the British government had degenerated to tyranny. In their efforts to overthrow their British "father," Americans believed they had come of age and now stood as independent citizens eligible to establish a political compact founded on consent, not command. Yet, as historian Jan Lewis has suggested, most Americans remained loyal to notions of "natural" hierarchy within the family and within society, essentializing the inferiority of women. According to historian Norma Basch, even in Revolutionary literature, "intimate and egalitarian constructions of marriage were persistently qualified and inevitably undermined by references to order and subordination."[3]

Patriarchy thus survived in the household even when overthrown in government. American writers and political theorists revised older analogies between a government based on the consent of its people and relations within harmonious families: women, it was asserted, now voluntarily chose their masters when they consented to a marriage contract just as virtuous citizens freely chose their legitimate rulers through the electoral process. Deference, then, was natural—for wives to husbands, and for the "little" people to those most worthy to occupy elected office. As a result, republican political theory stimulated the growth of democratic political institutions at the same time that female subordination in domestic relations remained unchallenged. Thus emerged "deferential domesticity."[4]

In the new republic and the states that constituted it, marriage law incorporated ideas about women's deference to men. Built upon British legal precedents, it remained largely unchanged, accepting the common law doctrine of coverture, the principle that, upon marriage, the wife's legal identity was subsumed into her husband's. In the eighteenth century, British jurist William Blackstone constructed his much-cited compilation and commentaries on the British common law on which colonial governments based their understanding that the married woman, or *feme covert*, lost her legal identity upon marriage. Some historians assert that Blackstone's codification actually strengthened the subordination expected of women; others believe he merely reproduced the practices of his contemporaries. Regardless of the origins of Blackstone's approach, all agree that the new states developed their laws largely based on his works.[5]

The first major American treatise on domestic relations published in 1816 by legal educator Tapping Reeve emphasized the inequality of the marriage relationship in its very title, *The Law of Baron and Femme, of Parent and Child, of Guardian and Ward, of Master and Servant . . . .* As document 4 reveals, Reeve documented the female subordination demanded in marriage, but he also recognized the traditional rights conferred on wives to demand support and maintenance, and the ways in which a single woman, known as a *feme sole*, might hold independent property and contract as an individual. Historians debate the extent to which coverture was challenged by a variety of legal techniques that allowed some married women to gain special status in order to hold property, to create trusts outside the control of husbands, or to negotiate property settlements before marriage. But in the end, coverture was a powerful statement of law and ideology in the early republic. The default position was that married women simply lacked standing before the law.[6]

Only in the third decade of the nineteenth century did coverture face serious challenges. Family dissatisfaction with the inability of wealthy women to protect their property from their husbands' creditors played a significant role in growing support for married women's property acts. By the 1830s, fathers as well as husbands found it in their interests to protect women's assets without endorsing general notions of equality. Fathers moved to shield their daughters' portions from spendthrift or untrustworthy husbands; in an era of economic instability, husbands wished to protect some of the family goods from creditors by settling them separately on their wives. The first state law, a Mississippi statute passed in 1839, specifically empowered married women to maintain their property in slaves. In the following decades, other states also passed legislation to set aside some of the resources and possessions married women brought to their unions or inherited during them. Such maneuvers served well women with significant resources but did little to ensure gender equality more broadly. Instead, in the name of family unity, they strengthened class position.

In the early republic, state laws provided little recourse to women trapped in marriages in which husbands failed to act the part of virtuous rulers. Divorce was difficult to obtain, even for reasons of adultery, desertion, or physical cruelty. Unlike the contract between an elected leader and his constituency, matrimony was seen as fundamentally a contract for life. Although procedures for divorce varied from state to state, all were hard to access, especially for women. Early in the antebellum period, special bills in the state legislatures granted most divorces. Only later in the period did statutory law move divorce proceedings into the courts in most states and then more rapidly in the northern states than in the South.[7]

With or without the introduction of what came to be called "judicial divorce," legal dissolutions of marriages remained rare and expensive. Since marriage presumed the subordination of women, wives could not easily protest men's failures. As Basch has written, judges reflected the general beliefs of society that women in well-regulated homes deferred to masculine authority; divorce litigation brought to the fore the battles over the limits to that authority. Wives who complained of violence, alcohol abuse, or the squandering of property rarely received a sympathetic hearing. In a peculiarly cruel twist, women's failures were presumed to provoke men to misbehave.[8]

Unreliable, incomplete, and scattered divorce statistics force historians to find creative ways to assess the prevalence of divorce in the early republic. Several studies for the early years of the century suggest a gradual increase in the number of formal divorce actions, which nonetheless remained very low, especially before the advent of judicial divorce. The South, with its support of patriarchal power in the slaveholding household, lagged behind the North in developing new divorce legislation; the state of South Carolina, for example, did not pass laws providing for judicial divorce law until after the Civil War ended enslavement.[9]

Because of the complications of legal action, some women and men turned as well to what historian Clare Lyons has called "self-divorce," actions even more difficult to document than legal separations. Moreover, lines between officially sanctioned partings and those that existed as extralegal actions were not always clear, as was the case for Rachel Donelson and Andrew Jackson, who believed that Donelson's divorce from her first husband had been completed when they married in 1791. When her first husband subsequently sued to finalize their divorce, now on the grounds of adultery, Jackson and Donelson discovered the error that would follow them throughout his political career. Jackson accused the critics who made his alleged adultery a public issue in his 1828 presidential campaign with causing the death of his beloved Rachel.[10]

Self-marriage, the counterpart of self-divorce, frequently took place in areas without settled local governments in the early republic. It also served participants in unions between people of different races. On the "Middle Ground," the areas of the frontier that brought together Native Americans with Euro-American traders, white men and indigenous women formed households that negotiated between cultures. In the constantly shifting borderlands, the local knowledge of wives and their kinship connections proved valuable to men from the outside; moreover, traditions of matrilineality and matrifocality further empowered some women in these relationships. But long contact between native nations and the state and federal governments undermined traditions of women's authority, diminishing female standing within native society and in the dominant society into which some Indian women married. In Indiana, pioneer trader William Conner separated from his first wife, Mekinges, when she was forced west with her Delaware band by the terms of the 1818 Treaty of St. Mary's, an agreement, ironically, that Conner had helped negotiate.[11] Among the Cherokees, women had traditionally pursued farming while men hunted, sustaining gendered equality and reciprocity; moreover, matrilineal clans organized society. But with the coming of trade, and under the influence of missionaries who sought to "civilize" the warriors in particular, women's standing suffered. Even Cherokee women who had married white men found themselves increasingly marginalized as federal and state decisions pushed them from their traditional lands.[12]

Marriage for people of African descent was also problematic. As historian Nancy Cott has written, "Slavery and marriage were so incompatible that a master's permission for a slave to be 'legally' married was interpretable as manumission." Largely prohibited in the South, interracial matrimony presumed the free status of both parties. White men might own women of color, but they could rarely accord them legal recognition as partners. Throughout the antebellum years, white men who acknowledged children resulting from stable unions with black women faced obstacles to achieving legal recognition of their family. African American statesman John Mercer Langston was born in 1829 in Virginia to a white man who had freed Langston's mother; when both died, Langston and his older brothers left the state to ensure their safety.[13]

Enslaved women who made families with men of color lacked the benefits of legally recognized marriage. A free person of color could not protect an enslaved partner from an owner's demands, and increasingly complex manumission laws might require that a newly freed man or woman leave the state. Hence, some protected their voluntary relationships by purchasing their mate, appearing in the law as their spouse's master or mistress. Similarly, some marriages between enslaved people survived despite, not because of, the law. Without recognition of their personhood, men and women of African descent struggled to create meaningful unions under oppressive conditions. While southern states referred to slavery as a "domestic institution," it profoundly differed from other relationships within the household; it included neither fictions of consent nor notions of legal capacity that could be conferred with age. Generations of urban and rural men and women, on plantations and in small, planter households, in cities and in the countryside, created customs and rituals, including "jumping the broom," to celebrate the partnerships they chose, "until death or the master" parted them. Hopping over the simple domestic tool used to clean and claim interior space, couples carved out their own room for familial intimacy. Tragically, as slave populations in the old South grew, and white migrants took up new lands in the Southwest, these unions proved increasingly fragile. Masters took young, healthy people born in settled areas away from partners, parents, and children to make the Cotton Kingdom.[14] Indeed, historian Michael Tadman argues that, for blacks in the Chesapeake between the ages of seventeen and thirty-five, the odds of sale were one in three.[15]

The disparities of gender and race thus shaped the lives of women in the early republic. The story of suffrage in the state of New Jersey underscores consolidation of the legal disabilities of gender in the early antebellum years. Between 1776 and 1807, New Jersey inhabitants "worth fifty pounds" could participate in elections; women—generally single women or widows whose status allowed them to hold property—could and did vote, as did men and women of color. Yet in 1807, the state legislature revised qualifications, explicitly excluding women and people of color from the electorate. Not long after, in 1811, New Jersey eliminated its property requirement. When all white men could vote, the stark exclusions on the basis of race and gender reinforced hierarchies that left women categorically in positions of subordination to men. White male democracy thus built on gender hierarchy.

Men were qualified to vote; women were excluded. Electors were white and male.[16]

This masculinization of electoral politics promoted and accompanied a feminization—and domestication—of "virtue." Virtue had a special meaning in Revolutionary America and the early republic. In the political theory embraced by the patriots during the American Revolution, virtue was the quality that prompted a citizen to act in the public interest, even at the expense of his personal happiness or potential gain. To the founders, only men held political responsibility, and men were the chief vessels of this politically defined virtue. For Revolutionary Americans, virtue was a safeguard against corruption, for corruption turned politicians away from the public good and toward their own selfish benefit at the expense of the state. Corruption made for tyranny, and tyranny was cause for rebellion. Property allowed citizens the independence that bolstered their virtue; with secure and independent property, the citizen would not be tempted by the spoils of corruption. Thus, public virtue was "active self-sacrificial service to the state on behalf of the common good."[17]

Yet, as Ruth Bloch has written, by the end of the eighteenth century, the meaning of virtue changed. With the rise of evangelical theology and the emergence of a new interest in literary sentimentalism, virtue was reinterpreted in a new, personal context. Now connected with personal morality instead of civic republicanism, virtue was no longer linked to sacrifice for the public good but rather with individual resistance to immorality and corruption. This personalized virtue nonetheless remained essential for society and government: citizens had to be able to stand firm against the temptations and blandishments offered by fraudulent and dishonest politicians; they had to be able to know morality, increasingly interpreted at the personal level. Training in such qualities was best accomplished by women, whose role in the creation of the state involved teaching their sons the virtues of self-restraint and abstention. Following the formulation of historian Linda Kerber, scholars have seen the efforts of the "Republican Mother" to produce virtuous sons as "a fourth branch of government."[18]

Sexual Restraint and the Demographic Revolution

Deferential domesticity created new dangers as well as new sources of power. Beginning late in the eighteenth century, domesticated virtue came to be most closely associated with a particular kind of resistance to corruption: the female struggle to defend chastity against male seduction. The emergent print culture of the early republic played a critical role in dispersing this new morality, providing an abundance of cautionary tales. Novels featured instructive accounts of cunning knaves who ensnared respectable, trusting young women through romantic deceptions, only to abandon them after completing their conquests. *The Power of Sympathy*, recognized as the first American novel, appeared in 1789; author William Hill Brown used the epistolary form—telling the story through correspondence between characters—to trace the dire effects of sexual transgressions including seduction and incestuous love. Susanna Rowson's *Charlotte Temple* (see document 1) followed, with its first American edition in 1794 capturing the imagination of the reading public and becoming the first American best seller. Its tale of transatlantic lust and deception concluded with the death of the "ruined" heroine.[19]

The emphasis on the restraint of women's passions in the postrevolutionary republic marked an important moment in the shift both in ideas about women's sexuality and in women's sexual behavior. Before the Revolution, popular images portrayed prodigious female appetites and lusts. Even the seduction novels recognized women's desires. But with the end of the Revolution came a transformation. An anonymous poem in 1785 captured the moment of transition, referencing the threat to the New England custom that had allowed unmarried men and women to spend the night together in a bed that placed a board between them, writing:

> Some maidens say, if through the nation,
> Bundling should quite go out of fashion,
> Courtship would lose its sweets; and they
> Could have no fun till wedding day.
> It shant be so, they rage and storm,
> And country girls in clusters swarm,
> And fly and buz [sic] like angry bees,
> And vow they'll bundle when they please.
> Some mothers too, will plead their cause,
> And give their daughters great applause,
> And tell them 'tis no sin or shame,
> For we, your mothers did the same.

Discussions of female sexuality soon disappeared from respectable publications. Influenced by the transatlantic religious revival known as the Second Great Awakening, and reflecting the larger reaction against women's autonomy, popular culture not only counseled restraint but also now disavowed that middle-class women had sexual curiosity or physical lust.[20]

Yet, as Cott argues, the construction of respectable womanhood as "passionless" also held some positive potential: with the reversal of "the tradition of Christian mistrust based on women's sexual treacherousness," women might gain some standing. Moreover, the implicit lack of interest in carnal acts endorsed women's refusal to engage in intercourse and hence provided opportunities for female reproductive self-determination. Historian Susan Klepp has suggested that the transformation meant that women developed the sense of self and notion of control over life that male Americans typically enacted in their understandings of the self-made man. Based on her readings of diaries and portraits of well-educated and economically prosperous women in the Philadelphia area, she stresses that women gained in bodily autonomy and control even as they lost avenues for sexual expression. Other historians, however, see new dangers, arguing instead that the "reconceptualization of female sexuality provided one promising avenue for bolstering the gender hierarchy," since it invited the policing of women's bodies to ensure their compliance and restraint.[21]

Regardless of their impact on the power of literate white women, the new standards for erotic and reproductive repression clearly reinforced boundaries that separated women by class and color even as they reasserted white, male dominance. Popular constructions of women of color continued to emphasize their lustfulness and hence banished them from respectability, subjecting them to particular risk for exploitation. White men justified their exercise of control over the bodies of women of color as defensive and explained their transgressions as caused by women who needed to be mastered. By attributing unnatural appetites to enslaved women as well as free women of color, men avoided taking responsibility for their sexual exploitation. Women of color—slave and usually free as well—thus found themselves excluded from the social constructions of virtuous womanhood. Little wonder that many communities of color in the North reacted by strictly enforcing standards of respectability in the hope of elevating the status of African American females.[22]

Class, too, was integral in categorizing and constructing women's sexual behaviors. In some cities where a robust sex trade had flourished during the late colonial era, the early years of the republic brought new restraint. In a society that increasingly constructed womanhood as sexually inert, the adventurous and expressive female behaviors that persisted as remnants of the earlier "permissive sexual culture" essentially became markers of class. By the 1820s, prostitution had become a well-organized trade in Boston and New York. Although the occupation brought wealth to some women, they bought their economic security at the price of their respectability. By definition, those women involved were simply not "ladies." Moreover, keeping a brothel was one of the few crimes for which a married woman could be held responsible in her own right; according to the law, a woman forfeited the "benefits" of coverture when she engaged in the sex trade. True women learned restraint. For women of all classes, sex outside marriage, once recognized with a "wink and a nod," became increasingly unacceptable.[23]

For many historians, this change in ideas about female sexuality appears to have driven the American demographic transition between the years 1790 and 1900, when the United States experienced the change from a "traditional" society with high levels of fertility and high mortality rates to a "modern" society of low fertility rates and low mortality. Changes in family size were key: the average number of children born to a white woman when she completed her reproductive career was cut in half, from about 7 to an average of 3.5 children ever born, with the greatest decline taking place before the Civil War. The transition began in the more settled areas of the Northeast and the South Atlantic regions, spreading slowly into the Old Northwest and south-central areas. Traditionally, demographers have attributed half of this early decline in white fertility to the rising age of marriage and the decline in the proportion of women who married; that is, for demographers, the lack of "exposure" to sexual intercourse explains much of the decrease in the birth rate in the nineteenth century. They note that, in a society without modern methods of contraception, the number of children ever born to a married woman could be expected to drop by one for every two years of delay in the age of marriage. Estimates suggest that white women married at about age twenty in 1800, with the age rising to nearly twenty-four by 1865. Since childbearing by single women was rare and highly stigmatized, the relatively large—and growing—proportion of women who never married also lowered the overall birthrate.[24]

Few of these changes could be attributed to new contraceptive technologies, which remained fairly rudimentary in the early republic. While the sale of equipment was not yet prohibited by antiobscenity laws that would limit their distribution after the Civil War, condoms had not significantly changed for nearly two hundred years. Still made of hand-stitched animal intestines, they offered, as an early, modern British mother had told her daughter, an "armour against enjoyment and a spider web against danger." The custom of washing and reusing these expensive devices did not add to their comfort or effectiveness. Finally, on the eve of the Civil War, the price of condoms began to drop, while cheaper and more effective male sheaths found their way into distribution with the introduction of vulcanized rubber. When Europeans began to experiment with cervical caps, pessaries, and "womb veils" in the 1840s, these inventions slowly made their way to the United States. Still, most had available only the traditional herbal douches and the practice of coitus interruptus (withdrawal) in their efforts to secure birth limitation. Faulty biological understanding unfortunately located a woman's "safe period" at the middle of a woman's menstrual cycle. If prevention failed, abortifacients and abortionists, especially in the hidden but flourishing sexual culture of the rough working class in cities, served some women who sought, as the expression had it, to "unblock" their menses. Access to contraceptive technologies, thus, was limited, but never entirely absent.[25]

Yet, even without the assistance of new devices, married women bore fewer children in the years between the founding of the republic and the coming of the Civil War. Why? In the classic explanation of demographic historian Ansley Coale, three critical factors need to be in place for couples to limit their childbearing within marriage: a desire to limit the number of children; a social acceptance of such limitation; and, finally, an understanding of the means by which to achieve it. Cultural and social historians have identified several factors that inclined men and women to make the effort to control their fertility, including rising literacy and education for women, and the increase in women's work outside home. Others argue that the decline in the number of children born was fundamentally a rational family response to the declining availability of land that could be provided to settle adult children into farming vocations as well as the greater cost of childrearing in urban environments, where education and amenities were expected. Historian Daniel Scott Smith suggests that the number of children born declined as women's power within households grew, sketching out how a "domestic feminism" empowered them to enlist men's help to control their exposure to intercourse, thus limiting the numbers of pregnancies and births to which they would be vulnerable. From a somewhat different perspective, Cott has argued that women accepted their definition as "passionless" in part in order to leverage men into self-restraint.[26]

Historians have evidence of premarital as well as marital restraint: according to one study, the number of first children born to newly married couples after only 8.5 months of marriage rose to nearly 30 percent in the years of the American Revolution and then fell precipitously through 1860 to under 10 percent. Did the enhanced restraint between couples during courtship indicate a new way that men and women thought about premarital sexual activity? Was it part of the larger reconstruction of notions of the "natural" desires attributed to men and women? If women gained reproductive self-determination by their renunciations of access to sexual expressiveness, did it reinforce or free them from domestic deference?

For enslaved women, reproduction and sexuality involved yet other factors. In work focusing primarily on the colonial period in both the American

South and the West Indies, scholar Jennifer Morgan has explored how the reproductive capacities of enslaved women lay at "the heart of the venture of racial slavery." As she explains, "slaveowners both relied upon and ignored the physiological realities of women's bodies." Throughout the New World, laws provided that children inherited the status of their mothers, so enslaved women literally reproduced slavery, often through nonconsensual relations, at the same time that slave owners exploited them as laborers, usually in agricultural work. Historians and demographers have long noted that enslaved women in the areas that became the United States had significantly higher levels of fertility than those held in the Caribbean and in South America. Such numbers meant that slavery in the United States could be self-sustaining even before the federal government barred continued American participation in the international slave trade in 1808. As early as 1740, the number of enslaved people born in what would become the United States outweighed the number born in Africa. This "Creole" majority made possible the ties between generations of enslaved peoples. By comparison, in the West Indies and South America, slave deaths outnumbered births well into the nineteenth century.[27]

Historians have celebrated the ability of the people of African descent in North America to establish a firm demographic foundation before the Civil War as evidence of the achievement of some degree of autonomy. Yet, slave families faced enormous obstacles. Mothers struggled to nurture infants under truly horrifying conditions. As one demographer has written, "Children's health was comparable to that in the poorest populations ever studied." Yet, despite these constraints, net population increase continued until the Civil War, with the established states of the Upper South, especially Virginia, as the birthplace for many enslaved peoples who were moved west with the spread of agriculture. In even the most conservative estimates, such forced migrations resulted in the disruption of 10 to 20 percent of all slave marriages, also tearing apart the relationships of parents to their children and of siblings to each other. Some demographic evidence suggests that the fertility of enslaved people on the United States mainland began to decline after 1830, with population growth continuing only because of the decline in mortality. Historians can speculate whether this decline was a result of such separations limiting the possibilities for women to bear children; the autonomous choices made to resist slavery by women who determined to limit the number of children they would bring into the oppressive institution; or a decline in the ability of women to conceive due to deteriorations in the conditions of slavery. Regardless of the conclusion, it is clear that enslaved women's private reproductive lives profoundly influenced the culture and politics of the antebellum South where lifetime heritable slavery persisted to the Civil War.[28]

While it persisted, northern slavery had its own constraints. Like southern bondage, slavery in the North was transmitted through the status of the mother. Especially in the Hudson Valley, some slavery involved agricultural labor, but much of the northern variant had a significant urban component. In Revolutionary New York, perhaps 20 percent of the city's population was black, with two-thirds of these people of color enslaved. Over half of those held in slavery were women, most in domestic tasks. During the closing decades of the eighteenth century and the opening years of the nineteenth, racial emancipation spread throughout the North. The first independent portion of the nation to provide for immediate emancipation, Vermont freed the small number of slaves within its boundaries in 1777. Rhode Island began the process of gradual emancipation in 1779, accelerating it in 1784. More significantly, led by a Quaker-dominated manumission movement in Philadelphia, Pennsylvania passed a state statute in 1780 providing for the emancipation of all persons held as slaves when they reached the age of twenty-eight. In Massachusetts, a 1783 state court ruling confirmed that, as the state chief justice William Cushing had ruled two years earlier, "the idea of slavery is inconsistent with our own conduct and Constitution." In 1784, Connecticut followed with its own gradual emancipation act. By 1817, New York finally concluded arrangements to abolish the entire institution of slavery after the passage of an additional decade, in 1827. Yet, New York was ahead of New Jersey where gradual emancipation left some people enslaved until the passage of the Thirteenth Amendment to the U.S. Constitution in 1865. Thus, between 1777 and 1804, most northern states at least began the process of emancipation, although some took several generations to complete it. Almost all northern women of color enjoyed freedom before the Civil War.[29]

Free people of color were the most urbanized population in the United States before the Civil War, with about one-third dwelling in cities. And women dominated the population of people of African descent. Both enslaved women and free women of color in the urban North generally experienced lives of grinding poverty and toil as domestic labor. Historian Leslie Harris has documented how New York's 1790 population of people of color found most women serving as domestics, a few free women working as seamstresses and milliners, and others working in the context of family businesses operating oyster cellars, restaurants, and dance halls. But, as she has discovered, even freedom did not bring family security. According to Harris's estimate, perhaps one-half of all black children aged ten to fifteen in postemancipation, antebellum New York City lived away from their parents, reflecting their mothers' live-in service, and their fathers' employments at sea or as domestic labor. Moreover, fertility rates were low, while mortality rates for black, urban infants and children aged one to four years were probably twice that experienced by the white population as a whole. Under such conditions, women of color struggled for survival and respectability. Women's deferential domesticity within African American households might offer a welcome alternative to racialized and sexualized subordination in service to whites. As James and Lois Horton wrote, domesticity was, for free women of color in the North, "freedom's yoke."[30]

Women and Work

If the early years of the American republic were a counterrevolution in female lives, during which women faced increasing restrictions, what did this mean for the labors of women, and representations of this work? Many historians now argue that the spread of market relations obscured the continuing importance of women's productivity within households. As exchanges that linked households to a wider economy accelerated, men's legally recognized ownership of family goods and services disguised women's roles in the economic development of the new republic. Especially for the emergent urban, middle class, labors once acknowledged as "work" became submerged into "domesticity"; that is, disguised by sentimentality, critical tasks still demanded the efforts of women but rarely received recognition as actual labor. As a result, contemporary observers as well as current scholars often relegate their analysis of such efforts to the category of the "private sphere."

But recognizing that domesticity and public life are not exclusive but rather interconnected, new questions emerge: what was the relationship of household production to the developing market, including the market for "free labor"—that is, compensation for particular tasks accomplished or time committed? Put another way, how was paid work that drew women out of their homes related to household work? Did differently situated women engage in the household production of goods for market in order to sustain family economies? In short, what particular gendered, classed, raced, and regionalized labors did women undertake both within and beyond their households, and under what conditions? How and why did American women in the early antebellum years bear the yoke of deferential domesticity?

One way to understand the transition was suggested in 1851 by Congregational pastor Horace Bushnell in an address, "The Age of Homespun," delivered at the centennial commemoration of his county, Litchfield, in

Connecticut. Celebrating the merits of the past as guides for the future, Bushnell recurred to the image of the home-produced cloth that had once been manufactured inside the household where it was made into clothing for the family; he contrasted it with the factory-made textiles that were, by midcentury, widely available. For Bushnell, this change signified multiple developments in economic and social relations that put at risk the relations that secured the family, and society more broadly. As he opined, the "transition from mother and daughter power to water and steam power is a great one . . . a complete revolution of domestic life and social manners." Bushnell believed that some women followed the work once done within their homes into factories, while others, more fortunately situated, had taken up unproductive "polite living," ceasing to engage in productive work. For Bushnell, the end of home manufacture meant the end of domestic virtue. As he saw it, leisure threatened to corrupt womanhood, and the relocation of women's work undermined the household.[31]

More than a century later, pioneering women's historian Gerda Lerner's path-breaking article "The Lady and the Mill Girl" also highlighted the impact of industrialization on women in antebellum New England. Like Bushnell, Lerner presumed that, for wealthy women, production moved out of the household. As Lerner explained, one critical result of industrialization was "increasing differences in life styles between women of different classes. When female occupations, such as carding, spinning and weaving, were transferred from home to factory, the poorer women followed their traditional work and became industrial workers. The women of the middle and upper classes could use their newly gained time for leisure pursuits: they became ladies." For Lerner, it was these middle-class women who became devotees of the "cult of true womanhood." And, citing the social theorist Thorstein Veblen, Lerner saw them as markers of a class for whom an idle "lady" was a mark of status achieved through "conspicuous consumption" of leisure.[32]

More recently, historians have questioned whether the New England home was, in fact, so precipitously stripped of its industrious female labor. In a volume drawing its title from Bushnell's "Age of Homespun," Laurel Ulrich argues that colonial America transformed weaving from a men's into a women's occupation and that "far from being in opposition to one another 'store-bought' and 'homemade' fabrics developed together." For Ulrich, women continued to engage in a variety of tasks that connected households to a burgeoning market economy. Her study of Martha Ballard, a woman who resided in the Maine frontier from 1785 until her death in 1812, demonstrated how, even in a remote rural location, female labor had long been involved in exchange beyond her household. As document 2 reveals, Ballard received payments for her special work as a midwife, hired others to work with her, and made exchanges to ensure the production of cloth and clothing for her family and other necessities for the members of her household.[33]

The rhythms of women's work and the exchanges between households described by Ballard persisted well into the antebellum period. Women's "out-work"—that is, their paid labor performed at home away from the employers' premises—involved making products destined for the market and could be found throughout the Northeast. As Thomas Dublin has documented, weaving continued as a lucrative home-based occupation for many New England women well into the antebellum period. Rural women also plaited straw and constructed palm-leaf hats—many destined for the southern market and slaves, as well as work on piecing together shirts for the developing men's ready-to-wear clothing market. In Lynn, Massachusetts, women worked at home as binders for the shoe industry.[34]

In the greater New York City area, the Ridgefield Shirt Company flourished by distributing materials for several thousands of shirts annually to women home workers along the routes of the stage line that connected Ridgefield, Connecticut, to Long Island Sound and the metropolis beyond. The "Butter Belt," encompassing Pennsylvania and Delaware farms, encouraged household production of dairy products managed by women for sale in Philadelphia. Further south, the free woman of color Molly Horniblow sold her crackers to augment her household's income in Edenton, North Carolina, with the hope that she could use her earnings to purchase freedom for additional members of her family. In sum, women's household production for exchange and sale persisted well into the antebellum period, even as gender ideology blinded contemporaries and historians alike to its ongoing significance. Industrious women might appear as "deferential domestics."[35]

The ideology of domesticity obscured women's important labor for both the market and home consumption. Market development did not terminate the need for many labor-intensive processes that substituted for the purchase of goods and services. But the growing sentimentalization of the home in conjunction with the gendered division of labor veiled the actual work involved in the cooking, cleaning, nursing, childrearing, lighting, heating, and washing that occupied middle-class women for whom these tasks were supposed to be "labors of love." As historian Jeanne Boydston suggested, "The pastoralization of housework, with its emphasis on the sanctified home as an emanation of woman's nature, required the articulation of a new way of seeing (or, more exactly, of not seeing) women as actors, capable of physical exertion." According to Boydston, the ideology that categorized domesticity as woman's sacred calling essentially blinded men and women from seeing the actual toil it required from women. For the vast majority of American women, North and South, urban and rural, their most time-consuming labors, in the service of the maintenance of their households, no longer appeared to be "productive."[36]

Women reared with understandings of the frugality required to balance the domestic economy not only kept gardens and domestic animals. Even in the 1840s, Massachusetts-born Lucy Stone continued to make her own soap and candles to save money for items only cash could purchase while she was a student at the Oberlin Collegiate Institute. Almost all women continued to sew their own simple clothes at home, even when they hired skilled needlewomen to cut and fit their garments. All but the wealthiest wives of southern planters not only oversaw but also participated in the chores necessary to maintain their farms. In cities, new standards of cleanliness challenged middle-class matrons to intensify their efforts. After midcentury, Harriet Beecher Stowe could still extol the virtues of "The Lady Who Does Her Own Work."[37]

Some historians have argued that, for enslaved women, the work of household maintenance provided to their own families and children might perhaps have offered one of the few areas in which their labors were not merely appropriated by those who claimed their service. Yet, such chores also allowed slaveholders to maintain tight control over—and profit from—additional labor expected above and beyond the fieldwork to which most enslaved women were assigned. Frequently, it fell to enslaved women to find ways to stretch and supplement the rations of food, clothing, and shelter to aid the survival of children and other kin. The rough equality with enslaved men they might thereby gain for their role as "providers" caused new gender tensions within the black community and in relation to the white world beyond. Angela Davis observed that slavery was an equal opportunity exploiter, excluding women of color from the antebellum conventions of gender and thereby "unsexing" them.[38]

Enslaved women primarily worked in agricultural labors, but many also aided in the work of white households in the South. In the North, both before and after emancipation, women of African descent concentrated in cities where they also worked in households. While domestic service was the most significant occupation for which women received pay, their work in this field differed in certain critical ways from that of most native-born white women during the early antebellum years. Typically, American-born domestics looked upon a period of work before marriage in the home of another as a way to advance their own skills in housewifery, assisting as "helps," not as servants. Such wage-earning work was a brief period in the female life cycle. Many historians see the celebration of these young women as apprentices in homemaking as part of the myth of the "Golden Age" of domesticity. They note that the "republican helps" described so lovingly by Catharine Beecher in her *American Woman's Home* had disappeared from American cities, replaced by long-term servants, particularly immigrants and women of color, by midcentury. Especially in the Northeast, the Irish migration that began in the 1830s, and swelled to a torrent in the 1840s and 1850s in response to the potato famine, brought large numbers of single women willing to work for room, board, and low wages that often helped continue the chain of immigrants to the United States. Employed to embellish and sustain the domesticity in other households, these workers relinquished their own homes. Their service demanded deference to those who hired them even as their work remained within the household.[39]

Ironically, in the payment of wages to women who performed domestic service, Americans recognized the economic value of housework in a way that the ideology of domesticity did not. Yet, earning cash through household work for others in a sense broadened the boundaries of women's domestic economies. While it remained the predominant form of women's employment throughout the nineteenth century, service was not the only remunerative occupation for women's employment outside the home. The urban economy offered the greatest range of opportunities for women. Even in the wake of the "revolutionary backlash," some women still maintained small stores and continued peddling and huckstering in the streets, although such outdoor work generally placed its practitioners beyond the scope of respectability. In Philadelphia, for example, African American women traditionally sold "pepper pot"—a soup—on the street. In New York, women of color peddled the Manhattan delicacy hot corn.[40]

Many urban women advertised their services. Among the most skilled were those who called themselves nurses, although training varied greatly in this period before the professionalization of the occupation. Some worked as cooks. A few straddled the home/work boundary as boardinghouse keepers, while others, with less capital, worked as washerwomen, sometimes in homes or taking their bundles to manage offsite; in an age before running water or sophisticated mechanical assistance, laundry was no small chore.[41]

The indistinct line between workplace and home particularly characterized unskilled sewing. While some "workrooms" existed, much was accomplished in outwork. In American cities as well as across the Atlantic, reformers bemoaned the fate of women who took up the needle only to find themselves unable to sustain their lives on its meager wages. Thomas Hood wrote the following in his poem "The Song of the Shirt" for London's satirical magazine *Punch* in 1843:

> Stitch—stitch—stitch,
> In poverty, hunger and dirt,
> Sewing at once, with a double thread,
> A Shroud as well as a Shirt.

Recent studies of the garment trades have emphasized the difference between the unskilled needlewomen and the well-trained women who proudly maintained a craft tradition. While men's clothing moved increasingly into mass production for a ready-to-wear market during the antebellum years, women's garments continued to command high levels of skills. Mantua makers, milliners, and dressmakers were accomplished artisans, at the very top of the hierarchy of the needle trades. In rural areas, skilled women made the rounds to help households cut and fit clothes that might later be sewn at home. The required expertise was often passed along in families through the female line, becoming a family tradition.[42]

Other respectable occupations for women included writing for the growing female audience who propelled what historians have called "the print revolution." This tiny fragment of the female workforce maintained an influence well beyond its numbers. The work of women writers was a powerful force, both in maintaining notions of domestic deference and in claiming new competence for women. Many literate women became teachers, an occupation that, particularly in New England, served as a bridge between childhood and adulthood. According to some estimates, as many as one-quarter of all native-born women in Massachusetts served as teachers during their youth in these antebellum years.[43]

Such young women represented one variation of the pattern whereby females in their teens and early twenties might alternate outwork, service, and other forms of employment. In New England, early industrial employers developed incentives to draw precisely this labor force into the first textile mills holding out the promise of genteel avocations and carefully supervised housing accommodations. In the city of Lowell, Massachusetts, built expressly to introduce mechanization but resist the creation of a permanent industrial working class, "mill girls" accepted textile work as one further option for securing cash. In studying the motives and the lives of such New England women, historians have debated whether these young, unmarried females saw themselves as working for the benefit of the households into which they were born, or for themselves, either as independent people or as future wives laying up money to establish households of their own. Dublin has suggested that, while gendered prescriptions encouraged young women to invoke the concept of familial loyalty and continued deference to parental authority, some achieved greater autonomy and mobility when they joined the female workforce beyond their homes. Yet, when mill owners found their profits squeezed and working conditions deteriorated, native-born females left factory employment. Massachusetts' "mill girls" sought out more options, proudly proclaiming themselves "the daughters of free men."[44]

The French social critic Alexis de Tocqueville reflected on the distinctive independence of young American women during his trip through the United States in 1831 (see document 7). Born into the French nobility in the wake of the French Revolution, Tocqueville was at once horrified and fascinated by the American experience with what he called the "providential fact" of democracy. In 1840, he looked specifically at the impact of the ethos of "equality" on the white women of America, drawing his most important distinction between females before and after marriage. To his eyes, "long before an American girl arrives at the marriageable age, her emancipation from maternal control begins; she has scarcely ceased to be a child when she already thinks for herself, speaks with freedom, and acts on her own impulse."[45] Tocqueville believed he saw these self-determining American women changed dramatically in later life, for "the independence of woman is irrecoverably lost in the bonds of matrimony. If an unmarried woman is less constrained [in America] than elsewhere, a wife is subjected to stricter obligations." He finally concluded,

> I never observed that the women of America consider conjugal authority as a fortunate usurpation of their rights, or that they thought themselves degraded by submitting to it. It appeared to me . . . that they attach a sort of pride to the voluntary surrender of their own will and make it their boast to bend themselves to the yoke, not shake it off. Such, at least, is the feeling expressed by the most virtuous of their sex.[46]

Tocqueville's notion that American women willingly accepted the appearance of subordination after marriage suggests the persistence of the view that virtuous women were, at least after marriage, in important ways, deferential domestics. But, by the 1830s, some women, in some situations, found places as collaborators and colleagues of men. In the realm of civil society—outside politics and government on the one hand, and beyond the household on the other—women worked with men in endeavors including education, religion, and voluntary organizations; even in acting as consumers in a market society, women explored new aspects.

Notes

1. Among the many works on women in the American Revolution, one early and critical piece remains Joan Hoff, "The Illusion of Change: Women and the American Revolution," in *The American Revolution: Explorations in the History of American Radicalism*, ed. Alfred F. Young, 385–445 (DeKalb: Northern Illinois University Press, 1976). Other important work includes Carol Berkin, *Revolutionary Mothers: Women in the Struggle for America's Independence* (New York: Knopf, 2005); Mary Beth Norton, *Founding Mothers and Fathers: Gendered Power and the Forming of American Society* (New York: Knopf, 1996); and Rosemarie Zagarri, *Revolutionary Backlash: Women and Politics in the Early American Republic* (Philadelphia: University of Pennsylvania Press, 2007).

2. Mary Lyndon Shanley, "Review: Public Values and Private Lives: Cott, Davis, and Hartog on the History of Marriage Law in the United States," *Law and Social Inquiry* 27 (Autumn 2002): 923–40; Berkin, *Revolutionary Mothers*.

3. Jan Lewis, "The Republican Wife: Virtue and Seduction in the Early Republic," *William and Mary Quarterly* 44 (October 1987): 689–721; Norma Basch, *Framing American Divorce: From the Revolutionary Generation to the Victorians* (Berkeley: University of California Press, 1999), 32.

4. The phrase "deferential domesticity" is ours, but for a related concept, see Shanley, "Review."

5. Richard H. Chused, *Private Acts in Public Places: A Social History of Divorce in the Formative Era of American Family Law* (Philadelphia: University of Pennsylvania Press, 1994); Hendrik Hartog, *Man and Wife in America: A History* (Cambridge, Mass.: Harvard University Press, 2000); Nancy F. Cott, *Public Vows: A History of Marriage and the Nation* (Cambridge, Mass.: Harvard University Press, 2000).

6. See the excerpt in this volume from Tapping Reeve, *The Law of Baron and Femme, of Parent and Child, of Guardian and Ward, of Master and Servant, and of the Powers of Courts of Chancery: With an Essay on the Terms, Heir, Heirs, and Heirs of the Body* (New Haven, Conn.: Oliver Steele, 1816); Linda K. Kerber, *No Constitutional Right to Be Ladies: Women and the Obligations of Citizenship* (New York: Hill and Wang, 1998), 11. See also Basch, *Framing American Divorce*; Joan R. Gundersen, *To Be Useful to the World: Women in Revolutionary America, 1740–1790*, rev. ed. (Chapel Hill: University of North Carolina Press, 2006), 202–3.

7. Cott, *Public Vows*.

8. Even in the twelve states that adopted terms for divorce that appeared not to differentiate between men and women, lack of access to funds made female supplicants more rare. See Cott, *Public Vows*; Joan E. Cashin, *A Family Venture: Men and Women on the Southern Frontier* (New York: Oxford University Press, 1991); and Basch, *Framing American Divorce*, 98.

9. Cott, *Public Vows*, 32. On the whole, state efforts in the 1830s and 1840s to create judicial divorce as well as safeguards for women's property bolstered notions of marriage as a contract. Yet, in his work on the origins of American family law, Michael Grossberg argues that this contractualism did not free women from subordination. Husbands and fathers consolidated their positions as the official heads of the family and managers of family property. With ownership generally dislodged from the hands of the *feme covert* in the early years of the American republic, few married women could access property, which, in the formative years, remained one key to public representation, independence, and power. In addition, the courts did not reject male authority, often agreeing with a point of view that historian Grossberg has called "judicial patriarchy." See Michael Grossberg, *Governing the Hearth: Law and the Family in Nineteenth-Century America* (Chapel Hill: University of North Carolina Press, 1985); and also Laura F. Edwards, "Law, Domestic Violence, and the Limits of Patriarchal Authority in the Antebellum South," *Journal of Southern History* 65 (November 1999): 733–70.

10. Clare A. Lyons, *Sex among the Rabble: An Intimate History of Gender and Power in the Age of Revolution, Philadelphia, 1730–1830* (Chapel Hill: University of North Carolina Press, 2006).

11. The story of William Conner and Mekinges is presented online at Timothy Crumrin, "Walking the Knife-Edged Path: The Life of William Conner," Conner Prairie Interactive History Park, http://connerprairie.org/Learn-And-Do/Indiana-History/America-1800-1860/William-Conner.aspx.

12. Ramón A. Gutiérrez, *When Jesus Came, the Corn Mothers Went Away: Marriage, Sexuality, and Power in New Mexico, 1500–1846* (Stanford, Calif.: Stanford University Press, 1991); Richard White, *The Middle Ground: Indians, Empires, and Republics in the Great Lakes Region, 1650–1815* (Cambridge: Cambridge University Press, 1991); Theda Perdue, *Cherokee Women: Gender and Culture Change, 1700–1835* (Lincoln: University of Nebraska Press, 1998); and Theda Perdue, *The Cherokee Removal: A Brief History with Documents*, 2nd ed. (Boston: Bedford/St. Martin's, 2005).

13. Cott, *Public Vows*, 33; and William F. Cheek and Aimee Lee Cheek, *John Mercer Langston and the Fight for Black Freedom, 1829–65* (Urbana: University of Illinois Press, 1989).

14. Peter D. McClelland and Richard Zeckhauser, *Demographic Dimensions of the New Republic: American Interregional Migration, Vital Statistics, and Manumissions, 1800–1860* (Cambridge: Cambridge University Press, 1982); Sally Gregory McMillen, *Southern Women: Black and White in the Old South*, 2nd ed. (Wheeling, Ill.: Harlan Davidson, 2002); Brenda E. Stevenson, *Life in Black and White: Family and Community in the Slave South* (New York: Oxford University Press, 1996).

15. Michael Tadman, *Speculators and Slaves: Masters and Traders in the Old South* (Madison: University of Wisconsin Press, 1989), Chapter 2, esp. p. 45.

16. Judith Apter Klinghoffer and Lois Elkis, "'The Petticoat Electors': Women's Suffrage in New Jersey, 1776–1807," *Journal of the Early Republic* 12 (Summer 1992): 159–93.

17. Ruth H. Bloch, "The Gendered Meanings of Virtue in Revolutionary America," *Signs* 13, no. 1 (Autumn 1987): 37–58, esp. 42; Rosemarie Zagarri, "The Rights of Man and Woman in Post-Revolutionary America," *William and Mary Quarterly* 55(April 1998): 203–30; Linda K. Kerber, *Women of the Republic: Intellect and Ideology in Revolutionary America* (Chapel Hill: University of North Carolina Press, 1980).

18. Bloch, "Gendered Meanings"; Kerber, *No Constitutional Right to Be Ladies*; see also Lewis, "The Republican Wife."

19. William J. Gilmore-Lehne, *Reading Becomes a Necessity of Life: Material and Cultural Life in Rural New England, 1780–1835* (Knoxville: University of Tennessee Press, 1989); Cathy N. Davidson, *Revolution and the Word: The Rise of the Novel in America*, expanded ed. (Oxford: Oxford University Press, 2004); Marion Rust, "What's Wrong with Charlotte Temple?" *William and Mary Quarterly* 60 (January 2003): 99–118.

20. "A New Bundling Song," *OAH Magazine of History* 18, no. 4 (July 2004): 12; Daniel Scott Smith and Michael S. Hindus, "Premarital Pregnancy in America 1640–1971: An Overview and Interpretation," *Journal of Interdisciplinary History* 5 (Spring 1975): 537–570; John D'Emilio, *Intimate Matters: A History of Sexuality in America*, 1st ed. (New York: Harper & Row, 1988).

21. Nancy F. Cott, "Passionlessness: An Interpretation of Victorian Sexual Ideology, 1790–1850," *Signs* 4 (Winter 1978): 228; Susan E. Klepp, "Revolutionary Bodies: Women and the Fertility Transition in the Mid-Atlantic Region, 1760–1820," *Journal of American History* 85 (December 1998): 910–45; Lyons, *Sex among the Rabble*, 289.

22. Jennifer L. Morgan, *Laboring Women: Reproduction and Gender in New World Slavery* (Philadelphia: University of Pennsylvania Press, 2004); Patrick Rael, *Black Identity and Black Protest in the Antebellum North* (Chapel Hill: University of North Carolina Press, 2002); Carol Lasser, "Enacting Emancipation: African American Women Abolitionists at Oberlin College and the Quest for Empowerment, Equality, and Respectability," in *Woman's Rights and Transatlantic Antislavery in the Era of Emancipation*, ed. Kathryn Kish Sklar and James Brewer Stewart (New Haven, Conn.: Yale University Press, 2007), 319–45.

23. Lyons, *Sex among the Rabble*, 280; Sharon Block and Kathleen M. Brown, "Clio in Search of Eros: Redefining Sexualities in Early America," *William and Mary Quarterly* 60 (January 2003): 5–12; Bruce Dorsey, *Reforming Men and Women: Gender in the Antebellum City* (Ithaca, N.Y.: Cornell University Press, 2002); Victoria E. Bynum, *Unruly Women: The Politics of Social and Sexual Control in the Old South* (Chapel Hill: University of North Carolina Press, 1992).

24. Michael R. Haines and Richard H. Steckel, eds., *A Population History of North America* (Cambridge: Cambridge University Press, 2000); Michael R. Haines, "Vital Statistics," in *Historical Statistics of the United States, Millennial Edition On Line*, ed. Susan B. Carter and Gavin Wright (Cambridge: Cambridge University Press, 2006); Susan Carter, Scott Gartner, Michael R. Haines, Alan Olmstead, Richard Sutch, and Gavin Wright, eds., *Historical Statistics of the United States: Millennial Edition*

(Cambridge: Cambridge University Press, 2002); McClelland and Zeckhauser, *Demographic Dimensions of the New Republic.*

25. Andrea Tone, *Devices and Desires: A History of Contraceptives in America* (New York: Hill and Wang, 2001), esp. 68–69; Janet Farrell Brodie, *Contraception and Abortion in Nineteenth-Century America* (Ithaca, N.Y.: Cornell University Press, 1994).

26. Ansley Coale, "The Decline of Fertility in Europe from the French Revolution to World War II," in *Fertility and Family Planning: A World View,* ed. S. J. Behrman and Leslie Corsa (Ann Arbor: University of Michigan Press, 1969); Helen Lefkowitz Horowitz, *Attitudes toward Sex in Antebellum America: A Brief History with Documents* (New York: Palgrave Macmillan, 2006); Daniel Scott Smith, "Family Limitation, Sexual Control, and Domestic Feminism in Victorian America," *Feminist Studies* 1 (Winter–Spring 1973): 40–57; Cott, "Passionlessness."

27. Morgan, *Laboring Women*, 4.

28. Richard H. Steckel, "A Dreadful Childhood: The Excess Mortality of American Slaves," *Social Science History* 10 (Winter 1986): 449; McClelland and Zeckhauser, *Demographic Dimensions of the New Republic*; see also Walter Johnson, *Soul by Soul: Life inside the Antebellum Slave Market* (Cambridge, Mass.: Harvard University Press, 1999).

29. James Oliver Horton and Lois E. Horton, *In Hope of Liberty: Culture, Community, and Protest among Northern Free Blacks, 1700–1860* (New York: Oxford University Press, 1997), 71 and elsewhere. See also Richard S. Newman, *The Transformation of American Abolitionism: Fighting Slavery in the Early Republic* (Chapel Hill: University of North Carolina Press, 2002).

30. Leslie M. Harris, *In the Shadow of Slavery: African Americans in New York City, 1626–1863* (Chicago: University of Chicago Press, 2003), 70–80; Steckel, "A Dreadful Childhood," 457; James Oliver Horton, "Freedom's Yoke: Gender Conventions among Antebellum Free Blacks," *Feminist Studies* 12 (Spring 1986): 51–76.

31. Horace Bushnell, "The Age of Homespun: A Discourse Delivered at Litchfield, Conn., on the Occasion of the Centennial Celebration, 1851," in *Litchfield County Centennial Celebration Held at Litchfield, Conn., 13th and 14th of August, 1851* (Hartford, Conn., 1851).

32. Gerda Lerner, "The Lady and the Mill Girl: Changes in the Status of Women in the Age of Jackson," (1969), reprinted in *The Majority Finds Its Past: Placing Women in History*, 10–34 (New York: Oxford University Press, 1979), 18.

33. Laurel Ulrich, *The Age of Homespun: Objects and Stories in the Creation of an American Myth* (New York: Knopf, 2001), 5; Laurel Ulrich, *A Midwife's Tale: The Life of Martha Ballard, Based on Her Diary, 1785–1812* (New York: Knopf, 1990).

34. Thomas Dublin, *Transforming Women's Work: New England Lives in the Industrial Revolution* (Ithaca, N.Y.: Cornell University Press, 1994).

35. Marla R. Miller, *The Needle's Eye: Women and Work in the Age of Revolution* (Amherst: University of Massachusetts Press, 2006), 197ff; Joan M. Jensen, *Loosening the Bonds: Mid-Atlantic Farm Women, 1750–1850* (New Haven, Conn.: Yale

University Press, 1986), 87; Harriet A. Jacobs, *Incidents in the Life of a Slave Girl: Written by Herself* (Cambridge, Mass.: Harvard University Press, 2000).

36. Jeanne Boydston, *Home and Work: Housework, Wages, and the Ideology of Labor in the Early Republic* (New York: Oxford University Press, 1990), 149; much of the interpretation in this volume draws on the astute analysis of Jeanne Boydston.

37. Carol Lasser and Marlene Deahl Merrill, eds., *Friends and Sisters: Letters between Lucy Stone and Antoinette Brown Blackwell, 1846–93* (Urbana: University of Illinois Press, 1987); the story by this name appears in Harriet Beecher Stowe, *House and Home Papers* (Boston: Fields, Osgood, 1865), 125ff.

38. Deborah G. White, *Ar'n't I a Woman? Female Slaves in the Plantation South,* 1st ed. (New York: Norton, 1985); McMillen, *Southern Women;* Angela Y. Davis, "Reflections on the Black Woman's Role in the Community of Slaves," *Black Scholar* 12 (1981): 2–15.

39. Carol Lasser, "The Domestic Balance of Power: Relations between Mistress and Maid in Nineteenth-Century New England," *Labor History* 28 (1987): 5; Faye E. Dudden, *Serving Women: Household Service in Nineteenth-Century America* (Middletown, Conn.: Wesleyan University Press, 1983); Catharine Esther Beecher, *The American Woman's Home: Or, Principles of Domestic Science; Being a Guide to the Formation and Maintenance of Economical, Healthful, Beautiful, and Christian Homes* (New York: J. B. Ford, 1869).

40. Erica Armstrong Dunbar, *A Fragile Freedom: African American Women and Emancipation in the Antebellum City* (New Haven, Conn.: Yale University Press, 2008); Harris, *In the Shadow of Slavery.*

41. Teresa L. Amott and Julie A. Matthaei, *Race, Gender, and Work: A Multicultural Economic History of Women in the United States* (Boston: South End Press, 1991); Alice Kessler-Harris, *Out to Work: A History of Wage-Earning Women in the United States* (New York: Oxford University Press, 1982); Christine Stansell, *City of Women: Sex and Class in New York, 1789–1860* (New York: Knopf, 1986).

42. Wendy Gamber, *The Female Economy: The Millinery and Dressmaking Trades, 1860–1930* (Urbana: University of Illinois Press, 1997).

43. Mary Kelley, *Learning to Stand and Speak: Women, Education, and Public Life in America's Republic* (Chapel Hill: University of North Carolina Press, 2006); Jo Anne Preston, "Domestic Ideology, School Reformers, and Female Teachers: School Teaching Becomes Women's Work in Nineteenth-Century New England," *New England Quarterly* 66 (December 1993): 531–51; Barbara Miller Solomon, *In the Company of Educated Women: A History of Women and Higher Education in America* (New Haven, Conn.: Yale University Press, 1985).

44. Thomas Dublin, *Women at Work: The Transformation of Work and Community in Lowell, Massachusetts, 1826–1860* (New York: Columbia University Press, 1979); see also his *Farm to Factory: Women's Letters, 1830–1860* (New York: Columbia University Press, 1981). See also Claudia Goldin, "The Economic Status of Women in the Early Republic: Quantitative Evidence," *Journal of Interdisciplinary History* 16 (Winter 1986): 375–404; and Claudia Goldin and Kenneth Sokoloff, "Women,

Children, and Industrialization in the Early Republic: Evidence from the Manufacturing Censuses," *Journal of Economic History* 42 (December 1982): 741–74.

45. Alexis de Tocqueville, *Democracy in America* (New York: Modern Library, 1981), 485.

46. Tocqueville, *Democracy in America*, 489.

Phase 2: Companionate Co-laborers

In the wake of the "Revolutionary Backlash," women in the early republic attended to their households and families, working with deference toward their male relatives to meet domestic needs. Yet, over the first three decades of the nineteenth century, these "deferential domestics" moved toward engagement with a rich network of women's voluntary organizations. What influenced the shift of women that brought them into more public positions? In what particular areas, and in what particular ways, did women begin to emerge as more public actors? And how did this engagement of women in reform organizations alter gender relations, society, and politics in the antebellum years? Further, how did the "positionality" of women—the intersections of race, class, gender, location, and age—shape their activities? And, finally, how and why did some women follow their increasingly politicized reform activities into a demand for full public participation as co-equals of men?

Women from different places, classes, and races understood their domestic duties to include engagement in a wider world where they often labored beside their male counterparts in emergent social movements. Significant numbers of men and women participated in voluntary, benevolent, and charitable organizations, sometimes seeking to mobilize support from the federal and state governments in matters they believed critical to the civic morality and religious health of the nation. Many women brought to this work the education that became increasingly accessible to them. Such learning provided skills that helped women use their gendered identities as virtuous and modest females to establish their civic presence. They turned especially to activities with moral and maternal connotations, including the moral and economic relief of the poor and the regulation of alcoholic beverage in order to enhance home life. They also viewed Indian removal and the problem of slavery as issues of benevolence and sin. With experience from these interventions and the organizations they generated, some northern women began to contemplate not only companionate co-work in reform but also co-equality that suggested their standing in the civil society and in the political process.

Education and Intellectual Empowerment

In 1825, the short-lived *Boston Monthly Magazine* published an article entitled "The Natural Rights of Women." Said to be written by a woman in the Boston area, the ten-page essay celebrated female progress:

> Ladies are no longer afraid, nor ashamed to be acquainted with history, with geography, with natural history, or with whatever has a tendency to enlarge their views, strengthen their understanding, improve their taste, or amend their heart. The sickening sensibility of romance, has given place to the genuine feelings of sympathy for real distress; and the idle, vain and showy accomplishments of the late boarding schools are, we believe, giving place to the solid and useful departments of practical knowledge.[1]

Education played a critical role for antebellum American women who sought to enhance their participation in public life by building upon, rather than renouncing, their domestic expertise. Just as household responsibilities often included remunerative work so, too, did home duties for women encompass training the young. Even as they deferred to male authority within their families, they assumed the task of educating daughters and sons as Christians and as citizens in the emergent public culture of the early republic. Leveraged by their veneration as mothers, they taught their own and other children. Moreover, Euro-American women in the North were increasingly well prepared to take on the mission; they joined with men to enjoy the revolutions in print and literacy. Free women of color also participated in the emergent associational opportunities, often seeking through them the respectability frequently denied to them because of their race. In the South, where white women's formal education lagged behind men, seminaries nonetheless offered some opportunity for a select female population to enter into public work. Western women built upon the traditions they brought with them, with publicly financed schooling following populations into regions claimed by Yankees and New Englanders, and lagging in the new southern states. All in all, however, the proliferation of women's educational opportunities provided the knowledge that allowed women to work for what they viewed as improvements that would benefit both home and nation.

Historian Mary Kelley has argued that, in the early republic, schooling helped women to redefine "themselves and their relationship to civil society." This development built upon the achievements of an earlier generation when, as the scholar Linda Kerber has written, the rationale for female schooling lay in the importance of women's roles as mothers to sons who required training to maintain the virtue of the new republic. Kerber posited the concept of "Republican Motherhood." In the wake of American independence, the nation needed knowledgeable women to transmit to future male citizens the wisdom and judgment they would be required to exercise to maintain a virtuous country; republican mothers served the state by raising sons who served it. Both Kerber and Kelley drew evidence from the writings of Philadelphia physician, philanthropist, and educator Benjamin Rush who urged early and thorough training so that women could take on responsibility for "instructing their sons in the principles of liberty and government." Rush maintained that American women should be taught to read, speak, and spell in English, and to write in "a fair and legible hand." Rush believed that young ladies might be schooled in the genteel pursuits of vocal music and dancing. But, explaining that the emergent nation distinguished itself as a country with early marriages, instability in property, and many business and professional ventures that took men from home, he also endorsed more vocationally oriented instruction in "geography and . . . chronology," as well as "figures and book-keeping."[2]

Rush joined others in stressing that women's education must encompass basic and useful skills in contrast to limiting them to ornamental polish. In the early years of the republic, female academies prepared wealthy and privileged daughters of the elite to preside over the domestic arrangements by developing their "accomplishments;" a few, however, also provided solid foundations in liberal learning. Among the best examples was Sarah Pierce's Litchfield Seminary, founded in 1791, to provide thorough academic education as well as decorative refinement for young women from wealthy families. Strategically located, the school often helped its students meet and marry young men completing their educations at Tapping Reeve's prestigious law school in the same town.

Beyond the few select institutions, a broader "revolution in literacy" reached even farmers' daughters in the early nineteenth century, spreading both the written word and aspirations for a new womanhood among female Americans. New England led the way. According to historian William Gilmore, all but the poorest of the region's inhabitants were functionally literate at an elementary level by the early years of the nineteenth century. An analysis of samples of the 1850 census, the first national poll that included relevant questions, suggests that 96 percent of the first generation of women born in the Northeast after the American Revolution achieved literacy.

While white, southern women's attainment lagged, estimates nonetheless peg their literacy level at nearly 80 percent at midcentury.[3]

Legal prohibitions barred enslaved women from learning to read and write in most parts of the South, with enforcement strengthened after Nat Turner's uprising in 1830, so the absence of such skills among people of color is hardly surprising. Adult literacy levels in the southern African American population (free and unfree) stood at less than 10 percent on the eve of the Civil War. A notable exception, Harriet Jacobs learned from her sympathetic mistress to read and write elegantly despite her slave status (see document 19). Free women of color in the South faced increasingly restricted opportunities for education as the antebellum period progressed. North Carolina, which had once been among the more liberal southern states, passed a law in 1835 that prohibited the public instruction of black children of either sex. Other states, like Mississippi, "solved" the problem of literate, free people of color by insisting that no free black person be permitted to reside within its boundaries.[4]

Literacy among northern, free women of color was undoubtedly greater than among their southern counterparts, but persistent racial poverty and school segregation even in postemancipation states nonetheless challenged their ability to pursue education. Sojourner Truth, the visionary African American activist who inspired antislavery and woman's rights activists, never learned to read despite spending her entire life in the North. Maria Stewart, the Connecticut-born, Boston-based activist spoke out on the advantages of education for both boys and girls, urging her free, black community:

> Let our money . . . be appropriated for schools and seminaries of learning for our children and youth. We ought to follow the example of the whites in this respect. Nothing would raise our respectability, add to our peace and happiness, and reflect so much honor upon us, as to be ourselves the promoters of temperance, and the supporters, as far as we are able, of useful and scientific knowledge. The rays of light and knowledge have been hid from our view. . . . Had we as a people received, one half the early advantages the whites have received, I would defy the government of these United States to deprive us any longer of our rights.[5]

Yet, schooling for African American girls remained rare. New England Quaker Prudence Crandall caused controversy when, in 1832, she welcomed into her female seminary in Canterbury, Connecticut, an African American farmer's daughter who wanted to train as a teacher. White citizens of the town withdrew their daughters in protest. In response, Crandall decided to

"Young Lady Graduates," Oberlin College 1855. (Source: Oberlin College Archives)

focus on instructing young women of color who sought to become educators. Her school closed only when a white mob attacked it.[6]

About the same time, the Oberlin Collegiate Institute in Ohio began to educate white men and white women together. In 1835, two years after its founding, Oberlin began to admit students of color of both sexes. Its first female student of color, Sarah Watson, arrived in 1842, and in 1862, Mary Jane Patterson became the first African American woman to receive a bachelor's degree. Those pioneering, black female students who attended before the Civil War overwhelmingly became teachers in black schools, frequently expressing their commitment to the elevation of their race; they were clearly extraordinary in their level of achievement. Their task was daunting since, according to some estimates, as late as 1900, barely a majority of the adult black population was literate, with women disproportionately represented among those who had not achieved the ability to read and write.[7]

Northern black women and southern white women benefited from the momentum generated in the Northeast, where female schooling became widely valued, promoting the literacy that, in turn, paved the vocational path to teaching. Originally, women's instructional work focused on early learning. In Massachusetts, publicly funded summer schools emerged from traditional "dame schools," where younger children of both sexes had attained the fundamentals of literacy. Older children whose labor could not be spared during the agricultural season attended winter schools, most frequently taught by men in the early years of the century but increasingly feminized in the antebellum period.[8]

In New England, as elsewhere, the turn to female teachers drew on both ideology and economy. While women were cheaper to hire, cultural orientations toward the desirability of female instruction played a special role. What Sarah Robbins has called "the domestic literacy narrative" envisioned nurturing, antebellum mothers who would best provide basic instruction to their own children as part of their maternal duties. Yet, this narrative also supported an "extradomestic dimension" that translated into the respectable employment of female teachers in the expanding United States and its territories on the North American continent—and even abroad. By 1860, three out of four teachers in the Northeast were female, while in the Old Northwest, nearly two out of every three teachers was female; even in the South, one out of three teachers was a woman, many of them trained in the rigorous schools developing in New England. New England teachers could also be found in Africa and in Asia, promoting versions of Republican Motherhood along with Christianity in what might be seen as a vast empire of American outreach.[9] Women teachers in the antebellum common schools thus widely disseminated the culture of the emergent American middle class with its gender forms while teaching literacy.

Female educators and their allies also supported the development of advanced educational opportunities for women. When educational pioneer Joseph Emerson opened his Byfield Academy in Massachusetts in 1818, he created an institution that profoundly influenced the ways in which women teachers would be prepared for many generations. Among his early students were farmer's daughters Zilpha Grant and Mary Lyon, who together founded the Ipswich Female Seminary in 1828, which Lyon subsequently left to open Mount Holyoke Female Seminary in 1836 (see document 16). Lyon's school expected its students to contribute their labor to household maintenance, thus keeping it affordable to women of modest means—and reinforcing the connection between women's accomplishments and their domestic roles. Another architect of the New England academy model, Emma Hart Willard, opened her first school, the Middlebury Female Academy, in 1814, followed by a school in Waterford, New York, founded in 1819. When the second school failed, citizens of Troy, New York, seeing an opportunity to enhance the education of their young women and the status of their emergent industrial city, specifically wooed Willard to their city with a promise of land and buildings. Her widowed sister Almira Hart Lincoln soon joined her there to help the Troy Female Seminary establish a reputation for excellence. When Lincoln married John Phelps in 1831, she moved with him to

Catharine Beecher, 1848. Sister to Harriet Beecher Stowe, Catharine earned her fame as an advocate for women's education. She did not support the public participation of women in the debate over slavery and engaged in a famous exchange over this issue with Sarah Grimke in the late 1830s. (Source: Schlesinger Library, Harvard)

Maryland where she opened her own female seminary, spreading the model further south.[10]

A second transformative impetus centered on Catharine Beecher. The daughter of one of New England's most important ministers, Beecher briefly attended Miss Pierce's school in Connecticut before beginning a career in teaching that led her to found the Hartford Female Seminary in 1823, where her younger sister Harriet—later the author of *Uncle Tom's Cabin*—received her education. The Beecher sisters followed their father to Cincinnati where, in 1832, Catharine established the Western Female Institute. The elder Beecher sister subsequently became associated with the Board of National Popular Education in Cleveland and the American Woman's Educational Association, organizations that helped to bring hundreds of female school-teachers from New England to the American "West"—the lands beyond the Appalachian Mountains.[11]

Women's education thus spread from New England throughout the antebellum United States with the migration of educators and the proliferation of women's academies. Single-sex institutions predominated at the advanced level, allowing women the opportunity to develop their own abilities to read and write, "stand and speak," and reason and argue. Yet, at the same time, the coeducational model established in the lower, common schools of New England provided a precedent for educating men and women together. Mixed-sex schools flourished in less populated regions where fledgling communities embraced the economy of funding a single institution, even at the upper levels of the curriculum. Among the first was the Oberlin Collegiate Institute; although, from the first, men training for the ministry sat in its classes with women preparing to teach, not until 1837 did the school officially grant women permission to pursue the BA degree. Before the Civil War, the University of Iowa was the only public institution to enroll women and men together. More commonly, coeducation characterized small, often denominational, colleges in the Midwest, including Olivet in Michigan, Knox in Illinois, and Antioch and the historically black college Wilberforce in Ohio. Working together, and studying together, men and women at these emergent centers of learning developed new relationships to each other, as companionate co-laborers serving together in the developments of their churches and communities.[12]

From Evangelical and Cultural Awakenings to Organized Benevolence

Church support for women's literacy, for their education at the collegiate level, and often for denominational coeducation formalized the long-standing connection between religion and women's empowerment. The spiritual momentum that swept through the young republic in the first decades of the nineteenth century spread from the evangelical revival that began in 1801 in Cane Ridge, in the Kentucky backcountry. Igniting a new religious enthusiasm, the revival spread to the east and south, drawing converts and concern among a vast cross-section of Americans. Fundamentally democratic in orientation, the Second Great Awakening as it came to be called in the 1830s and 1840s (the first Great Awakening having occurred before the American Revolution) preached a message of personal salvation; individuals could and should, through their own effort, establish a relationship directly with God, through which they could secure their grace. Women and men examined their responsibilities for their own sins, embraced their churches and their religious communities, and then reached out to help in the conversion of others. This revitalized Christianity sacralized the virtue that the civic republic explained in secular terms; in the process, it placed women at the center of the religious experience. Women were deemed especially religious, thus mothers were particularly suited to teach children the ways of righteousness. While "naturally" inclined to sympathy and sensitivity, women needed education in order to better comprehend their religious duties and more effectively minister appropriately to the young, weak, and needy. Training for their moral mission, middle-class women sought out Sabbath schools as well as higher learning.

The evangelical movement of the early nineteenth century stimulated a rapid growth in church membership. Methodists and Baptists, in particular, gained new adherents, appealing particularly to hardworking rural people and urban laborers; their religious messages stressed the availability of salvation to all, even the unlettered, and presented the gospel as a fundamentally egalitarian opportunity. Without requiring their clergy to display academic credentials—or even literacy—these denominations occasionally supported female preachers, sometimes even women of color who felt called to ministry. After joining the Baptists in Cranston, Rhode Island, in 1820, Elleanor Knight claimed a dream sent to her by God led her to become his prophetic instrument; Jarena Lee was recognized by the African Methodists for her call to the pulpit.[13] Congregationalists were more hesitant to overthrow all aspects of the standing order that, in some parts of New England, continued to privilege their denomination as the official church until disestablishment concluded in 1833. Congregationalists nonetheless joined with Presbyterians to spread a liberalized theology into the Old Northwest, and with it came some empowerment for women—although within limits. Not until 1853 was a woman, Antoinette Brown, ordained as a Congregational or Presbyterian minister. Yet, whether formally empowered to the ministry or as participants more broadly in a culture that valued religion and specified for women critical roles in ministering their families, the Second Great Awakening provided new opportunities for women.

This enhanced female standing in the religious culture, combined with growing women's literacy, opened the world of print to specialized publications—books, magazines, and periodicals—for women, as well as pamphlets and periodicals printed for a "family" audience. Print products specifically for a female audience announced their intentions with names like *Godey's Lady's Book*, the *Magnolia*, the *Casket*, or the *Ladies Miscellany*. In addition, newspapers wrote about and for women, and female writers published books and articles. Publications from the *Ohio Cultivator* to the *Liberator* included specific women's columns. Such newspapers and family magazines graced the domestic tables of the genteel household, the country cottage, and the frontier home.

With the proliferation of print, women—like men—formed literary societies, and at the same time, women joined men at lyceums and lectures.

In Concord, the lyceum founded in the 1830s sold tickets to individuals as well as families; young women enjoyed the social outing that came with the cultural participation.[14] In Oberlin, the Collegiate Institute sponsored both men's and women's literary societies for its students. In South Carolina, the females who formed the Sigourney Club read widely and presented essays on topics including the study of nature, Socrates, and the sciences. In Lowell, Massachusetts, "mill girls" formed a society to discuss literature and publish their own writings. Moreover, such organizations often promoted more than simple reading. As Erica Armstrong Dunbar has recounted, "Literary societies were among the first sociopolitical organizations formed by and for African American women." According to Martha S. Jones, literary societies, lyceums, and print all supported a "public culture" in which African American women began to explore political issues, often as part of gatherings that included men and women together as co-workers in struggle. Literacy thus encouraged women to join with men in their engagement in a larger world of reform and religion.[15]

Empowered by education and an evangelical awakening, many women in the 1820s and 1830s began to participate in a variety of reform organizations that drew them into the public in complicated new ways. Their experience in organizing, recruiting, fund raising, petitioning, and challenging male authority led to an expansion of women's self-representation in public. Women began to claim the right to participate in civic conversations as concerned citizens and morally driven Christians. They responded to their critics by highlighting a multilayered public status—as human beings, Americans, mothers, and women. They thoughtfully articulated a sense of responsibility toward the larger civic community that moved well beyond family, friends, and neighborhood. In other words, they began to see themselves as women and reformers, mothers and activists, and Christians and citizens. These roles did not, for them, seem separate, or bounded by a "sphere." In joining reform groups they acted on this new sense of civic accountability, and they represented themselves in increasingly multifaceted public ways. They saw their work as part of a larger public effort and themselves as companionate co-laborers.

Initially, much of women's reform activism was linked to the notion of Christian "uplift"—virtuous, middle-class white women were motivated to help other less fortunate women. With the rise of an increasingly complicated market economy and new urban centers, poverty became more visible and widespread. Women, fortified with a energetic evangelical dedication to making the world a more perfect place, determined that they could play a role in easing the burdens of poor widows, orphans, abandoned wives, and ailing elderly. In this "uplifting" process benevolent women also imposed a degree of social control on those they sought to aid, hoping and expecting that those who benefited from their generosity—newly employed widows and school-going orphans—would embrace the values and cultural norms of the middle-class North.[16]

While benevolent women sought to "share" their world order with the needy, others began to expand beyond charitable concerns. By the 1830s women joined reform groups focused on aiding Indians, slaves, and fugitives. In the process of advocating for the rights of the disempowered, white women sometimes glimpsed the limitations in their own lives. Denounced for violating the sacred "woman's sphere," they wondered how they could achieve their goals without renouncing their claims to womanhood. Black women provided a source of inspiration—their unyielding resistance to slavery and racism offered white women role models and pragmatic partners. They learned simply to "do" and "act" without concern for boundaries, spheres, or prescribed roles.[17]

As women joined benevolent and reform organizations and developed knowledge, skills, and confidence, they also looked to men for support, guidance, and collaboration. Men and women worked in separate as well as mixed-sex groups. Even when they held separate meetings they tended to coordinate, negotiate, and organize in conjunction with each other. Reform and benevolent organizations offered men an opportunity to act on the same evangelical impulses that drove women and embrace the same notions of morality that were increasingly linked to womanhood. Women, for their part, honed public skills in areas closely linked to men—finance, policy making, and partisanship. The civic world became increasingly relevant and important to these women as they built a wider foundation for their activism.

Relying on popular assumptions about women's moral superiority and innate virtue, reform-oriented women quietly gained skills and knowledge to become astute players in city politics and community development. As historian Lori D. Ginzberg explains, "Virtually all women who employed the language of moral change—those active in charity work, moral reform, temperance, and abolition—moved casually into organizing for legislative action." Decades before women began flooding the U.S. capitol with antislavery petitions—and with much less controversy—benevolent women paved the way. Using the comfortable notion of family life as their model, women eased into civil society. Mother-daughter team Isabella Marshall Graham and Joanna Graham Bethune founded the New York Society for the Relief of Poor Widows with Small Children in 1797. Their activism became a family endeavor and a part of their daily routine. It was as if their domestic circle simply grew to include the problems and challenges of a larger group of women and children. As Anne Boylan shows, women's organized activities "were neither fully private nor fully public, neither wholly integrated with nor fully separate from their domestic lives." This growing "family" required women like Joanna Bethune to interact with civil society in new ways. She negotiated with the state legislature to expand the grounds of her Orphan Asylum Society in 1806. A few years later, her mother circulated a petition addressed to the mayor of New York City requesting financial assistance for her Society for the Promotion of Industry among the Poor. With little fanfare these women strolled into the world of politics to confer, collaborate, and bargain.[18]

African American women also entered the world of benevolence during the early decades of the nineteenth century. Like Euro-American women, they coordinated their benevolent work with and through churches. Ministers encouraged this charity work, and women activists were emboldened by the sisterly connections they developed in their congregations. Black women organized groups focused on aiding the disempowered in their community— including widows, orphans, and the indigent. Similar to their white sisters, they imposed notions of respectability and femininity on those they hoped to "uplift." As Dunbar argues, "African American women formed their own mutual aid societies and associations not only to assist the community, but also to chaperone it." The women who ran the Philadelphia-based Daughters of Africa, for example, provided critical aid to the sick and indigent even as they made sure to exclude those members of their community who drank too much, fought, or committed adultery. Charitable women in the African American community tended to combine paid labor with their benevolent work, and they also included a focus on fugitives. This meant that their activism was more grounded in the chronic and persistent challenges confronting blacks daily in a deeply racist and often dangerous society. Henrietta Green Regulus Ray was a freeborn woman who attended the New York Abyssinian Baptist Church in the 1820s. She became active in a variety of African American women's organizations, including the African Dorcas Association, a mutual aid and sewing society that provided clothes to the children attending free African schools (see document 12). Ray was also involved with the New York Female Literary Society, which raised funds for runaway slaves. Her benevolent work allowed her to acknowledge and promote notions of proper female behavior even as it brought her into legal debates, economic challenges, and politics. Combining common assumptions about female virtue with a pragmatic recognition of the needs of their disempowered community, black women negotiated both racial and gender politics to make real improvements for their families, friends, and larger community.[19]

Engaging in charitable work, black and white women entered the world of politics with a deferential attitude. Girls and women learned deference in their youth through their parents, teachers, neighbors, and relatives. They understood that they had a prescribed role in the world. They also learned that despite these prescriptions their increasingly "disordered" communities demanded that they step beyond their homes—even if only to ensure that other women had homes. Deference was a useful tool that allowed women to acknowledge their subordinate status even as they made requests that brought them into political debates and financial transactions. They reminded public authorities that their efforts were designed to benefit others, not themselves, and that they were grateful and humbled by the attention and aid of policy makers. Often addressing their petitions and requests to "the respected guardians and rulers of our city," these women purported to seek not power but influence. As Anne Boylan contends, "Deferential politics wrapped its practitioners—and, by extension, their organization—in the mantle of domesticity, their voluntarism encircled within the bounds of 'woman's sphere.'" These deferential relationships that benevolent women developed with powerful men in their communities were heavily reliant on personal connections developed through socioeconomic ties. This meant that women outside of elite circles had much less access to policy makers and power brokers. African American activists, for example, often had to find other avenues to pushing forward their agendas.[20]

The Rise of Women Reformers

By the 1830s, an increasing number of women became involved with organizations outside their homes. Many still joined local charity groups, but others embraced the emergent reform-oriented causes including temperance, colonization, Indian removal, and antislavery. Although reform women still claimed to be driven by a selfless desire to help the less fortunate, these newer causes proved more controversial. While everyone might agree that orphans deserved shelter and support, the same was not true in relation to the evil of drink, the sin of slavery, or the immorality of Indian removal. People disagreed about such issues. Female temperance advocates and abolitionists challenged male authority more directly—whether as husbands or politicians—and resistance to women's impact on public policy and civil society grew.

Men dominated the antebellum temperance movement. Although ministers and other male temperance leaders encouraged women's support, it was in a carefully constructed and subordinate role. Even when women created separate auxiliaries, as with the Daughters of Temperance, they were not allowed to participate in national temperance conventions, hold office, or vote. At the 1853 World's Temperance Convention in New York the all-male Credentials Committee refused to seat female delegates. Nonetheless, African American and white women supported temperance with exuberance, arguing that drunkenness led to family disorder, poverty, gambling, and illness. As with benevolent groups, temperance women emphasized the moral issues at stake. Drinking caused otherwise dependable men to act irresponsibly. Morally superior women needed to step in and clean up the mess—the failures of men required women to work in civic spaces and negotiate public policy. In Elizabethtown, New Jersey, five hundred women signed a petition in 1834 requesting that their local representatives limit the spread of liquor shops in their communities. A few years later, more than a thousand women signed a petition to the state legislature of Maine requesting legal help in supporting temperance. In Cincinnati the Daughters of Temperance organized an employment bureau to aid abandoned wives in finding work. This activity placed women in the center of their community. They negotiated for their clients and collaborated in public spaces for the financial benefit of their martyred sisters. While some southerners joined the movement, it was primarily a northern phenomenon.[21]

By the 1850s, some temperance women moved from careful negotiations with local leaders over issues of public policy to violent demonstrations. "Respectable" women in various communities took to the streets in a public expression of their frustration and carried out acts of civil disobedience. They used axes and hatchets to attack saloons and destroy private property. Abraham Lincoln defended a group of nine women in Marion, Illinois, comparing their actions to the Boston Tea Party. Men and women interpreted the actions of these female vigilantes as virtuously motivated and patriotic. They were defending their families, communities, and even their nation. Empowered women reformers took their moral concerns into civil society.[22]

As some reformers focused on the evil of drink, others turned to the injustice of Indian removal. When President Andrew Jackson's 1830 Removal Bill mandated that Georgia's Cherokee population move off increasingly valuable land, many considered this a violation of basic rights and Christian responsibility. Catharine Beecher, then director of the Hartford Female Seminary, catalyzed the first national, female petition campaign by circulating an anti-removal petition to benevolent groups across the nation. When she presented the printer with the original petition and asked him to create copies for distribution, she made him promise to keep her identity a secret because she feared possible retribution. Women reformers understood that their political activism might engender opposition, so they worked diligently to construct their activism as an expression of Christian morality and there-fore a proper extension of womanhood.

An anti-removal petition presented by a group of Ohio women focused on defending their decision to engage in political activity:

> Your memorialists would sincerely deprecate any presumptuous interference on the part of their own sex, with the ordinary political affairs of the country, as wholly unbecoming the character of American Females. Even in private life we may not presume to direct the general conduct, or control the acts of those who stand in the near and guardian relations of husbands and brothers, yet all admit that there are times when duty and affection call on us to advise and persuade, as well as to cheer or to console.[23]

These efforts to construct their activism as Christian, moral, and supplicating proved successful. As historian Alisse Portnoy points out, only one politician spoke out against the petitions. Women anti-removalists found themselves supported by their husbands, brothers, fathers, and communities. This sup-port was a reaction to the gentle manner of the petitions but also, as Portnoy reveals, a response to the positive depiction of Native Americans in popular culture. Unlike African Americans who were commonly constructed as passive and inhuman, authors and journalists described Native Americans as complex, thoughtful people with skills and intelligence. This primed the American public to be sympathetic to their plight. Women took advantage, continuing their quiet expansion of skills, knowledge, and political savvy.[24]

While northern women edged toward political action in Indian removal, southern women also became increasingly active in civic society through their efforts in the American Colonization Society (ACS). Founded in 1816, the ACS sought to encourage voluntary emancipation and emigration of slaves. From its inception, women supported the ACS with the hearty ap-proval of its male leaders. Henry Clay, Whig presidential candidate in 1844 and an ACS vice president, proclaimed that colonization was "countenanced and aided by that fair sex, which is ever prompt to contribute its exertions in works of charity and benevolence, because it always acts from the gener-ous impulses of pure and uncorrupted hearts." Female support for the ACS increased throughout the 1820s and 1830s, particularly in Virginia. Women donated their own money, bequeathed large legacies, and even manumitted and colonized their own slaves. Margaret Mercer, the daughter of Maryland governor John Francis Mercer and an enthusiastic supporter of colonization, practiced what she preached. She manumitted her sixteen slaves and sent them to Liberia. Southern women, like their counterparts in the temperance movement, formed female auxiliaries to the ACS and adopted some of the same methods for raising money including hosting fairs. Mary Blackford formed the Fredericksburg and Falmouth (Virginia) Female Auxiliary to the ACS that raised over five hundred dollars in a short period of time. Blackford claimed that the work of her auxiliary occurred "in the domestic circle, around our own or the firesides of our neighbors, without the sacrifice of time or the proprieties of our sex."[25]

Female colonizationists used the same rationale for their public activism as did northern reformers. They emphasized the religious nature of their concern, and they proclaimed that their efforts were moral not political. As historian Elizabeth Varon explains, "For Virginia's most prominent female colonizationists, the conviction that Africa should be Christianized went hand in hand with the conviction that the institution of slavery was sinful and should, on moral grounds, be gradually dismantled." By emphasizing the religious benefit of colonization both in the United States and in Liberia, southern women hoped to prove that their activity remained purely "female" and, although "public," outside the realm of male-dominated politics.[26]

Following the 1831 Nat Turner rebellion in Virginia that resulted in the deaths of sixty whites, the political climate in the South changed. Women colonizationists veered much more directly into politics and with fewer apologies. Virginia women submitted several petitions to the state legislature calling for emancipation in order to avoid such violent revolts in the future. These women asserted it was their patriotic duty to protect their families from the potential danger of the slave population. They further claimed that civic society was simply a grander version of domestic life. "What is a nation but a family upon a large scale?" As Elizabeth Varon asserts, "Rather than advancing the notion that woman's sphere operated according to rules and values all its own, the women [petitioners] portrayed the domestic sphere as a microcosm of the public one." Women did not simply leave their petitions in the hands of male politicians and walk away. Many attended the renowned debates in the state legislature about the future of slavery in Virginia. Although the House declined to emancipate Virginia slaves, women continued to participate in political debates about slavery through the Civil War.[27]

Women and men worked together to take American antislavery in a radical direction after 1830. The emergence of immediate emancipation as an alternative to colonization galvanized evangelicals to recognize and renounce the sin of slavery. Americans of faith joined with Quakers who had pioneered the renunciation of both the slave trade and the enslavement of Africans. From the founding of the American Anti-Slavery Society in 1833, women and men worked together to forge an outspoken critique of the legality of race-based American hereditary servitude. [28]

During the 1830s, hundreds of female antislavery societies emerged across the North. These groups organized monthly prayer meetings, wrote and published antislavery pamphlets, raised funds, hosted sewing groups (document 17), and engaged in a whole spate of increasingly public activities. Women's abolitionist sewing societies, for example, served as locations for political education. As participants plied their needles they also read antislavery newspapers out loud, conversed about the latest political developments in Congress, and planned antislavery activities. One such activity was the annual antislavery fair. These well-attended events involved selling a variety of donated goods, from elegant European imports to locally made cheese, over the course of two or three days, usually around the Christmas holiday. Fairs allowed women to raise funds, educate the public, and socialize, all within a gorgeous, inviting setting. At the same time, as historian Deborah B. Van Broekhoven shows, abolitionist fairs "propelled female participants into a public activity outside the family, church, and neighborhood. Selling their goods in the market brought female workers, however motivated by charity, into the same physical space in which men worked."[29]

Women's participation in the antislavery petitioning campaign put them even more squarely into a public space. Petitioning was one of the few political avenues open to women in the antebellum period. They could not vote or hold office, but they could write, sign, and submit a petition to any legislative body.[30] Although their sister reformers in benevolent and charitable causes had also petitioned legislative bodies, abolitionist women experienced much more resistance. Even though antislavery petitions were often framed in respectful and obsequious language, the nature of their requests combined with the sheer number of petitions they sent to Congress raised hackles all around. The "Fathers and Rulers" petition, as revealed in document 14, politely asked congressmen to abolish slavery in the District of Columbia. Female antislavery societies across the North, from Rhode Island to Illinois, printed, copied, and circulated this petition with a zeal that shocked the nation. So successful was this campaign that it helped to catalyze the first national meeting of women abolitionists in 1837. Modest and self-effacing, the "Fathers and Rulers" petition offered a "humble memorial" to the "honorable body" that represented the "guardians of a Christian people."[31] Coating its demand in religion and morality, the petition on one level embraced women's domesticity. Yet, making demands on politicians and presuming political knowledge, it also clearly articulated a public concern. Frustrated politicians responded to this vast mound of unwanted antislavery petitions by passing the infamous "gag rule" in 1837, automatically tabling all such petitions without even reading them.[32]

Although women abolitionists grounded their petition in female virtue, they understood that they would be criticized for violating feminine custom. In presenting their petition to the larger community for circulation, they forthrightly argued that it was woman's "right, privilege and duty to petition Congress to abolish slavery in the District of Columbia." One determined petitioner warned her sister activists that they would experience opposition because of their sex, but this should not affect their passion. "The sphere of female action has been so narrowed down, as to cause us sometimes to inquire, if the shadows of the dark ages are returning to dim our hemisphere, and shut out the faint glimmerings of millennial glory?" Abolitionists, she averred, should not be "bantered from the field because we are women." She concluded, "God holds us accountable for all the talents which he has committed to our keeping."[33]

Petitioning did in fact bring women into political action. Although motivated by moral outrage at slavery, this antislavery method required political knowledge and oratory skills.[34] Women had to explain to their neighbors, friends, and relatives that Congress had authority over slavery in the District of Columbia and the territories and that their petitions sought to encourage Congress to use this authority to end slavery in these areas. They also had to respond to fears that such petitions would lead to conflict with the South or encourage a slave uprising. Certainly, women had political knowledge prior to petitioning. But reading a newspaper article about slavery was quite different from engaging in a heated political discussion with a neighbor about the constitutionality of slavery. Petitioning placed women in the middle of a nationwide political debate. It made them active participants in a civic contest over the most important political issue of the antebellum period.

Though petitioning brought women directly into politics, the most controversial activity of female abolitionists proved to be public lecturing. By the late 1830s, a few women abolitionists entered the lecturing field and encountered vehement opposition. When Sarah and Angelina Grimké began speaking to small audiences of women about the atrocities of slavery they knew of what they spoke. The South Carolina sisters grew up on a plantation as the daughters of slave owners. Their intimate knowledge of southern slavery and their skilled oratorical style drew increasingly large audiences.

Eventually, men began attending their presentations. These "promiscu-ous" mixed-sex audiences engendered widespread opposition. A group of Presbyterian ministers published a pastoral letter (document 15) censuring the Grimkés for "adopting the place and tone of a public reformer." The sisters brought "shame and dishonor" to womanhood. Ironically, Catharine Beecher concurred and engaged in a public exchange of letters with the Grimkés over the appropriate role of women in public; despite her earlier role as anonymous author of the petition for Cherokee Indian removal, she now sought to restrain woman's entry into the antislavery controversy. Not only did the sisters insist on continuing their activism, but also Sarah penned the first pamphlet in support of woman's rights in the United States, *Letters on the Equality of Sexes*.[35]

While the Grimkés defended their right to participate equally in the antislavery movement, Abby Kelley, a young Quaker from Massachusetts, followed in their footsteps and became an antislavery lecturer. Her first pub-lic speech occurred at the second National Female Anti-Slavery Meeting in Philadelphia where she spoke against the backdrop of a loud and angry mob raging outside the building. Within a few years, Kelley became one of the most skilled lecturers in the movement. With fearlessness and dogged determination, Kelley quietly crisscrossed the Northeast speaking to audi-ences about the sinfulness of slavery. In reward for her exhausting activism, a few male leaders of the American Anti-Slavery Society nominated her to the business committee at their national meeting. A significant minority opposed women's leadership in the organization, and they walked out when Kelley's nomination proved successful.[36]

Those antislavery men who left after Kelley's election founded a "New Organization" that increasingly focused on political intervention. Delin-eating a subordinate status for women within this "American and Foreign Anti-Slavery Society," they moved ahead into electioneering, including an alliance with the nascent Liberty Party. As historian Elisabeth Griffith once noted, it made sense to cut women loose from the movement as they moved into mainstream politics. Women could not vote. Thus, they maintained a consistency when they formally excluded women from membership. Mean-while, within the "Old Organization," William Lloyd Garrison and his fol-lowers embraced woman's rights even as they maintained a commitment to the tactics of moral suasion for the conversion of public opinion to eliminate slavery. Women were welcome to participate fully, although the American Anti-Slavery Society continued to denounce voting in a nation founded with a Constitution that recognized slavery.[37]

Woman's Rights and Co-equality

Traditionally, historians have argued the American woman's rights movement emerged directly from the antislavery movement, awarding credit to
"the school of antislavery" for providing antebellum women with training
in organizing meetings, for honing rhetorical skills, and for establishing the
intellectual foundations for notions of women's emancipation.[38] Certainly,
ideology as well as personalities firmly tied the two together; within the anti-
slavery movement, women developed a language of equality and confronted
opposition to their public activities. Yet, while closely related, antebellum
woman's rights activities merit attention for their own course of development. Classic accounts of the origins of the 1848 convention in Seneca
Falls, cited as the first woman's rights convention in the United States,
explain that seeds had been planted at the World's Antislavery Convention
in London in 1840. Held just after the rancorous convention that split the
American movement, the London convention reenacted the conflict. The
venerable Quaker Lucretia Mott, an elected representative of the Pennsylvania Antislavery Society, watched as the male delegates from Britain and
the United States determined not to seat women on the convention floor.
"Fenced off behind a bar and curtain," Mott struck up a friendship with
newly married Elizabeth Cady Stanton, the daughter of an upstate New York
judge whose law books had early revealed to her the injustices suffered by
wives. Stanton's recent groom, Henry Brewster Stanton, a veteran abolitionist radical since the early 1830s, now associated himself with the political
"new organization."[39]

In her narrative of the convention, activist Matilda Jocelyn Gage, writing for the official *History of Woman Suffrage*, recounted the debates in
which Wendell Phillips asserted the Massachusetts "principle of admitting
women to an equal seat with men, in the deliberative bodies of anti-slavery
societies." Opponents included British delegates as well as Philadelphian
reverend Henry Grew, who argued that "the reception of women as a part of
this Convention would, in the view of many, be not only a violation of the
customs of England, but the ordinances of Almighty God." With the session
concluded,

> As Lucretia Mott and Elizabeth Cady Stanton wended their way arm in arm
> down Great Queen Street . . . they agreed to hold a convention on their return
> to America, as the men to whom they had just listened had manifested their
> great need of some education on that question. Thus a missionary work for the
> emancipation of woman in "the land of the free and the home of the brave"
> was then and there inaugurated.

Stanton later wrote, "Mrs. Mott was to me an entirely new revelation of womanhood. . . . She fed my hungering soul. . . . She told me . . . of Mary Wollstonecraft, her social theories, and her demands of equality for women. . . . I had been reading . . . Wollstonecraft . . . but I had never heard a woman talk what . . . I had scarcely dared to think."[40]

Eight years later, the Seneca Falls convention reunited the two in their woman's rights activism. The first gathering to focus explicitly on elevating the status of women, as document 21 shows, the Seneca Falls convention interwove the lessons women had learned in the antislavery movement with other potent forces in the world of upstate New York. As Judith Wellman has written, the nearby Erie Canal galvanized the forces of the market revolution with its impact on family economies and women's roles, while local gatherings of egalitarian-minded Quakers engaged in reform activities that brought together women as well as men to discuss gender and politics. Meanwhile, statewide issues before the New York Constitutional Convention of 1846 spread "rights talk" throughout the area. By the time Stanton visited with the Quaker Hunt family in nearby Waterloo to renew her conversation with their guest Mott and her sister Martha Coffin Wright, woman's rights ideas had become, as Lori Ginzberg has written, "available in the language of the day."[41]

The two-day convention at Seneca Falls, chaired for the nascent movement by sympathetic James Mott, husband of Lucretia, received the support of African American activist Frederick Douglass, who publicized the gathering in his paper. Attendees debated, drafted motions, and ultimately endorsed the "Declaration of Sentiments" that Stanton had modeled on the Declaration of Independence. Resolutions called for revision of laws that prevented women from the exercise of conscience, demanding "the right and duty of woman, equally with man, to promote every righteous cause by every righteous means, and especially in regard to the great subjects of morals and religion." Most controversial was their demand for suffrage. Yet, in the end, the convention accepted that "inasmuch as man, while claiming for himself intellectual superiority, does accord to woman moral superiority, it is preeminently his duty to encourage her to speak and teach." Historian Nancy Isenberg has argued that the vision of these "first wave feminists" embraced "co-equality" as its cornerstone, accepting the differences between the sexes while at the same time asserting a similarity in their claim to sacred rights. Antebellum woman's rights advocates, then, argued that men and women were both the same and different, while also holding that they each needed to work fully in their own ways, becoming companions in the great reform struggles of the day.[42]

Seneca Falls initiated a new era in organizing for woman's rights, yet it did not, by itself, create American feminism. Even in the first years of the early republic, Americans had read Mary Wollstonecraft with approval. Elizabeth Drinker of Philadelphia wrote, in 1796, "In very many of her sentiments, she, as some of our friends say, speaks my mind." Abigail Adams called her husband John "a disciple of Wolstoncraft [sic]." Indeed, when Lowell's "mill girls" first protested against wage cuts their leader delivered "a flaming Mary Wollstonecraft speech on the rights of woman and the inequities of the 'monied aristocrats.'" Other intellectual influences included Scottish-born freethinker Fanny Wright, who traveled extensively in the United States in the 1820s, lecturing against slavery and for the advancement of women. With support from Robert Dale Owen, founder of a utopian community in New Harmony, Indiana, Wright established her own settlement, Nashoba, envisioning a community in which enslaved men and women would demonstrate that they could work to earn their freedom. Nashoba did not survive, and critics spurned her abolitionism as well as her feminism. But elements of her ideas survived.[43]

In 1836, Polish-born Ernestine Rose took to the platform in New York to speak on abolition, woman's rights, and other progressive causes. Rose, too, had been influenced by Owenite socialism. By the 1840s, Rose was directing her attention toward redressing the grievances about the loss of control over their property women suffered upon marriage. She later became a mainstay of the antebellum woman's rights movement. Massachusetts-born Margaret Fuller made her mark on American feminism by adding a gendered dimension to the teachings of New England transcendentalism. Writing in 1843 in the movement's journal the *Dial*, she set forth ideas about male and female complementarity and mutuality, asserting, "There is no wholly masculine man, no purely feminine woman." Fuller's subsequent career as an author and reporter for the *New York Tribune* prepared her for adventures in revolutionary Italy. Yet, tragically, Fuller, her Italian husband, and her young son all died in 1850 when the ship that was to bring them to the United States ran aground off Long Island.[44]

The Seneca Falls convention in July 1848 was followed by a woman's rights convention in nearby Rochester, New York, and another in the abolitionist hotbed of Salem, Ohio, in April 1850. The convention in Worcester, Massachusetts, in October 1850, however, was the first woman's rights gathering to claim "national" attendance. Announced by a "call" signed by eighty-nine prominent men and women, the convention drew over nine hundred people from eleven states. Antislavery and woman's rights lecturer Lucy Stone captured the spirit of her colleagues when she proclaimed, "We

Lucy Stone, between 1840 and 1860. An antislavery and woman's rights lecturer after graduating from Oberlin College in 1847, Stone embodied the connections between the abolition and woman suffrage movements. (Source: Library of Congress)

Sojourner Truth, carte de visite, ca. 1864. Truth sold her images to provide
for herself. As she said, "I sell the Shadow to support the Substance." (Source:
Courtesy of the Library of Congress).

want that Woman should be the coequal and help-meet of Man in all the interests, and perils and enjoyments of human life."[45] As Elizabeth Cady Stanton explained, "The violence, rowdyism, and vulgarity which now characterize our Congressional Halls, show us clearly that 'it is not good for man to be alone.'"[46] The Worcester convention established a pattern and a rhetoric that carried the woman's rights movement to the Civil War. As American feminism developed in the 1850s, it drew on a range of notions about rights and duties, sex differences and human equivalence, and reciprocity and identity, to argue for women's empowerment. Yet, the movement took no formal associational shape. Meeting in national conventions every year between 1850 and 1860, except 1857, supporters also gathered at smaller local and regional meetings without official institutional apparatus. With all of their engagement in structured associations for religious work, education, and reform, women did not lack for knowledge. Rather, the fluidity of the convention form allowed for flexibility and exploration.[47]

In a bold move that further tied together woman's rights and abolition, women of color participated in some gatherings. Then living in Northampton, Massachusetts, former slave Sojourner Truth journeyed to Worcester in 1850 and ventured to Akron, Ohio, for a regional gathering in 1851. At the later meeting, she rebuked the opponents of woman's rights, using her own situation to illustrate the class and racial biases encompassed in their fragile notions of femininity, explaining,

> I have as much muscle as any man, and can do as much work as any man. I have plowed and reaped and husked and chopped and mowed, and can any man do more than that? I have heard much about the sexes being equal; I can carry as much as any man, and can eat as much too, if I can get it. I am strong as any man that is now.
>
> As for intellect, all I can say is, if woman have a pint and man a quart—why can't she have her little pint full? You need not be afraid to give us our rights for fear we will take too much—for we won't take more than our pint'll hold.[48] (See document 25.)

Although Truth remains the best known, other women of color articulated support for woman's rights. The Philadelphians Margaretta Forten and Harriet Forten Purvis worked with white women for the rights of their sex. Outspoken Mary Ann Shadd Cary moved from Delaware to Canada where she edited a newspaper, demonstrating formidable capacities. And Frances Ellen Watkins Harper spoke widely against slavery and for women.[49]

Yet, the gatherings and the agitation on behalf of women remained distinctly northern; they also continued to be self-consciously unaffiliated with partisan politics. Just as not all antislavery women became woman's rights supporters, it was clear that only a few women in the nascent woman's rights movement of the antebellum era moved from visions of co-equality to activism based on notions of identical rights. Some of those who did developed from "compassionate co-workers" who labored with men for educational, professional, and legal opportunities into "passionate partisans," willing to risk the perils of political engagement. Yet, many women continued to develop public networks and affiliations outside parties and unconnected with elections. And many women remained deferential to men. Nonetheless, the rise of partisan women marked a new development for American politics and for American women.

Notes

1. D'Anville, "The Natural Rights of Women," *Boston Monthly Magazine* 1 (August 1825): 135. The "Note to Patrons and Correspondents" in the same issue identifies "D'Anville" as a Boston-area woman.

2. Mary Kelley, *Learning to Stand and Speak: Women, Education, and Public Life in America's Republic* (Chapel Hill: University of North Carolina Press, 2006), 2; Linda K. Kerber, *Women of the Republic: Intellect and Ideology in Revolutionary America* (Chapel Hill: University of North Carolina Press, 1980); and Benjamin Rush, *Thoughts upon Female Education, Accommodated to the Present State of Society, Manners, and Government, in the United States of America. Addressed to the Visitors of the Young Ladies' Academy in Philadelphia, 28 July, 1787, at the Close of the Quarterly Examination* (Philadelphia: Prichard & Hall, 1787), 6.

3. William J. Gilmore, *Reading Becomes a Necessity of Life: Material and Cultural Life in Rural New England, 1780–1835*, 1st ed. (Knoxville: University of Tennessee Press, 1989), 5; Joel Perlmann, *Women's Work? American Schoolteachers, 1650–1920* (Chicago: University of Chicago Press, 2001), 61–63.

4. Jacqueline Jones Royster, *Traces of a Stream: Literacy and Social Change among African American Women* (Pittsburgh, Pa.: University of Pittsburgh Press, 2000), 142; Carter Godwin Woodson, *The Education of the Negro prior to 1861* (New York: Arno Press, 1968), 163–71.

5. Maria Stewart, "Address Delivered at the African Masonic Hall. Boston," February 27, 1833, www.historyisaweapon.com/defcon1/stewartmason.html. On Sojourner Truth, see Carleton Mabee and Susan Mabee Newhouse, *Sojourner Truth: Slave, Prophet, Legend* (New York: New York University Press, 1993); Nell Irvin Painter, *Sojourner Truth: A Life, A Symbol* (New York: Norton, 1996); and Margaret Washington, *Sojourner Truth's America* (Urbana: University of Illinois Press, 2009).

6. Susan Strane, *A Whole-Souled Woman: Prudence Crandall and the Education of Black Women* (New York: Norton, 1990).

7. On Oberlin, see Robert Samuel Fletcher, *A History of Oberlin College from Its Foundation through the Civil War* (Oberlin, Ohio: Oberlin College, 1943); Shirley Wilson

Logan, "Literacy as a Tool for Social Action," in *Nineteenth-Century Women Learn to Write*, ed. Catherine Hobbs (Charlottesville: University Press of Virginia, 1995), 181.

8. Perlmann, *Women's Work?*, 19–22.

9. Sarah Robbins, *Managing Literacy, Mothering America: Women's Narratives on Reading and Writing in the Nineteenth Century* (Pittsburgh, Pa.: University of Pittsburgh Press, 2004), 224; Perlmann, *Women's Work?* 37.

10. Barbara Miller Solomon, *In the Company of Educated Women: A History of Women and Higher Education in America* (New Haven, Conn.: Yale University Press, 1985).

11. Kathryn Kish Sklar, *Catharine Beecher: A Study in American Domesticity* (New Haven, Conn.: Yale University Press, 1973); see also http://ocp.hul.harvard.edu/ww/people_beecher.html.

12. Solomon, *In the Company of Educated Women*, 50–53.

13. Catherine A. Brekus, *Strangers and Pilgrims: Female Preaching in America, 1740–1845* (Chapel Hill: University of North Carolina Press, 1998), 134–35, 162–68, 178–79.

14. Erin Durham, "Self-Culture and Controversy within the Community Lyceum" (honors thesis, Oberlin College Department of History, May 2009).

15. Kelley, *Learning to Stand and Speak*; Erica Armstrong Dunbar, *A Fragile Freedom: African American Women and Emancipation in the Antebellum City* (New Haven, Conn.: Yale University Press, 2008), 97; Martha S. Jones, *All Bound up Together: The Woman Question in African American Public Culture, 1830–1900* (Chapel Hill: University of North Carolina Press, 2007), 4.

16. Mary P. Ryan, *Cradle of the Middle Class: The Family in Oneida County, New York, 1790–1865* (Cambridge: Cambridge University Press, 1981).

17. See Nancy Hewitt, *Women's Activism and Social Change: Rochester, New York, 1822–1872* (Ithaca, N.Y.: Cornell University Press, 1984); and Jones, *All Bound up Together*.

18. Lori D. Ginzberg, *Women and the Work of Benevolence: Morality, Politics, and Class in the Nineteenth-Century United States* (New Haven, Conn.: Yale University Press, 1990), 71–78; Anne M. Boylan, *The Origins of Women's Activism: New York and Boston, 1797–1840* (Chapel Hill: University of North Carolina Press, 2002), 110.

19. Dunbar, *A Fragile Freedom*, 52.

20. Boylan, *The Origins of Women's Activism*, 152–53.

21. Scott C. Martin, *Devil of the Domestic Sphere: Temperance, Gender, and Middle Class Ideology, 1800–1860* (DeKalb: Northern Illinois University Press, 2008). Susan Zaeske, *Signatures of Citizenship: Petitioning, Antislavery and Women's Political Identity* (Chapel Hill: University of North Carolina Press, 2003), 23; Anne Firor Scott, *Natural Allies: Women's Associations in American History* (Urbana: University of Illinois Press, 1991), 45; Holly Berkley Fletcher, *Gender and the American Temperance Movement of the Nineteenth Century* (New York: Routledge, 2008).

22. Jed Dannenbaum, *Drink and Disorder: Temperance Reform in Cincinnati from the Washingtonian Revival to the WCTU* (Urbana: University of Illinois Press, 1984); Scott, *Natural Allies*, 45.

23. Susan Zaeske, *Signatures of Citizenship*, 23, 25.

24. Alisse Portnoy, *Their Right to Speak: Women's Activism in the Indian and Slave Debates* (Cambridge, Mass.: Harvard University Press, 2005), 229.

25. Elizabeth R. Varon, *We Mean to Be Counted: White Women and Politics in Antebellum Virginia* (Chapel Hill: University of North Carolina Press, 1998), 43–44, 46, 61–62.

26. Varon, *We Mean to Be Counted*, 44–45.

27. Varon, *We Mean to Be Counted*, 51.

28. There is an extensive literature on women abolitionists. Among the more recent books, see Julie Roy Jeffrey, *The Great Silent Army of Abolitionism: Ordinary Women in the Antislavery Movement* (Chapel Hill: University of North Carolina Press, 1999); Beth Salerno, *Sister Societies: Women's Antislavery Organizations in Antebellum America* (DeKalb: Northern Illinois University Press, 2005); Stacey M. Robertson, *Hearts Beating for Liberty: Women Abolitionists in the Old Northwest* (Chapel Hill: University of North Carolina Press, 2010); Deborah Bingham Van Broekhoven, *The Devotion of These Women: Rhode Island in the Antislavery Network* (Amherst: University of Massachusetts Press, 2002); and Zaeske, *Signatures of Citizenship*.

29. Deborah B. Van Broekhoven, "Needles, Pens, and Petitions: Reading Women into Antislavery History," in *The Meaning of Slavery in the North*, ed. David Roediger and Martin H. Blatt (New York: Garland, 1998), 140. For more on antislavery sewing societies and fairs see Lee Chambers-Schiller, "'A Good Work among the People': The Political Culture of the Boston Antislavery Fair," in *The Abolitionist Sisterhood: Women's Political Culture in Antebellum America*, ed. Jean Fagan Yellin and John C. Van Horne, 249–74 (Ithaca, N.Y.: Cornell University Press, 1994); Beverly Gordon, "Playing at Being Powerless: New England Ladies Fairs, 1830–1930," *Massachusetts Review* 26 (September 1986): 144–60; Debra Gold Hansen, *Strained Sisterhood: Gender and Class in the Boston Anti-Slavery Society* (Amherst: University of Massachusetts Press, 1993); Nancy Hewitt, "The Social Origins of Women Antislavery Politics in Western New York," in *Crusaders and Compromisers: Essays on the Relationship of the Antislavery Struggle to the Antebellum Party System*, ed. Alan Kraut, 205–33 (Westport, Conn.: Greenwood Press, 1983); Julie Roy Jeffrey, "'Stranger, Buy . . . Lest Our Mission Fail': The Complex Culture of Women's Abolitionist Fairs," *American Nineteenth Century History* 4 (Spring 2003): 1–24; Carolyn J. Lawes, *Women and Reform in a New England Community, 1815–1860* (Lexington: University of Kentucky Press, 2000); Jean R. Soderlund, "Priorities and Power: The Philadelphia Female Anti-Slavery Society," in *The Abolitionist Sisterhood: Women's Political Culture in Antebellum America*, ed. Jean Fagan Yellin and John C. Van Horne, 67–88 (Ithaca, N.Y.: Cornell University Press, 1994); Alice Taylor, "Selling Abolitionism: The Commercial, Material, and Social World of the Boston Antislavery Fair, 1834–58" (PhD diss., Western Ontario University, 2007); Deborah B. Van Broekhoven, "'Better than a Clay Club': The Organization of Anti-Slavery Fairs, 1835–60," *Slavery and Abolition* 19 (April 1998): 24–45; Debora B. Van Broekhoven, "'Let Your Names Be Enrolled': Method and

Ideology in Women's Antislavery Petitioning," in *The Abolitionist Sisterhood: Women's Political Culture in Antebellum America*, ed. Jean Fagan Yellin and John C. Van Horne, 179–99 (Ithaca, N.Y.: Cornell University Press, 1994).

30. Women's antislavery petitions covered a variety of topics. Some were addressed to Congress and requested an end to the war in Mexico or the elimination of slavery in the District of Columbia. Others were directed to state representatives and dealt with racial bias in the laws. See Zaeske, *Signatures of Citizenship*.

31. "Petition of the Ladies Resident in the State of Ohio," *Philanthropist*, June 24, 1836. There is a slightly different version of this petition in the papers of Theodore Dwight Weld. See Gilbert H. Barnes and Dwight L. Dumond, eds., *The Letters of Theodore Dwight Weld, Angelina Grimké Weld, and Sarah Grimké*, vol. 1 (Gloucester, Mass.: Peter Smith, 1965), 175–76. For more on "Fathers and Rulers" petition see Robertson, *Hearts Beating for Liberty*, 33–36.

32. Zaeske, *Signatures of Citizenship*, 69–74.

33. "Preamble and Resolutions of the Ohio Female A. S. Society," *Philanthropist*, May 27, 1836. "Address to the Females in the State of Ohio," *Philanthropist*, June 24, 1836.

34. Gerda Lerner, "The Political Activities of Antislavery Women," in *The Majority Finds Its Past: Placing Women in History* (New York: Oxford University Press, 1979), 112–28.

35. Dorothy Sterling offers an excellent description of the Grimkés' first "promiscuous" lecture in Lynn, Massachusetts. See *Ahead of Her Time: Abby Kelley and the Politics of Antislavery* (New York: Norton, 1991), 51–55. See also Stephen H. Browne, *Angelina Grimké: Rhetoric, Identity, and the Radical Imagination* (East Lansing: Michigan State University Press, 1999); Gerda Lerner, *The Grimké Sisters from South Carolina: Rebels against Slavery* (Boston: Houghton Mifflin, 1967); and Katharine DuPre Lumpkin, *The Emancipation of Angelina Grimké* (Chapel Hill: University of North Carolina Press, 1974).

36. On Abby Kelley see Dorothy Sterling, *Ahead of Her Time*.

37. Elisabeth Griffith, *In Her Own Right: The Life of Elizabeth Cady Stanton* (New York: Oxford University Press, 1984), 37–44.

38. Ann D. Gordon, ed., *The Selected Papers of Elizabeth Cady Stanton and Susan B. Anthony: Volume 1: In the School of Anti-Slavery, 1840 to 1866* (New Brunswick, N.J.: Rutgers University Press, 1997).

39. Elizabeth Cady Stanton, Susan B. Anthony, and Matilda Joslyn Gage, eds. *History of Woman Suffrage*, vol. I (New York: Fowler and Wells, 1881), 60.

40. Mari Jo Buhle and Paul Buhle, eds., *The Concise History of Woman Suffrage: Selections from the Classic Work of Stanton, Anthony, Gage, and Harper* (Urbana: University of Illinois Press, 1978), 80, 86–87; Kathryn Kish Sklar, *Women's Rights Emerges within the Anti-Slavery Movement, 1830–1870: A Brief History with Documents* (Boston: Bedford/St. Martin's, 2000), 166–67.

41. Judith Wellman, *The Road to Seneca Falls: Elizabeth Cady Stanton and the First Woman's Rights Convention*, (Urbana: University of Illinois Press, 2004); Lori D.

Ginzberg, *Untidy Origins: A Story of Woman's Rights in Antebellum New York* (Chapel Hill: University of North Carolina Press, 2005), 56.

42. Sklar, *Women's Rights Emerges*, 174–75; Nancy Isenberg, *Sex and Citizenship in Antebellum America* (Chapel Hill: University of North Carolina Press, 1998), xviii.

43. Drinker is quoted in Mary Beth Norton, *Liberty's Daughters: The Revolutionary Experience of American Women, 1750–1800* (Boston: Little, Brown, 1980); Eleanor Flexner, *Century of Struggle: The Woman's Rights Movement in the United States*, enl. ed. (Cambridge, Mass.: Harvard University Press, 1996); Gail Bederman, "Revisiting Nashoba: Slavery, Utopia, and Frances Wright in America, 1818–1826," *American Literary History* 17(Autumn 2005): 438–59; Celia Morris, *Fanny Wright: A Biography* (Cambridge, Mass.: Harvard University Press, 1984).

44. Carol A. Kolmerten, *The American Life of Ernestine L. Rose* (Syracuse, N.Y.: Syracuse University Press, 1999); Bell Gale Chevigny, *The Woman and the Myth: Margaret Fuller's Life and Writings* (Old Westbury, N.Y.: Feminist Press, 1976).

45. Lucy Stone, *New York Daily Tribune*, October 26, 1850.

46. Elizabeth Cady Stanton, *The Proceedings of the Woman's Rights Convention* (Boston, Mass.: Prentiss & Sawyer, 1851), 53.

47. Buhle and Buhle, *Concise History of Woman Suffrage*; Flexner, *Century of Struggle*; Wellman, *The Road to Seneca Falls*; Sklar, *Women's Rights Emerges*.

48. Buhle and Buhle, *Concise History of Woman Suffrage*; Painter, *Sojourner Truth*; Washington, *Sojourner Truth's America*.

49. Janice Sumler-Lewis, "The Forten-Purvis Women of Philadelphia and the American Anti-Slavery Crusade," *Journal of Negro History* 66 (Winter 1981–1982): 281–88; Jones, *All Bound up Together*; Frances Ellen Watkins Harper, *A Brighter Coming Day: A Frances Ellen Watkins Harper Reader* (New York: Feminist Press, 1990); Nell Irvin Painter, "Voices of Suffrage: Sojourner Truth, Frances Watkins Harper, and the Struggle for Woman Suffrage," in *Votes for Women: The Struggle for Suffrage Revisited*, 42–55 (Oxford: Oxford University Press, 2002).

Phase 3: Passionate Partisans

By the 1850s, women's political participation had become increasingly widespread. Although the ebb and flow of this activism varied across party and region, it spread with a consistency that surprised even women. As one Ohio abolitionist wrote to a friend, "All Ladies have politics now."[1] How did popular assumptions about women's domestic nature expand to include partisanship? Why did male politicians invite women to attend partisan rallies and campaign for candidates? How did this new partisanship affect women's lives at the local level? Although advocates often explained female partisanship by linking it to moral concerns, women's participation in the political arena eventually spread beyond the boundaries of moral issues.

Women's antebellum political activism was not unprecedented. As discussed earlier, the Revolution helped to create an opening for women to act in electoral politics. Although this opening proved temporary and resulted in a backlash against outspoken politically opinionated women, it illuminated the fluidity of ideas about gender and governance in the new nation. Despite such recoil, between 1800 and 1830, women garnered increased political power through collective women's organizations—those charitable and benevolent groups discussed earlier. By 1840, a "mass mobilization" of politically minded women occurred. Mostly reformers and abolitionists, these post-1840 women engaged in political activities "frankly oriented toward influencing votes and mobilizing for broad-based political change." Women of all types—African American and Euro-American, southern and northern, working class and privileged—initiated petition drives and hosted national meetings to address large-scale political goals. Whether working with the Liberty Party, Whigs, Free Soilers, Republicans, or even Democrats, women seized on their authority as moral arbiters to empower themselves within the political system. And their participation in politics was not exclusively limited to moral issues, as Ronald and Mary Zboray have shown. Some women espoused a particular party because it best represented their economic, racial, and regional interests. These female partisans were motivated by "a blend of kin and neighborhood affiliation, party loyalty, and rational judgment of current economic and political issues."[2]

By the 1850s, the range of women's political endeavors widened. They published pamphlets and penned letters to newspapers. A few edited political newspapers. They lobbied local, state, and national political bodies. They spoke out about slavery, Indians, temperance, and even woman's suffrage. Partisanship did not require access to the vote. Recent studies by Melanie Gustafson, Sylvia Hoffert, Michael Pierson, Alisse Portnoy, and Elizabeth Varon have shown that women found a wide variety of methods for expressing their political positions.[3] Their activism, by its very breadth and diversity, became legitimized. Certainly, women continued to find themselves criticized for expressing radical political opinions or publicly speaking at partisan events. But women's presence at political rallies, conventions, picnics, parades, and meetings did not cause a public uproar in the decade preceding the Civil War.[4]

Third parties associated with the antislavery movement provided a relatively smooth path from morally motivated political action to a more electoral-driven partisanship that emerged in the 1850s. The nationwide

discussion about slavery—which was defined in the North as a moral issue—immediately allowed room for women's participation. As the virtue and
conscience of the nation, woman's voice had power in this debate.

From Deference to Partisanship

Long before the emergence of antislavery third parties, the ideals of the
Revolution ignited a wide-ranging discussion about the meaning of equality,
freedom, and political rights in the newly created United States. Though
most assumed that both voting and office holding would be limited to white
propertied men, some challenged that notion. As discussed earlier, New
Jersey lawmakers in 1790 enfranchised property-holding women in seven of
the state's thirteen counties, and seven years later, this law was extended to
all eligible women. Because married women could not hold property, only a
small number of women, mostly widows, met the necessary property qualifications. Rosemarie Zagarri estimates that about one hundred New Jersey
women voted in any election, most of whom were Federalists, suggesting that
wealth and standing influenced who participated in politics. Even then, the
New Jersey law sparked much criticism. Opponents contended that female
voters upset the balance of both politics and familial relationships. Critics
nonetheless acknowledged the legitimacy of the principle behind the law:
no taxation without representation. Propertied women, like men, earned the
right to express their political opinion.[5]

The New Jersey experiment, which ended in 1807 when the state legislature disenfranchised both women and free blacks, did not repeat itself
in other states. Yet, American women found other avenues in the first few
decades of the new nation to communicate their political opinions. Inspired
by the New Jersey situation as well as the example of Revolutionary women
who boycotted, petitioned, and forthrightly expressed their convictions, a
small group of highly educated, privileged women voiced their ideas about
elections, parties, laws, and rights, through letters, publications, and social
interactions. As literacy rates increased and print culture exploded, women
had more access to political discussions and more opportunities for convey-
ing their opinions. They read political newspapers and talked about politics
in newly created literary societies. Mercy Otis Warren published a three-
volume history of the American Revolution and penned political plays.
Judith Sargent Murray wrote an essay entitled "On the Equality of the Sexes"
in 1790 and enthusiastically supported the Federalist Party. Political wives of
Washington, D.C., including Dolley Madison and Louisa Catherine Adams,
began to play an important role in the affairs of the state through "parlor

politics," using the private and social sphere of their parlors to influence national policy decisions.[6]

By 1830, these experiments with women's increased participation in politics once again provoked a reaction and retrenchment. As divisiveness grew between the Federalists and the Republicans in the first decades of the 1800s, women's political position became increasingly fraught with gendered fears about the effects of conflict. Families divided over politics—were women's political voices to blame? Prescriptive literature warned women to remain out of the fray—and embrace their "proper" role as virtuous models of family harmony. As more and more white men gained access to the franchise with the elimination of property qualifications, women as well as black men were seen increasingly as unwelcome interlopers in politics. As Zagarri asserts, "The passage of laws that limited the franchise to 'free white males' solidified women's exclusion from government and gave that prohibition the force of law."[7] Women did not simply leave politics to men, however. They found they had to be more creative and subtle as they negotiated their way through partisan politics.

Women in the early national period understood that politics affected their lives. As discussed earlier, they initially worked at the local level in "feminine" endeavors focused on charitable work. Through this activism women learned to negotiate the political system in their towns and states. As Anne Boylan has shown, these women employed a deferential attitude to convince local politicians to support and even fund their efforts. Claiming ignorance, inexperience, and virtuous motives, women appealed to powerful male patrons to help them. They did not seek political power but instead focused on influence. Like other citizens looking to maneuver within the American democratic system, they understood that finding an influential politician to support their cause was critical to their success. Ironically, by 1840, the so-called democratization of American politics disadvantaged white, Euro-American women. It undercut the patronage system and, with it, women's entrée to individuals on whom they could rely. Deferential politics no longer offered women access to political influence. As this shift in political access occurred, women's relationship to the political system also began to change. Women transitioned from thinking about politics as an avenue for achieving a specific reform-oriented goal such as public funding for an orphanage to thinking about politics as legitimate partisan activity.[8]

The acceptance of woman's "natural" virtue and selflessness became the avenue for women's increasing partisanship in the 1840s. This happened through the combination of women's eagerness to become political actors and parties' welcoming attitude. With no access to the vote and thus limited appeal to political parties, women were perceived as having no self-interest when it came to partisanship. Their political position appeared to be entirely driven by unadulterated patriotism and republican virtue. While men could be persuaded to exchange their votes for ambition or gain, women allegedly remained altruistically above the fray. So women might attend a political rally or barbeque with the excuse that her presence was driven by a devotion to the betterment of the nation—not the quest for political power or favors. Women's virtue also appealed to parties because they could use female virtue for improved public relations. As a result, women symbolized the morality of each party. Democrats and Whigs competed for female support as a sign of their superior virtue.[9]

Historians have debated the meaning and importance of women's increased partisanship in the 1840s. Mary Ryan argues that women's presence at parades, dinners, parties, and public meetings was primarily symbolic and characterized by passivity. Varon and others disagree, contending that women were active participants at these events. They assert that women did not simply wave handkerchiefs and smile for their favorite candidates. Like male partisans, females identified as Whigs, Democrats, or Libertyites. In the 1840 Whig campaign female supporters were labeled "Harrison women."[13] They understood the difference between their candidates and their opponents. They discussed policy issues with their husbands, brothers, sisters, and friends. They carefully perused campaign literature. Some housed visiting politicians and campaigners, providing them with food and conversation. In some instances, women even tendered campaign speeches. Increasing evidence of the depth and variety of women's partisan activism in various parts of the country suggests that women made "vital contributions to party politics by serving as both partisans and mediators in the public sphere."[10]

Women's partisan activism infiltrated both major parties, though the Whigs proved more welcoming to female political influence. Beginning in 1840, the Whigs boasted of women's preference for their party. They invited women to attend partisan events, and they publicized female participation. Even in the South, where resistance to women's public role was stronger, Whigs encouraged women to vocalize their partisan support in the 1840 and 1844 presidential campaigns. Jayne Crumpler DeFiore has shown that the growth of frontier evangelism in the South, which brought outdoor religious camp meetings to communities across the region, helped convey women into the public sphere. Political campaigns adopted the techniques of camp meetings, thus allowing women to move smoothly from religious gatherings to partisan assemblies. Just as some evangelical gatherings continued for hours, animated by fevered religious conversions, so too did some political meetings thrive through long hours of energetic speeches. Baltimore Whigs in the 1840 presidential campaign hosted an all-night political meeting that included women. Though undoubtedly serving in some traditional roles—cooking and cleaning for the crowd—their attendance at this meeting revealed women as keen political enthusiasts.[11]

As Whig women entered the political world, their participation was wide ranging. In many cases, Whig assemblies welcomed and entertained entire families. Food, games, outdoor activities, music, and even courtship oc- curred at political gatherings. Unmarried Tennessee women swooned during a speech by presidential candidate Henry Clay, while others were afforded the opportunity to speak before large crowds when they awarded banners to "deserving military companies." Miss Jane Field offered a public address before the Fayette County, Illinois, Whig delegation, declaring her support for "'Harrison and Liberty.'"[12]

Whig men promoted this active participation. Famed Massachusetts senator Daniel Webster addressed a group of nearly 1,200 Whig women in Richmond, Virginia, in 1840, encouraging their partisan support. Women's loud and visible presence at Whig events, he averred, helped to mold sons and husbands into good Whig men. Like those who advocated Republican Motherhood at the turn of the century, Webster understood women's politi- cal influence as manifesting primarily within the family. But Webster moved beyond simply advocating that women educate their sons in republican citizenship. He and other Whig politicians argued that women, like men, "shared an intense interest and stake in electoral contests."[13] Whig women, like Whig men, were devoted partisans who encouraged their families, friends, and communities to vote for their party. Whig womanhood became an important element of Whig Party identity.

In the 1844 presidential election, Ladies Clay Clubs proclaimed their preference for Whig candidate Henry Clay in 1844, hoping to link female righteousness to their party. So common was women's presence at Clay events that he began his speeches by greeting the "ladies" in his audiences. Some unmarried Clay women attended rallies with sashes that read, "'Whig husbands or none.'"[14] Linking chaste womanhood to the Whig Party, female supporters made clear the connections between politics and family. Ladies preferred to marry men who carried the same values that they did, as was clearly represented by the Whig Party.

Women's support for the Whigs may have been popularly linked to female virtue, but tangible economic and political issues also attracted women to the party. Like their husbands, brothers, fathers, and neighbors, women tended to support the party that represented their class, ethnic, and social standing.

Mary Pierce of Massachusetts was an earnest Whig loyalist who followed the elections throughout the 1840s and 1850s. She circulated petitions, kept up with campaign literature, and participated in Whig processions. She made political contacts with men to whom she had no familial or other relationship. She eventually married a man whose Whig commitment rivaled her own. Her devotion to the Whig Party was grounded in her values, economic interests, and political convictions.[15]

Though popular ideals of femininity helped to pave the way for women to become more politically educated and active, many women also found that partisanship allowed them to move beyond traditional domesticity. They voiced concerns about local institutions, economic issues, legal debates, and larger political questions. Partisanship opened the public world to women. Being a Whig woman meant that you should know about the public school conflict stirring in your community as well as the national question of the constitutionality of slavery. Certainly, there were limits to how women could express their political opinions. Abby Kelley and the Grimké sisters were deemed "monstrous" and abhorrent for public speaking.[16] They were perceived as aggressively violating the "woman's sphere," which made them easy targets for critique. By 1840, with the emergence of the Liberty Party, women had developed creative and subtle methods for impacting partisan politics and minimizing public opposition.

Abolition, Politics, and the Liberty Party

The emergence of the Liberty Party pushed notions about women's political engagement to new levels. In the 1830s, before the party's emergence, abolitionists had attempted to distance their movement from partisan politics, arguing that the most effective method for ending slavery was through voluntary emancipation. Employing "moral suasion" techniques, they sought to persuade southerners that slavery was a sin that should be immediately renounced. This emphasis on morality and Christianity certainly created an avenue for women's participation in a public movement that might otherwise have been perceived as political and therefore inappropriate for women. As the Jackson, Michigan, Ladies Benevolent and Antislavery Association declared, "We shall operate by using moral and christian persuasion to convince all of the sin and iniquity of slavery, of their duty to use every proper means in their power to promote emancipation and to exhibit their influence in all proper ways, and at all times, against slavery, and in behalf of Liberty."[17] These frontier women understood that it was critical for "ladies" to exhibit "proper" influence if they expected to be effective in a society that deemed their sex as inherently virtuous.

The Liberty Party took both antislavery and antebellum politics in new directions. Priding itself on being different from the two major parties, Liberty was dedicated not to winning political office but instead to ending slavery. Liberty leaders intended to force the Whigs and the Democrats to recognize the increasing antislavery sentiment in the North. They did not hope to compete for national office. The sinfulness of slavery was their platform. Most Libertyites considered themselves an "antipolitical" political party. This provided women with a perfect opportunity to engage in politics without seeming to be political. As Gustafson writes, Liberty "fused the civic world of benevolent and reform organizations with the electoral world of voting and legislating."[18]

Liberty also proved welcoming to women due to its local focus—which contrasted with the more centralized and nationally concentrated major parties. Because the party accentuated the importance of small-town campaigns—with their church fund-raisers and local meetings—women found a comfortable niche for themselves. Emphasizing the intimacy of family and community, Liberty organizers constructed the party as relaxed and safe (see document 20). Owen Lovejoy, an Illinois minister and brother to martyred abolitionist Elijah Lovejoy, gently prodded women to hold "neighborhood meetings" and chat with local friends about Liberty. The Michigan Liberty Party invited entire families to attend Liberty dinners and thanked Liberty women for providing attendees "with the richest of Michigan's bountiful dinners to cater for the body." The editor of the Indiana-based Liberty paper *Free Labor Advocate and Anti-Slavery Chronicle* emphasized the importance of local organizing when he called on both men and women to create "Liberty associations" in "each township and school district." Huldah Wickersham, the outspoken leader of the Henry County (Indiana) Female Anti-Slavery Society, referred to herself as a "humble and obscure country girl" in a letter to an esteemed male friend even as she confidently cited historical facts and religious motivations in a defense of the Liberty Party.[29] Illinoisan Mary Davis concluded a letter to the Chicago-based *Western Citizen* praising the progress of the Liberty Party with a scene from the dining room: "As a proof that the principles of the Liberty Party are advancing, permit me to say I have the pleasure of sitting at table with from ten to fifteen gentlemen boarders at the house where I board, who are, with one or two exceptions, liberty men." Blending the warm, comforting environment of the dining room with Liberty Party politics, Davis constructed a vision of partisan politics particularly inviting for women.[19]

As Davis and other leading abolitionist women carefully constructed a domesticated Liberty Party, they also negotiated an increasingly public space for themselves within the party. This public space first involved carefully timed female conventions that overlapped with state Liberty Party gatherings. The Illinois State Female Anti-Slavery Society, for example, met at the same time and location as the Liberty Party for four years. The timing of these two assemblies was no coincidence—they were intentionally scheduled to occur in the same location and during the same week. This was both practical and calculated. It allowed antislavery families across Illinois to make only one trip for everyone—male and female—to go to their abolitionist meetings. More surreptitiously, it also created an avenue for women to attend a "masculine" political meeting under the guise of a separate female organization.

Soon, however, women found themselves directly invited to participate in Liberty Party meetings, just as Whig women were attending partisan meetings. The call for the Chicago-based Northwest Liberty Convention in 1846, which included participants from across the Old Northwest, invited anyone interested in a "peaceable" overthrow of the "Slave Power" without "reference to sex, class, or condition" to participate. Four of the eleven male signers of the call for the convention were related to women who participated in the Illinois State Female Anti-Slavery Society. Eager to ensure women's presence, the organizers did more than offer an invitation. They guaranteed housing for all out-of-town female participants: "Ladies, and gentlemen with their wives, will be provided with places in private families." Lone men were warned to come prepared to find lodging for themselves. Women attended the meeting in large numbers, and on occasion, male speakers directly addressed them. Guy Beckley, a Michigan abolitionist, encouraged the "ladies" to focus on "persuading pro-slavery husbands to act rightly." Owen Lovejoy asked if the great throng before him were all "Liberty men." After cries of "yes, yes!" he then seemed to remember the women and asked, "Was every woman a Liberty man?" Lovejoy—in the heat of the moment and with the keen encouragement of the audience—walked a fine line in suggesting that Liberty women might identify themselves as Liberty men. This passionate impromptu call to women to find their inner masculinity was exactly what opponents feared. Where would this call end? What other masculine activities or traits might women desire?[20]

The Liberty women who attended both the political convention and the annual Illinois State Female Anti-Slavery Society gathering recognized that they would be vulnerable to attack for violating feminine propriety. When prominent men at the Liberty convention repeatedly acknowledged and applauded their presence, this gave the women pride and strength, but it also highlighted their presence. In order to contain any uproar their political activities might cause, the female group self-consciously and for the first time denoted officers by reference to their husband's names in the published minutes of their meeting. "Mrs. Lydia Lewis" became "Mrs. William Lewis."[21] The published account of their 1846 meeting was brief and vague, as if they preferred little attention. Liberty women sensed the highly charged environment and responded with a sensible, practical change in tactics.

The 1840s witnessed a dramatic rise in women's partisan activism, both through the Whig and Liberty parties. But this growth did not eliminate the opposition to women's involvement in politics. As members of the Illinois State Female Anti-Slavery Society recognized, it remained necessary to disguise and rationalize women's increasingly passionate political voices. In the late 1840s, with the rise of a new political party, women continued to negotiate a place for themselves in the partisan debates and expanded the range of their activities.

The Liberty Party never managed to gain significant support, and by 1848, it was largely supplanted by another antislavery third party, the Free Soilers. Historians have argued that, by the late 1840s, many northern antislavery Whigs and Democrats became increasingly dissatisfied with their parties' stance on slavery. These disgruntled citizens joined former Libertyites to construct a new party that favored abolition but also emphasized the detrimental impact of slavery on free labor in the North. Hardworking white men, they argued, simply could not compete with slave labor. Free Soilers were especially concerned with preventing the extension of slavery into the new territories, hoping to preserve the West for virtuous free labor. The Free Soil Party did not boast the same commitment to racial equality as its predecessor, causing some disenchanted Libertyites to maintain a version of their party in the form of the "Liberty League." Women by and large made the transition from the Liberty Party to the Free Soil Party. Indeed, as Pierson shows, women developed a more public role in the Free Soil Party and labored to strengthen the party's commitment to racial equality and widespread abolition.[22]

Following the lead of Liberty women like Davis, who consistently focused on the sinfulness of slavery and racial discrimination as the heart of abolitionist politics, women Free Soilers reminded party organizers and politicians that slavery was a moral issue, not a political tool. These women—and many men—worried that the party would sacrifice the slave for electoral success and political power. Jane Swisshelm and Clarina Nichols, two independent and thoughtful abolitionists, carried their commitment to emancipation into the political arena by editing their own partisan newspapers. Swisshelm, a Pennsylvania resident, embarked on a political career by writing letters to newspapers in support of the Liberty Party. By 1847, she was editing her own Liberty Party newspaper, the *Pittsburgh Saturday Visiter*, which she quickly switched over to the Free Soil Party. Nichols, who lived in Vermont, also established a Free Soil newspaper, the *Brattleboro Wyndham County Democrat*. Both women used their editorial voices to remind party leaders of the sinfulness of slavery by adopting a "higher law" position in their papers in relation to slavery (see document 23). God's law, they argued, superseded all other laws, including the Constitution, and so whenever God's law conflicted with human law, as in the case of slavery, one was morally bound to follow God. Although this higher law argument appealed to only a minority of Free Soilers, Swisshelm and Nichols developed a strong following among abolitionists, and they wielded influence within the party. Other Free Soil newspapers copied their editorials, and their voices were heard far and wide across the North. Famed abolitionist Frederick Douglass proclaimed that "'women are beginning to have much influence in politics. There are few papers exerting greater influence than the *Saturday Visiter*, edited by Mrs. Swisshelm, and the *Brattleboro Democrat*, edited by Mrs. Nichols.'"[23]

No woman writer had more political influence than Harriet Beecher Stowe, the author of the wildly successful *Uncle Tom's Cabin*. This novel, which also advocated a higher law position, was first published in serialized form in a Free Soil newspaper, the *National Era*, in 1852. Though, as Pierson points out, most scholars have not interpreted *Uncle Tom's Cabin* as a political document, its appearance in a Washington, D.C.–based third-party newspaper cannot be overlooked (see document 24). Stowe's emphasis on a morally driven, Christian-based antislavery movement forced male Free Soil editors to recognize and discuss its importance as an issue. A poignant expression of Stowe's position occurs in her novel when an Ohio state senator who reluctantly supported his state's fugitive slave law is converted to the higher law position by the arguments of his abolitionist wife and the presence of a fugitive mother and her son at his door. Unable to adhere to the very law that he helped pass, this politician instead followed his Christian impulse to aid escaping slaves. Gamaliel Bailey, the editor of the *National Era*, acknowledged that Stowe's influence pushed him to address the morality of slavery more directly in his newspaper. By publishing a novel that clearly promoted the idea that God's law trumped all human law, Bailey risked alienating those readers who believed that the Constitution was the highest law in the land and that, even though it protected a much-despised slave system, it had to be respected. Bailey carefully negotiated this potential problem by constructing the higher law argument as a "feminine" and moral position, and the constitutionality of slavery as "male" legalism. Women like Swisshelm, Nichols, and Stowe were thus able to dive into the political arena as morally driven females, not power-seeking politicians. By the early 1850s, when *Uncle Tom's Cabin* became an international best seller, the nation was increasingly aroused over slavery. The Compromise of 1850 had introduced a new, more intrusive fugitive slave law that required northern citizens, no matter what their feelings about slavery, to aid in the recapturing of escaped slaves. It increased the fines and jail time associated with aiding freedom seekers, and it offered more financial reward to judges who sided with southerners in fugitive cases. Free and fugitive blacks in the North were subject to kidnapping by slave catchers, and in response, thousands immigrated north to Canada. When Congress passed the Kansas-Nebraska Act in 1854, many northerners became fully convinced that the southern "Slave Power" sought to dictate its will to the North. Because the Kansas-Nebraska Act eliminated the Missouri Compromise 36°30' line, which had been the upper geographic limit of slavery for thirty years, it seemed to antislavery-leaning northerners that compromise had simply failed. The territory of Kansas, whose position on slavery would be decided by popular vote, became a battleground. Proslavery southerners and antislavery northerners raced to the plains to defend their position.[24]

Rallying Republican Ladies

The Kansas-Nebraska Act ignited antislavery sentiment in the North and resulted in a dramatic shift in the political landscape. As historian Richard H. Sewell writes, "Before the [Kansas-Nebraska] tempest subsided it had splintered the Democratic party, smashed the last remnants of organized Whiggery, and crystallized antislavery elements from all parties into a formidable new political coalition."[25] The resultant Republican Party absorbed Free Soilers and attracted thousands of new adherents, including women. With the demise of the Whigs, the Republican Party emerged as a major contender in the national political arena. Following the tradition of the Liberty and Free Soil parties, women's political activities were wide ranging but largely centered on the powerful idea that women embodied harmony and purity. Amidst a time of rising regional hostility and violence, this emphasis on virtue proved increasingly important.

In the Republicans' first presidential campaign, women were front and center, due in part to the candidate's wife, Jessie Frémont. An intelligent and beautiful woman, Jessie worked closely with party organizers in the

campaign for her husband, explorer and military commander John C. Frémont. Popular and articulate, Jessie pulled women into the political arena by
modeling acceptable feminine partisanship. Depicted as both a supportive
helpmate and a savvy political insider, Jessie made Republican advocacy
seem a natural choice for true-hearted northern women. The daughter of
Missouri senator Thomas Hart Benton, Jessie had defied her father to elope
with Frémont, thus revealing her independent streak. Benton opposed his
daughter's suitor not because he identified with the North but rather because
Frémont seemed to have few career prospects. This played beautifully into
the hands of Republican Party strategists, who contrasted the wealthy, arrogant Democrat Benton with John and Jessie, egalitarians dedicated to the
free labor system. John Frémont, they argued, worked his way up using only
his own talents and perseverance, relying on the opportunities afforded by
the free North. Jessie faithfully supported her hardworking spouse, occasionally using her wit and loyalty to aid him.[26]

Jessie Frémont was much more than a symbol in the 1856 election. As
Republican Party historian William E. Gienapp argues, she was a brilliant
political strategist and organizer. She served on the exclusive committee that
had the difficult job of preventing her husband from making political blun-
ders by carefully limiting his public exposure. John Frémont was an explorer
and soldier with little political experience or aptitude. He spent his time preceding the election "fencing, riding, and exercising," while Jessie and other
close advisors managed the day-to-day campaign. Jessie's calm demeanor and
her political acumen convinced several party insiders that she was a better
presidential prospect than her husband.[27]

Jessie Frémont impressed Republican leaders, but she mesmerized women
activists (see document 27). Amidst tensions in the North over increasing
southern aggressiveness—as evidenced by the violent caning of Republican
senator Charles Sumner by southern congressman Preston Brooks—Jessie
Frémont offered northern women hope that female virtue might guide the
White House. Historians have pointed out that she inspired thousands of
women to become active in partisan meetings, parades, picnics, and dinners.
According to Pierson, Republican women's activism outpaced and outsized
earlier women's partisan efforts. The gender ideal represented by Jessie—
feminine beauty and intelligence—was mirrored in rank-and-file women's
activism among Republicans. During a mass rally in Beloit, Wisconsin, a
float featured thirty-two attractive, young, single women. All of them wore
white save one, who wore black and represented Kansas. The message they
shared with their audience was a sophisticated critique of southern violence
and slavery. Republican women at this same mass rally also raised funds for

antislavery Kansas settlers by selling dinners to attendees. They eschewed political endorsements at their table in order to appear nonpartisan. Despite their wary negotiation of gender expectations, these Republican women worked closely with party organizers and definitely engaged in self-conscious partisanship. In raising money to aid "Free Soil Kansas," they inherently promoted the goals of the Republican Party. The symbolic Beloit float became a popular tool at Republican rallies across the North. Dozens of communities eagerly elected thirty-two young beauties to ride atop a float—representing the thirty-one states and Kansas.[28]

The conflict in Kansas, with its extensive violence and lawlessness, offered Republican women an opportunity to enter the fray as the voice of virtue and morality. Though not officially linked to the Republican Party, Kansas Aid groups organized to help "'feed and clothe the destitute in Kansas—especially widows and orphans,'" and also promoted Republican electoral goals. The leadership of such groups frequently included the wives of leading Republican politicians. Kansas women themselves pushed at the boundaries of appropriate female behavior. Abolitionist and Republican newspapers highlighted stories of physical bravery among the women of Kansas. Under the headline, "The Ladies of Lawrence," the Ohio-based *Anti-Slavery Bugle* reprinted an article about the critical role played by "Free State ladies" in the defense of Lawrence against anti-abolitionist "invaders." In contrast to proslavery women, who abandoned the town once violence began, the abolitionist women refused to leave. "Forty ladies of Lawrence enrolled their names secretly, with the determination of fighting by the sides of their husbands and sons as soon as the fighting commenced!" Many of the women practiced shooting with pistols, and one "young girl (a beauty of nineteen years)," even reported that she "dreamt last night of shooting three invaders." This emphasis on the youth and beauty of female abolitionist warriors paralleled the treatment of Jessie Frémont and likewise reassured readers that, although these women adopted manly characteristics—strength, courage, and determination—they remained feminine. The article concluded by telling the story of two "ladies" who risked their lives to sneak gunpowder and rifle cartridges into the town, using their femininity to fool the opposition. When an enemy scout stopped their wagon he "saw only a work-basket, which had purposely been filled with sewing materials." He did he not notice the enormous pillows—filled with gunpowder—beneath their skirts and he allowed them to pass through to the town. Skirts and pillows—female accoutrements—became tools for supporting the virtuous cause of Republican emancipation.[29]

Amidst the broad range of political activities Republican women engaged in during the second half of the 1850s, black women participated alongside white women. Some joined Kansas Aid groups, while others focused on local elections. Still others took to the lecture circuit. These skilled and articulate women usually spoke in support of Republican policies though not formally associated with the party. By promoting Kansas, or critiquing the fugitive slave law, abolitionist speakers inevitably advanced the party. But in the volatile environment of the Kansas period, black women also took risks simply by standing at the podium. When African American orator Frances Ellen Watkins lectured in Ohio during the late 1850s, she found herself occasionally subject to protests and mob opposition. Commenting in his diary, Salem resident Daniel Hise praised the female orator writing, "Miss Watkins, a colored lady made as good a speech as I ever listened to." In Fairfield, Ohio, a group of "rowdies" surrounded the lecture hall as Watkins spoke, yelling obscenities and breaking windows. Local citizens were so appalled by this behavior that they made sure that the "ruffians" were brought to justice. During the leader's trial, he revealed his own intolerance by referring to abolitionists as "maggoty-brained friends of the slave"; he was convicted of disturbing the peace.[30]

Watkins was not the only outspoken African American female who encountered intense opposition. When Sojourner Truth spoke in Indiana in June 1861 she also met a mob. She was there simply to visit friends, but according to abolitionist Josephine Griffing, who witnessed the aggressive encounter that followed, local abolitionists in Angola, Indiana, requested that Truth speak about the war in the local courthouse. Two months following Fort Sumter, but before the first battle of Bull Run, tensions ran high across the country. Truth began her lecture with the confession that she wished she could join the brave troops on the battlefield. "At this moment," according to Griffing, a mob "rushed up the stairs, and like a pack of hounds, with ears well rubbed, set upon this patriotic, noble woman, and with insolent threats and yells choked her down." The following night, the mob surrounded the home of Truth's host, "one of the oldest and wealthiest men in the county," and only failed to carry through on their "hellish plan" of violence because "they were soon too drunk for a riot." Still determined to run Truth out of the state, the leaders of the mob prosecuted her for violation of the Black Laws. Griffing explained that Truth was arrested for "coming into the State, being black; next, as a mulatto; then, for coming in; then, for remaining in the State!" This involved four different trials, all of which resulted in Truth's triumph. " The most influential and noble-hearted women" of the county attended the trials and "produced a marked impression." Even though Griffing herself had encountered innumerable violent opponents during her years as a Garrisonian lecturer, she concluded, "In my experience with mobs, I have never seen such determination. No dog ever hung to a bone as have these hungry hounds to Sojourner."[31]

The mobbing of both Truth and Watkins is evidence of continuing deep racism in the North but also ambivalence about women's intrusions into civic spaces. The questioning of Truth's femininity reveals that many still equated public oratory with manhood, assuming that any woman who excelled in this arena was either a disguised man or a promiscuous female. Despite the powerful disincentive of public censure, many Republican women hit the lecture circuit in the hope that their voices might help to protect and even free other women victimized by the sinful institution of slavery.

By 1859, when John Brown raided Harpers Ferry, women had become quite adept at articulating their political opinions. Abolitionist editor Lydia Maria Child wrote Virginia governor Henry Wise asking for permission to nurse Brown, who had been injured in the failed uprising, proposing to serve as "a mother or a sister to dress his wounds, and speak soothingly to him." She hailed him as a "martyr to righteous principles." Yet Child drew the ire of the southern matron Elizabeth Margaretta Chew Mason, the wife of the author of the Fugitive Slave Bill, who charged that Child's sympathy with Brown was misplaced. Rather, Mrs. Mason staked her own political claim by pointing to the care and devotion that southern mistresses lavished on their "servants," tending consumptives, sewing for the "motherless child," and softening "the pang of maternity" for mothers in childbirth. She believed Child's "sympathy" for Brown—using quotation marks to emphasize her point, actually "whet the knives for our throats." Unrepentant, Child responded with biblical quotations, then turned the politicized language of motherhood back on Mason when she asserted that New England women also sewed for the poor, watched the sick, and attended women giving birth, pointedly concluding, "And here in the North, after we have helped the mothers, we do not sell the babies."[32] (See document 28.)

Republican women like Ohio resident Amanda Sturtevant invoked their adherence to a "higher law." Accused by a Cleveland newspaper of abetting Brown, Strurtevant responded that she "invited and cordially welcomed" Brown to her home and was "glad [to have] entertained so worthy a man." She openly admitted that she had knowledge of Brown's violent rescue of fugitives in Missouri before inviting him to her home, concluding, "I am free to say that I approve it." While Sturtevant denied any foreknowledge of the Harpers Ferry raid, she defiantly announced that, even if she had "aided him in any way in his praiseworthy efforts to liberate the slaves," she would not have violated the laws of Ohio. As to federal laws, she stated, "Any law, enactment, or custom which forbids me to aid suffering humanity wherever found, I utterly reject and despise." She then dared her enemies "to find a grand jury . . . who will indict me."[33]

Other women followed her lead. "How in the name of common sense do Christians propose to do away with this enormous sin if not with John Brown's method?" one woman asked. "You know very well and every body knows that southern slaveholders will not allow any kind of Christian teaching in all their borders only the christianity of devils and how is the great southern heart to be reached but by God's ministers of vengeance." Griffing, a Garrisonian abolitionist from Salem, Ohio, also outspokenly recognized Harpers Ferry as "a necessary and lawful penalty for violated rights." Although, she concluded, the attack was "less beautiful than the sunshine, the rain, and the dew, of moral influence, it had nevertheless a place in the counsels of Heaven, as well as the whirlwind, the Earthquake and the Fire, in the physical economy of nature."[34] (See also document 28.)

In the wake of Harpers Ferry, the 1860 presidential campaign saw vocal female partisanship in support of the Republican Party. Women supported the quasimilitary "Wide Awake" groups that emerged across the North. Youthful, well organized, and very energetic, Wide Awakes held picnics, marches, meetings, and celebrations in order to arouse the North's support for the Republican presidential candidate Abraham Lincoln. Elizabeth Cady Stanton and other Seneca Falls women presented their local Wide Awake group with a banner in September 1860. As document 29 shows, the following evening the eager, young male Wide Awakes honored Stanton, Susan B. Anthony, and other guests at the Stanton household with martial music followed by dancing and celebrating. It was a memorable event that illuminated the increasing partisanship of women in the new party. Side by side, arm in arm, militaristic young men and partisan women challenged the status quo and helped to bring victory to the Republicans.[35]

So common had the idea of the partisan woman become by the early 1860s that the rise of young Anna Dickinson as a brilliant Republican speaker raised very few objections (see document 30). Dickinson attracted thousands of people to her lectures and established herself as one of the most persuasive, successful, and talented partisan orators in the nation. In 1863, the New Hampshire Republican Party paid her to lecture across the state during a critical election. The twenty-year-old electrified audiences, and most political strategists credited her with ensuring a Republican victory.[36] In January 1864, at the request of leading congressmen in Washington, D.C., she gave a speech in the House Chamber. The large contingent of the nation's most powerful men and women gave her "tremendous applause" for her powerful oratory.[37]

While Anna Dickinson thrilled audiences across the North, a contingent of southern women became politically active as well. Louisa McCord was a well-educated, wealthy plantation mistress and author who passionately defended secession, slavery, and the Confederacy. Her published essays argued that blacks were better off in slavery and that God had ordained this position for the African race. She joined other South Carolinian "fire eaters" in pushing for southern states to rebel against the Union. Maryland resident Anna Ella Carroll became well known for her political writings in support of the anti-Catholic Know Nothing party during the 1850s. When the South seceded she took a completely different position than her southern sister McCord. Carroll strongly advocated for the Union and even claimed to have conceived of the "Tennessee Plan" to invade the South through the Cumberland and Tennessee rivers. She also published essays in support of Lincoln and his policies throughout the war. Though taking very different political positions, these two southern women found avenues for voicing their political opinions.[38]

Thus, women entered partisan politics through a variety of paths in the 1840s and 1850s. Some joined Whig picnics, serving pies to attendees and listening closely to political speeches. Others edited Free Soil newspapers, reminding party leaders that antislavery was an inherently moral movement. Still others stood before crowds and added their voices to the growing antislavery chorus across the North. The antislavery movement offered women access to partisan politics through its intensely moral focus. Women did not, however, perceive of themselves only as moral actors in the partisan world. Their familiarity with electoral campaigns resulted in an increasing political savviness that served them well as they negotiated for their party and their values. Southern women soon joined their northern counterparts and added their voices to the growing contingent of "passionate partisans" who believed they had a stake in policy making and governing.

Notes

1. A. D. Hawley to Betsey Mix Cowles, July 6, 1840, Betsy Mix Cowles Papers, Box 1, Folder 9, Department of Special Collections and Archives, Kent State University Library.

2. Anne M. Boylan, *The Origins of Women's Activism: New York and Boston, 1797–1840* (Chapel Hill: University of North Carolina Press, 2002), 137, 158; Ronald J. Zboray and Mary Saracino Zboray, "Whig Women, Politics, and Culture in the Campaign of 1840: Three Perspectives from Massachusetts," *Journal of the Early Republic* 17 (Summer 1997): 277–315, 281.

3. Melanie Susan Gustafson, *Women and the Republican Party, 1854–1924* (Urbana: University of Illinois Press, 2001); Sylvia D. Hoffert, *Jane Grey Swisshelm: An Unconventional Life, 1815–1884* (Chapel Hill: University of North Carolina Press, 2004); Michael Pierson, *Free Hearts and Free Homes: Gender and American Antislavery Politics* (Chapel Hill: University of North Carolina Press, 2003); Alisse Portnoy, *Their Right to Speak: Women's Activism in the Indian and Slave Debates* (Cambridge, Mass.: Harvard University Press, 2005); and Elizabeth R. Varon, "Tippecanoe and the Ladies, Too: White Women and Party Politics in Antebellum Virginia," *Journal of American History* 82 (September 1995): 494–521.

4. Gustafson, *Women and the Republican Party*, 6; and Hoffert, *Jane Grey Swisshelm*, 104–5.

5. Rosemarie Zagarri, "Gender and the First Party System," in *Federalists Reconsidered*, ed. Doron Ben-Atar and Barbara B. Oberg, 118–34 (Charlottesville: University Press of Virginia, 1998).

6. Rosemarie Zagarri, *Revolutionary Backlash: Women and Politics in the Early American Republic* (Philadelphia: University of Pennsylvania Press, 2007), 46–81; Catherine Allgor, *Parlor Politics: In Which the Ladies of Washington Help Build a City and a Government* (Charlottesville: University of Virginia Press, 2002).

7. Zagarri, *Revolutionary Backlash*, 180.

8. Boylan, *Origins of Women's Activism*.

9. Rebecca Edwards, *Angels in the Machinery: Gender in American Party Politics from the Civil War to the Progressive Era* (New York: Oxford University Press, 1997).

10. Varon, "Tippecanoe and the Ladies, Too," 495, 499; Edwards, *Angels in the Machinery*, 17.

11. Edwards, *Angels in the Machinery*, 17; Jayne Crumpler DeFiore, "COME, and Bring the Ladies: Tennessee Women and the Politics of Opportunity during the Presidential Campaigns of 1840 and 1844," *Tennessee Historical Quarterly* 51 (1992): 204.

12. DeFiore, "COME, and Bring the Ladies," 201.

13. Varon, "Tippecanoe and the Ladies, Too," 502.

14. DeFiore, "COME, and Bring the Ladies," 201.

15. Zboray and Zboray, "Whig Women, Politics, and Culture."

16. Dorothy Sterling, *Ahead of Her Time: Abby Kelley and the Politics of Antislavery* (New York: Norton, 1991).

17. "Ladies Benevolent and Antislavery Association, of Jackson," *Signal of Liberty*, June 20, 1846. For more on women and the Liberty Party, see Robertson, *Heart Beating for Liberty*, 37–66.

18. Gustafson, *Women and the Republican Party*, 7.

19. On Liberty Party organizing at the local level, see Bruce Laurie, *Beyond Garrison: Antislavery and Social Reform* (Cambridge: Cambridge University Press, 2005), 63; and Reinhard O. Johnson, "The Liberty Party in Massachusetts, 1840–1848: Antislavery Third Party Politics in the Bay State," *Civil War History* 28 (Fall 1982): 246; "Notice," *Western Citizen*, March 21, 1844; "The Ladies of Michigan," *Signal of Liberty*, September 26, 1846; "Political Convention," *Free Labor Advocate and*

Anti-Slavery Chronicle, May 20, 1843; Letter from Huldah Wickersham to Charles H. Test, n.d., Indiana State Library, Indiana Division, Manuscripts Collection, Charles H. Test Letters, 1840–1843, S1296. Reprinted in Thomas D. Hamm, *The Antislavery Movement in Henry County, Indiana* (New Castle: Indiana County Historical Society, 1987), 62–65; Mary B. Davis, "For the Western Citizen," *Western Citizen*, May 9, 1848.

20. "A Call for a North-Western Liberty Convention at Chicago," *Western Citizen*, March 18, 1846; "A Call for a North-Western Liberty Convention." The four men included Charles V. Dyer, Luther Rossiter, Ichabod Codding, and Owen Lovejoy; "North-Western Convention," *Western Citizen*, June 30, 1846.

21. "Female Anti-Slavery State Society," *Western Citizen*, June 20, 1844; "State Female A. S. Society," *Western Citizen*, August 11, 1846.

22. On the Free Soil Party, see Jonathan Earle, *Jacksonian Antislavery and the Politics of Free Soil* (Chapel Hill: University of North Carolina Press, 2003); and Pierson, *Free Hearts and Free Homes*.

23. Pierson, *Free Hearts and Free Homes*, 57. On Swisshelm, see also Hoffert, *Jane Grey Swisshelm*; and Frederick J. Blue, *No Taint of Compromise: Crusaders in Antislavery Politics* (Baton Rouge: Louisiana State University Press, 2005).

24. Pierson, *Free Hearts and Free Homes*, 62–63. For more on Stowe, see Joan D. Hedrick, *Harriet Beecher Stowe: A Life* (New York: Oxford University Press, 1994); on the politics of the 1850s, see William H. Freehling, *The Road to Disunion: Volume 1: Secessionists at Bay, 1776–1854* (New York: Oxford University Press, 1991); William H. Freehling, *The Road to Disunion: Volume 2: Secessionists Triumph, 1854–1861* (New York: Oxford University Press, 2007); and Elizabeth R. Varon, *Disunion! The Coming of the Civil War* (Chapel Hill: University of North Carolina Press, 2008).

25. Richard H. Sewell, *Ballots for Freedom: Antislavery Politics in the United States, 1837–1860*, reprint (New York: Norton, 1980 [1976]), 254.

26. Pierson, *Free Hearts and Free Homes*.

27. William E. Gienapp, *The Origins of the Republican Party, 1852–1856* (New York: Oxford University Press, 1988), 376–77.

28. Pierson, *Free Hearts and Free Homes*, 142–47.

29. Pierson, *Free Hearts and Free Homes*, 148; "The Ladies of Lawrence," *Anti-Slavery Bugle*, January 12, 1856. See also Robertson, *Heart Beating for Liberty*, 198.

30. Daniel Hise diary, October 17, 1858, Ohio Historical Society, Columbus, Ohio; "Border Ruffianism in Fairfield Township," *Anti-Slavery Bugle*, November 27, 1858. See also "Letter from Frances E. Watkins," *Anti-Slavery Bugle*, November 13, 1858.

31. For more on Truth's lecturing experiences see Victoria Ortiz, *Sojourner Truth: A Self-Made Woman* (Philadelphia: Lippincott, 1974), 68–73. See also two recent biographies of Truth: Carleton Mabee and Susan Mabee Newhouse, *Sojourner Truth: Slave, Prophet, Legend* (New York: New York University Press, 1993); and Nell Irvin Painter, *Sojourner Truth: A Life, A Symbol* (New York: Norton, 1996). For references to Truth's early lectures in the Old Northwest, see *New Lisbon Aurora*, August 27,

1851, and March 3, 1852; "Treason in Disguise," *Liberator*, June 21, 1861; "Shameful Persecution," *Liberator*, June 28, 1861.

32. Lydia Maria Francis Child, *Letters of Lydia Maria Child* (Boston: Houghton, Mifflin, 1883), 135.

33. On the Missouri rescue, see Stephen Oates, *To Purge This Land with Blood: A Biography of John Brown* (New York: Harper & Row, 1970), 260–64; "Mrs. Sturtevant," *Anti-Slavery Bugle*, November 19, 1859.

34. Sarah Everett to "Jennie," December 31, 1859, John Brown Papers, Kansas State Historical Society, quoted in Oates, *To Purge This Land with Blood*, 317; "The Salem Quarterly Meeting of Human Progress," *Anti-Slavery Bugle*, May 26, 1860.

35. Jon Grinspan, "'Young Men for War': The Wide Awakes and Lincoln's 1860 Presidential Campaign," *Journal of American History* 92, no. 2 (September 2009): 357–78; Ann D. Gordon, ed., *The Selected Papers of Elizabeth Cady Stanton and Susan B. Anthony: Volume 1: In the School of Antislavery, 1840 to 1860* (New Brunswick, N.J.: Rutgers University Press, 1997), 441–44.

36. On Dickinson, see J. Matthew Gallman, *America's Joan of Arc: The Life of Anna Elizabeth Dickinson* (New York: Oxford University Press, 2008); Gustafson, *Women and the Republican Party*; James McPherson, *The Struggle for Equality: Abolitionists and the Negro in the Civil War and Reconstruction* (Princeton, N.J.: Princeton University Press, 1967), 128–31; and Wendy Hamand Venet, *Neither Ballots nor Bullets: Women Abolitionists and the Civil War* (Charlottesville: University of Virginia Press, 1991), 35–59.

37. Gallman, *Joan of Arc*, 37.

38. On McCord, see Leigh Fought, *Southern Womanhood and Slavery: A Biography of Louisa S. McCord, 1810–1879* (Columbia: University of Missouri Press, 2003). On Carroll, see Janet L. Coryell, *Neither Heroine nor Fool: Anna Ella Carroll of Maryland* (Kent, Ohio: Kent State University Press, 1990).

Conclusion

By moving beyond "separate spheres," the field of American women's history is now developing a rich and complex historiography that suggests a new periodization and new questions about women's lives—in the economy, in society, and in politics. The fledgling United States celebrated the "women patriots" of the Revolution, even in the midst of a "revolutionary backlash" that curtailed general approval for women's engagement in civic culture. A new ideal for women that mandated sexual restraint and domestic devotion seemed to offer at once constraints as well as compensatory opportunities. Yet, women in various classes and regions continued their interactions beyond their households—in producing for the market or marketing their labor, as students, educators, and authors, and as advocates for widows, orphans, slaves, and Native Americans. They appeared as informal arbitrators in the emergent political world of the new nation. This elite female political domain emerged in the early years of the two-party system but ebbed in influence with the spread of universal white manhood suffrage. Meanwhile, women gained influence in a myriad of voluntary organizations. Bolstered by claims of superior moral sensitivity, middle-class wives and mothers asserted the needs of others and, in the process, established the legitimacy of their presence. For most free African American women, the politics of respectability dominated; those who could participated actively in the auxiliaries to autonomous black organizations that emerged in churches, school, and the black convention movement. A few found a broader audience as they crafted gendered arguments for the morality of racial equality.

By 1840, some women—overwhelmingly white and northern but including women in the South and the Midwest, and including some free women of color—began to stake their claim to an enhanced political status within and beside political parties. Fueled by notions of the necessity of a "moral politics," women became partisans, finding their places in the "antipolitics" partisanship of the 1840s and 1850s, especially in the third-party challenges of the Liberty Party and then the successor Republicans. Antislavery women helped redefine the terrain of politics and its relationship to domestic values. In so doing, they challenged the masculine gendering of politics, with its corrupt and corrupting activities, and its psychological and sometimes even physical violence. Increasing numbers of women and men believed that elections could accomplish what moral suasion had failed to achieve: an end to the enslavement of African Americans and, with this, the material and ideological basis for American prosperity at home. Yet, by embracing the passions of politics, women partisans became participants in the inflammatory

conflicts at the polls; they were not the calm, companionate force of modera-
tion that had coolly reminded middle-class men of their habits of self-control.
The Second Party System—the rivalry between Democrats and Whigs that
had characterized American politics since the era of Andrew Jackson—was
undermined when enthusiastic women partisans left behind restraint to join
their male counterparts to accomplish through their political activities the
reformation of home and country.

Did the incursion of women into party politics bring about the Civil War?
Certainly, no event of such complexity had a single cause, but the mobilization of a new and energetic constituency may have raised the stakes of
the political conflict, making its resolution within the existing system even
more difficult. Certainly, the vituperation that "female politicos" received,
especially at the hands of southern critics, escalated tensions and excited
some to call for the return of women to their "separate sphere." Yet, as this
volume argues, women's concern for home and family had never been merely
a private matter, and the moral issues that were gendered female always had
a public dimension. Throughout the years between the ratification of the
Constitution and the outbreak of the Civil War, women's public activities
developed in conjunction with their domestic concerns. In different ways,
in diverse regions, and within particular intersectionalities of race and class,
American women had always combined private, public, and political.

Primary Documents

Phase 1: Deferential Domestics

1. Susannah Rowson, Excerpts from *Charlotte Temple*, 1791

Originally published in England, *Charlotte Temple* by Susanna Rowson (1762–1824) became the first American "best seller," with reprintings in the United States beginning in 1794. The novel told the story of a virtuous but impulsive young woman lured away from her loving parents by her evil French teacher, Mademoiselle La Rue, conspiring with a dashing British military lieutenant Montraville and his dissolute fellow officer Belcour. Transported for service across the Atlantic, Montraville convinces Charlotte to follow but abandons the now-pregnant runaway to wed another, having become convinced by Belcour that Charlotte has been unfaithful to him. Belcour, however, furthers Charlotte's fall with his own debauchery, pocketing the funds supplied by Montraville and leaving her penniless. Charlotte seeks aid from a respectable neighbor, Mrs. Beauchamp, but loses contact when she is turned out of her lodgings. Her former French teacher, now posing as a respectable Mrs. Crayton, rebuffs her. A compassionate maidservant, however, shelters Charlotte who gives birth to her daughter. This extract begins after the doctor called to attend to the failing Charlotte enlists the help of Mrs. Beauchamp without knowing that she had previously befriended his patient.

The archetypical seduction novel, *Charlotte Temple* appealed to a large American audience because it emerged amidst a time of changing assumptions about female sexuality. Women in the prerevolutionary period were constructed as highly sexual and uncontrollably seductive. In the early national period, new ideas began to take hold, emphasizing women's virtue and asexual nature that might be defiled by licentious men.

*   *   *

Chapter XXXIII: Which People Void of Feeling Need Not Read

WHEN Mrs. Beauchamp entered . . . , she started back with horror. On a wretched bed, without hangings and but poorly supplied with covering, lay the emaciated figure of what still retained the semblance of a lovely woman, though sickness had so altered her features that Mrs. Beauchamp had not the least recollection of her person. . . . The infant was asleep beside its mother, and, on a chair by the bed side, stood a porrenger [sic] and wooden spoon, containing a little gruel, and a tea-cup with about two spoonfulls [sic] of wine in it. Mrs. Beauchamp had never before beheld such a scene of poverty; she shuddered involuntarily, and exclaiming— "heaven preserve us!" leaned on the back of a chair ready to sink to the earth. . . . Charlotte caught the sound of her voice, and starting almost out of bed, exclaimed—"Angel of peace and mercy, art thou come to deliver me? Oh, I know you are, for whenever you was near me I felt eased of half my sorrows; but you don't know me, nor can I, with all the recollection I am mistress of, remember your name just now, but I know that benevolent countenance, and the softness of that voice which has so often comforted the wretched Charlotte."

Mrs. Beauchamp had . . . seated herself on the bed and taken one of her hands; she looked at her attentively, and at the name of Charlotte she perfectly conceived the whole shocking affair. . . . "Gracious heaven," said she, "is this possible?" and bursting into tears, she reclined the burning head of Charlotte on her own bosom; and folding her arms about her, wept over her in silence. "Oh," said Charlotte, "you are very good to weep thus for me: it is a long time since I shed a tear for myself: my head and heart are both on fire, but these tears of your's [sic] seem to cool and refresh it. Oh now I remember you said you would send a letter to my poor father: do you think he ever received it? or perhaps you have brought me an answer: why don't you speak, Madam? Does he say I may go home? Well he is very good; I shall soon be ready."

She then made an effort to get out of bed; but being prevented, her frenzy again returned, and she raved with the greatest wildness and incoherence. Mrs. Beauchamp . . . contented herself with ordering the apartment to be made more comfortable, and procuring a proper nurse for both mother and child; and having learnt the particulars of Charlotte's fruitless application to Mrs. Crayton from honest John, she amply rewarded him for his benevolence, and returned home with a heart oppressed with many painful sensations, but yet rendered easy by the reflexion [sic] that she had performed her duty towards a distressed fellow-creature.

Early the next morning she again visited Charlotte, and found her tolerably composed; she called her by name, thanked her for her goodness, and when her child was brought to her, pressed it in her arms, wept over it, and called it the offspring of disobedience. Mrs. Beauchamp was delighted to see her so much amended, and began to hope she might recover, and, spite of her former errors, become a useful and respectable member of society; but the arrival of the doctor put an end to these delusive hopes: he said nature was making her last effort, and a few hours would most probably consign the unhappy girl to her kindred dust.

Being asked how she found herself, she replied—"Why better, much better, doctor. I hope now I have but little more to suffer. I had last night a few hours sleep, and when I awoke recovered the full power of recollection. I am quite sensible of my weakness; I feel I have but little longer to combat with the shafts of affliction. I have an [sic] humble confidence in the mercy of him who died to save the world, and trust that my sufferings in this state of mortality, joined to my unfeigned repentance, through his mercy, have blotted my offences from the sight of my offended maker. I have but one care—my poor infant! Father of mercy," continued she, raising her eyes, "of thy infinite goodness, grant that the sins of the parent be not visited on the unoffending child. May those who taught me to despise thy laws be forgiven; lay not my offences to their charge, I beseech thee; and oh! shower the choicest of thy blessings on those whose pity has soothed the afflicted heart, and made easy even the bed of pain and sickness."

She was exhausted by this fervent address to the throne of mercy, and though her lips still moved her voice became inarticulate: she lay for some time as it were in a doze, and then recovering, faintly pressed Mrs. Beauchamp's hand, and requested that a clergyman might be sent for.

On his arrival she joined fervently in the pious office, frequently mentioning her ingratitude to her parents as what lay most heavy at her heart. When she had performed the last solemn duty, and was preparing to lie down, a little bustle on the outside door occasioned Mrs. Beauchamp to open it, and enquire the cause. A man in appearance about forty, presented himself, and asked for Mrs. Beauchamp.

"That is my name, Sir," said she.

"Oh then, my dear Madam . . . tell me where I may find my poor, ruined, but repentant child. . . . Tell me, Madam," cried he wildly, "tell me, I beseech thee, does she live? shall I see my darling once again? . . . Lead, lead me to her, that I may bless her, and then lie down and die."

The ardent manner in which he uttered these words occasioned him to raise his voice. It caught the ear of Charlotte: she knew the beloved sound: and uttering a loud shriek, she sprang forward as Mr. Temple entered the room. "My adored father." "My long lost child." Nature could support no more, and they both sunk lifeless into the arms of the attendants. . . .

When Charlotte recovered, she found herself supported in her father's arms. She cast on him a most expressive look, but was unable to speak. A reviving cordial was administered. She then asked in a low voice, for her child: it was brought to her: she put it in her father's arms. "Protect her," said she, "and bless your dying—"

Unable to finish the sentence, she sunk back on her pillow: her countenance was serenely composed; she regarded her father as he pressed the infant to his breast with a steadfast look; a sudden beam of joy passed across her languid features, she raised her eyes to heaven—and then closed them for ever.

Chapter XXXIV: Retribution

In the mean time Montraville having received orders to return to New-York, arrived, and having still some remains of compassionate tenderness for the woman whom he regarded as brought to shame by himself, he went out in search of Belcour, to enquire whether she was safe, and whether the child lived. He found him immersed in dissipation, and could gain no other intelligence than that Charlotte had left him, and that he knew not what was become of her.

"I cannot believe it possible," said Montraville, "that a mind once so pure as Charlotte Temple's, should so suddenly become the mansion of vice. Beware, Belcour," continued he, "beware if you have dared to behave either unjust or dishonourably to that poor girl, your life shall pay the forfeit:—I will revenge her cause."

. . . After much enquiry [Montraville] at length . . . learnt the misery Charlotte had endured from the complicated evils of illness, poverty, and a broken heart, and that she had set out on foot for New-York, on a cold winter's evening. . . .

Tortured almost to madness by this shocking account, he returned to the city, . . . entering the town he was obliged to pass several little huts, the residence of poor women who supported themselves by washing the cloaths [sic] of the officers and soldiers. It was nearly dark: he heard from a neighbouring steeple a solemn toll that seemed to say some poor mortal was going to their last mansion: the sound struck on the heart of Montraville, and he involuntarily stopped, when, from one of the houses, he saw the appearance of a funeral. Almost unknowing what he did, he followed at a small distance; and as they let the coffin into the grave, he enquired of a soldier who stood by, and had just brushed off a tear that did honour to his heart, who it was that was just buried. "An please your honour," said the man, "'tis a poor girl that was brought from her friends by a cruel man, who left her when she was big with child, and married another . . . she went to Madam Crayton's, but she would not take her in, and so the poor thing went raving mad." Montraville . . . struck his hands against his forehead with violence; and exclaiming "poor murdered Charlotte!" ran with precipitation towards the place where they were heaping the earth on her remains. "Hold, hold, one moment," said he. "Close not the grave of the injured Charlotte Temple till I have taken vengeance on her murderer."

"Rash young man," said Mr. Temple, "who art thou that thus disturbest the last mournful rites of the dead, and rudely breakest in upon the grief of an afflicted father."

"If thou art the father of Charlotte Temple . . . —I am Montraville." Then falling on his knees, he continued—"Here is my bosom. I bare it to receive the stroke I merit. Strike—strike now, and save me from the misery of reflexion [sic]."

"Alas!" said Mr. Temple, "if thou wert the seducer of my child, thy own reflexions [sic] be thy punishment. I wrest not the power from the hand of omnipotence. Look on that little heap of earth, there hast thou buried the only joy of a fond father. Look at it often; and may thy heart feel such true sorrow as shall merit the mercy of heaven." . . . Montraville . . . at that instant remembering the perfidy of Belcour, flew like lightning to his lodgings. Belcour was intoxicated; Montraville impetuous: they fought, and the sword of the latter entered the heart of his adversary. He fell, and expired almost instantly. Montraville had received a slight wound; and overcome with the agitation of his mind and loss of blood, was carried in a state of insensibility to his distracted wife. A dangerous illness and obstinate delirium ensued, during which he raved incessantly for Charlotte: but a strong constitution, and the tender assiduities of Julia, in time overcame the disorder. He recovered; but to the end of his life was subject to severe fits of melancholy, and while he remained at New-York frequently retired to the church-yard, where he would weep over the grave, and regret the untimely fate of the lovely Charlotte Temple.

Source: Susanna Rowson, *Charlotte: A Tale of Truth* (1791, First American Edition: Philadelphia: Mathew Carey, 1794, cited here from Project Guttenberg, 2006), www.gutenberg.org/dirs/1/7/171/171.txt.

2. Martha Ballard's Diary:
Two Months in the Life of a Maine Midwife, 1800

Between 1785, when the government of the fledgling United States still struggled to establish itself under the awkward Articles of Confederation, until 1812, when the country entered into its second war against Great Britain, the Maine midwife Martha Ballard (1734–1812) recorded the daily events of her life in a carefully written journal. Like many women in the rural North, Ballard filled her hours with household chores, visits with family and neighbors, and exchanges of services within her community. In the year 1800, from which this selection excerpts two months, Thomas Jefferson was elected to the American presidency in the nation's capitol, but the sixty-five-year-old Ballard, married for over forty-five years to a sometime mill manager, surveyor, and tax collector, manifests greater concern for the lives of her five children, all but the youngest married, and most nearby raising their own growing families. In addition to her engagement in this dense network of family relations, as the diary demonstrates, Ballard also undertook in multiple exchanges of labor, commodities, and cash to help maintain a family economy. The two months covered here—January and May 1800—include nine of the twenty-seven births Ballard attended that year; they also reveal the seasonal rhythms of her life, with her January days filled with nursing the ill and knitting, while May saw her "fatogued" by working in her garden planting vegetables, as well as milking, churning, and baking.

January 1800

[1]	4	Clear and Cold. Son Ephm Clapboarding ye South End of our house. I have been at home kniting.	at home.
[2] [Birth Davenport Dagt.]	5	Clear and pleast. I was Calld at 1h 30m morn to See the wife of Thos Davenport who was Safe Deld of her 3d daugt & 5 Child at 12 O Clock in ye day. I returnd home at 4 pm. Sons Lambd and Ephm here, finisht the outside of our house.	at mr Davenports. Birth 1st
[3]	6	Clear. I have been at home unwell. Son Jonas wife took Tea with me.	at home.
[4]	7	Cloudy. I have been at home mending Cloaths, feel unwell. Hepsy has a Soar throat. mr Ballard, Gilly and Jack Pierce to the meddow. Ephm has made Sellar Stairs, Bedroom partition &C, &C. Dagt Lambd Sent mr Ballards newGt Coat home.	at home.
[5]	1	Clear and Cold. my famely all attend worship Except my Self. I have felt very unwell.	at home.
[6]	2	Clear and Cold. I have been at home, helpt do house work. we killd all of our hens. mr Ballard been to meeting of Bridg proprieters, Cyrus to mr Hamlins Store, recd 9/ there by order of mr Stulely springer.	at home.
[7]	3	Clear and Cold. mr Ballard had a Collic ye morn, got better Soon. I have been at home, not so well as Could be wisht. mrss Edson Dind here.	at home. mrs Edson & Dagt Ballard here.
[8]	4	Clear. mr Ballard at Varsalboro Surveying for mr Stephens. Son Ephm Came and took a pigg, which wd 65 lb, for mr Lambd. I have been at home. we made Some mins and apple Pies. Cyrus giting wood.	at home
[9]	5	Clear. mr Ballard giting timber to mend Sleads and mending them, had threats of ye Collic. I have been at home, mended [Crocery]. mr Hains Learned here at Evng.	at home.

Date		Diary entry	Summary
[10]	6	Clear. I was Calld at 1h morn to See a mrss Hrriman, Shee was Deld of a Son before I reacht there, which wd 10 lb 5 oz. I Drest the inft and was then Calld by mr Elias Cragge to go and See his wife who was in Labour. Shee was Deld before Day of her 2nd Child and first Dagt. I was there and at mr Herimans till 4h pm when mr Cragge Sett out to Conduct me home. the Sleigh over Sett, the fills broke but we were not hurt. I went to mrs Dutins till another hors and Sleigh were procured and Came home Saffe. mr Crage bestowed 12/ as a reward. this inft 3rd Child.	at mr Herimans. Birth 2nd. mr Craggs. Birth 3d. recd 12/ as a rewd.
[X. Birth Elis Craggs Dagt. X.]			
11	7	Clear. I have been at home, finisht Allin Lambds mitts.	at home.
12	1	Snowd. I was Calld to Son Lambds to See Thoms, he being very unwell. we Gave him Senna and he Seemd better. I wrode home with mr Ballard at Evng.	at Son Lambds. Thomas is unwell.
13	2	Cloudy, Snowd at night. I have been at home. Hepsy past an operation for ye itch. mr Ballard and Jona mending Slead. Cyrus went to mill and to Son Lambds. Thomas is much better.	at home.
14	3	Snowd. Polly Faught here, left 1-2/1 busl Corn for Son Lambd. I have been kniting mitts for Cyrus. I wrote to Sister Waters and Sent to mr Burtun to Carrie to Boston	at home. wrote to Sister Waters.
15	4	Clear and Pleasant. Brother Moore, his wife & 2 of his Sons, Son and Dagt Lambd, mr Truant and Lady, Son Jona & wife here. I have been at home.	at home, had Compy.
16	5	Clear fore n, Cloudy aftern. I went to mr Parkers and mrs Welches foren, have been Kniting ys aftern. Jonas wife in here. mrs Welch Sent my Cloath, 20 and 1/2 yards.	at mr Parkers and mrs Welch es.
17	6	Snowd. I have been at home, finisht the 3d pair mitts which I have knit the prest weak.	at home. Death old mrss Littlefield.
18	7	very rainy. I have been at home Sewing.	at home.

19 1 X Birth James Herimans Dagt. XX.	Clear, a pleast Son but windy. mr Ballard, Jon a and his wife attended worship. we went there at Evng. Shubal Pitts & wife there. I was Calld from there at 9h Evn to See the wife of mr Heryman, Shee was Deld very Soon after I arivd, of a Dagt. Shee wrode in a Sleigh 13 miles after 7, her illness was on her when Shee Sett out from Doct Quimbys. I went to See mrss Robinson, Shee is very ill with a Cold.	at Son Jon as & mr Herimans. Birth 4th.recd a Letter of Decr 6th fm Sister Waters with News ytBror Jonas Dagt Sophia was Dead.
20 2	Clear till noon then over Cast. mr Ballard and Jona been to ye meddow, Cyrus Breakng flax. the widdow Farewell and mrss Pierce here. I have been kniting on a Stockin for mr Ballard, Hepsy washt.	at home.
21 3	Clear. I was at Son Jonas. mrss Titcomb and her Son there. mr Ballard got wood.	at Son Jonas.
22 4	Clear. I have been at home kniting. mrs Saunders & Silva Edson here. mr Benn Browns wife took Tea with me. Son Jona & wife to Sleigh ride.	at home.
23 5	Clear. I have been kniting, finisht a Stockin for my husband; at home all day.	at home.
24 6	Clear and Pleast. mr Ballard, my Self, Cyrus, Hepsy and her Bror Wilm, and Son Town Supt with Son Jon a on a fine Turkey roasted. Son Town, Hains Learned and Wm Brown Slept here.	at Son Jonas.
25 7	Snowd and windy. mr Ballard went down in Town, our Company Each to their homes. Josiah Parker Calld me and dagt Ballard to See his wife at dusk. Shee was not very ill when we arivd.	at mr Parkers.
26 1 X. Birth Josiah Parkers [3d] Son & 7th Child. X.	Clear and Cold. my Patient was Safe Deld at 5h this morn of a fine Son, her husband went and Conducted mrss Stone there and my Dagt & I Came home at 8h morn. I went to bed after I reacht home and Slept. mr Ballard wt to meeting.	at Josiah Parkers. Birth 5th. recd 8/ at Crosbys Store.
27 2	Clear and Cold. I have been at home.	at home.
28 3	Clear and Cold. I have been at home kniting.	at home.
29 4	Clear and very Cold. I have been at home, finisht a pair hoes for mr Ballard. Jona & his wife went to Son Pollards. Hepsy went there, came home at midnight. it is Colder then it has been this winter.	at home.

| 30 | 5 | Clear and a very Cold morn. I had fire put into our Seller. Son Pollard and Lambd, with their wives and Babes, and Rhoda Came here. we had meet and beens for Diner. Son Jona and his wife Joind us at Tea. Rhoda went home with them and their dagt Hannah tarries there this night. | at home. Sons Ballard, Pollard, Lambard & wives here. |
| 31 | 6 | Clear. Rhoda Pollard & Hanh Ballard here foren. I was Calld at 1h pm to go and See the wife of James moore at Read field, find her very unwell. mrss Gould and Taylor tarried there this night. | at James Moores. |

MAY 1800

1	5	Clear. I have been at home, workt in my gardin; feel fatagued	at home.
2	6	rainy. I kept house, my hands are so Soar with working in the gardin that I Could do no work butt Sort my beens.	at home.
3	7	Cloudy morn. I have been mooving dirt in my Gardin. mr Ballard and Son Jona Ploughd it this fore n. they then went to mr Spragues for hey. Hepsy went to See Huldy Hatch who is Sick at mr Mosiers, they think Shee is better. mr Dingly detr to Seeds 2/. Fredric Faught to 1 oz. Parsnip, and Dito Carrot Seed 2/. Old mrs Shaw to 1 oz Carrot, 1 do parsnips and Sundry other kinds 3/	at home. my Faught and Old mrs Shaw had Gardin Seeds
4	1	Clear and Cool. mr Ballard, my Self and Cyrus and Ephm attended worship. Jonas wife and Betsy Cowen took Tea here. I was at mr Blacks at intermition, his daught Dorkis has the mumps. Revd mr Stones Text forin was St John XIXC, 30V, aftern 11 Corinthns VII C, 2 vers.	at meeting, it was Communion day.
5	2	Clear. mr Ballard Surveying for mr Benn Petingail. I have planted potatoes, Beens and Sowd Peas in my Gardin. my Sister Barton came here, informs our friends at the west were well when Shee left there, I recd a Letter fm Bror Elijah. mrs Pitts, Son and Dagt Ballard, mr Cypher and Betsy Cowen took Tea here.	at home. Sister Barton Came here, Brot me a Letter from Brr Elijah. O ye Joy in [Seeing] & hearing fm my [dear] friends.

7	4	Clear but Cool. my Daughters and Son Pollard attinding ym Came foren here to welcom their dear aunt. we visited Son Jon a aftern where Son Lambd joind us. may our meeting be for our good as I Can truly Say it is a Comfort to me.	at Son Jon as. my Dagts here. mrs Crage [therel, gave me Tea and [ ].
8	5	Clear rainy forenn. Dagts Lambd and Ballard Dind and took Tea with me. Son Lambd took Tea and Sett out for home with their Childn. I have been at home, Planted Some beens.	at home. mrs Hamln & others here.
9	6	Clear and Cold. Old Lady Hamlin, mrs Pitts and Dagt Ballard here to Tea. mr Carter waited on his marm Hamlin to and from here.	at home. mrs Hamln & others here.
10	7	Clear and Pleast. I have workt in my Gardin, Planted Beens, Sowd Cabbage, French Turnip, Pepper grass, Sage & Parsley. mr Ballard Sowd Parsnips. I do feel fatagued. Richd Foster Sleeps here.	at home.
11	1	Clear. mr Ballard, Cyrus & Ephm went to meeting. Sister Barton Sett out with her Son Foster to go to his house. [I] Cookt the head and harslett of a Veall which we killd yesterday.	at home. Sister Barton went home withher Son Foster
12	2	Clear. I workt very hard in my Gardin, then had my Evning work to do by reason of Hepsys going to walk Streat with Lydia Nudd. I went to bed at 10.	
13	3	Clear. I have had my house work to do and, wors than all my hard work, to bear frowns (from one who Calls him Self my friend) and taunts from Hepsy for takeing proper Care of my house, may God forgiv their Erer and enable me to perform the trust reposed in me as the head of a famely, as he Dictates to me is right.	at home and O my Trouble.
14	4	Clear. I have been So unwell that I Could not Sett up till 2 or 3 o Clock aftern, whin Jonas wife Came in and got water for me to bath my feet and made me a dish of Tea. I had not had So much as a drop of water given me to wet my mouth till my husband Came to dine, when he gave me a little which had been in the house 2 days.	at home, very unwell. Hepsy left with out Saying Good by.
15	5	Clear. I have been at home but have but little Comfort. God grant me grace & patience to Sufer what he is pleased to inflict upon me.	at home, did my house work.

Day		Entry	Note
16	6	Clear. I have Done my house work alltho I have Sufered much pain. O God, if it is Consistant with thy will let this Cup depart, but not my will but thine be done.	at home.
17	7	Clear. mr Ballard Cleand flax Seed and Sowd it. he has Seen 75 years. I have Bakt and done my other work. O Parent allmighty, give me [Strength] to bear all that thou art pleased to Lay upon me, and may all things work for good to my immortal Sole. mr Capin and wife Dind here on their way to Son Lambards.	at home. mr Capin & wife here.
18	1	Cloudy and Some rain. my husband went to meeting but finds time to keep up the afair of Hepsy and torment me. I had no Sleep this night. he lay before the kitchen fire, he Compared me to Everdon. O God, pardon his Sin in this Cruel Conduct towards me.	at home.
19	2	Cloudy morn. mr Capin, his wife and Son Ephm Came here, took Breakfast. I [rose] early, put on a kettle of [yn] to boil, then milkt and got breakfast and did my washing; then went to ye Spring for water but, alass, how fatagued was I when I reacht my house. mrs Cypher and Son Jonas fife here.	at home.
20	3	Clear. I have been at home, workt some in the gardin and did my house work. God grant me Strength to bear my toil and affliction.	at home.
21	4	Clear. I have done my work, planted Potatoes, squash and musk mellons. mrs Farewell and Saunders and Dagt Ballard to See me yesterday. mrs Ballard is gone to Son Pollards ys day.	at home.
22	5	Clear. Dagt Ballard returnd, Dagt Polld Came with her. they are gone to ye Stores ys aftern, mr Ballard to meet a road Committee. I went in to Jonas with my Dagt Pollard.	at Jonas.
23	6	Clear. I have Done my hous work and plantd Cucumbers of the Long kind at ye N End of the hous. I Planted Cramby Beans. Nabby Andrw and Dagt Ballard took Tea with me. Nabby informd me Hepsy was at her Dadys and not at mr [Browains] as Shee pretended.	at home. workt Some in ye gardin. Dagt Pollard went home this morn.

24	7	Clear. I have Bakt, Churnd, made a Chees, Irond my Cloaths and done my other hous work. Dagt Ballard, Son Ephm took Tea with us. I Churned 7 lb butter.	at home.
25	1	Clear. I was Calld at the first h morn to See mrs Gill who is unwell. mrs Pitts there, went home at Evng and Old mrs Gill Came and tarried all night.	at mr Gills.
26	2	Clear. I have been at mr Gills all day.	At Ditoes.
27	3	Clear Except Showers. Son Lambd brot his wife and babe to mr Gills, tarrie there ys night. mrs Parker Sett out for Boston with her famely.	at Ditoes. my Patient unwell ye
28	4	Clear. I left mrs Gill more Comfortable, Came home at 10h morn; attended to my work. mrs Trask and dagt Ballard here. mr Ballard and I took Tea there.	at Ditoes & at mr Craggs.
29	5	Clear. I have, thro much pain, Done my work. been on the bed a great Part of the day. O God, if it be thy will let the Cup of affliction depart from me, but thy will be done.	at home, was very unwell.
30	6	Clear and warm. I have Done my house work, Bakt and Brewd; feel more Comfortable than I did yesterday. Cyrus went to mr Bonds for Some rice which Son Ephm procured for us, 16 lb.	at home.
31	7	rainy. I have been at home, Done my work in ye house and Some in ye Gardin, but feel unfitt.	at home.

Source: Martha Ballard's Diary Online: http://dohistory.org/diary

3. Eliza Leslie, "The Slaves," a Short Story from *The Young Ladies' Mentor*, 1803

Born in Philadelphia, Eliza Leslie (1787–1858) spent much of her first twelve years in London, returning to her native city in 1799. In the excerpt that follows, nineteen-year-old "Miss Leslie" composed a tale that highlights the pervasive culture of deference, structured by gender and race, that permeated the early years of the nineteenth century. White women as well as African American men and women, both free and enslaved, were expected to show respect and esteem for white males. In this story, the slave trader is depicted as a heroic figure and the slave woman shows appropriate respect for her superior. Britain and America both finally withdrew from the Atlantic slave trade in 1808. Later in her life, Leslie became well known as the author of household manuals and recipe books, as well as didactic tales for children and adults.

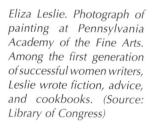

Eliza Leslie. Photograph of painting at Pennsylvania Academy of the Fine Arts. Among the first generation of successful women writers, Leslie wrote fiction, advice, and cookbooks. (Source: Library of Congress)

THE SLAVES, OR THE VICTIM RESCUED.

CAPT. SNELLGRAVE commanded an English vessel, in the African slave trade, and was remarkable for his humanity. Custom alone can authorise this commerce, offensive to nature, and which cannot be carried on, but at the utmost peril; since injustice and tyranny, generally produce despair and rebellion: for this reason, the Europeans are obliged to put the unhappy negroes they buy, in chains during the night, and most part of the day: notwithstanding which precaution, they often find means to unite, and conspire the destruction of their masters.

Snellgrave, bought many negroes on the banks of the river Collabar; among whom he observed a young woman, seemingly overwhelmed with affliction. Affected by her tears, he desired his interpreter to question her, and learned, that she wept for an only child she had lost the evening before.

She was taken on board the vessel, and, the very same day, Snellgrave received an invitation to visit the king of the district. Snellgrave accepted the invitation; but knowing the ferocity of the people, he ordered ten of his sailors and the gunner to accompany him, well armed. He was conducted to a place at some distance from the shore, and found the king placed on an elevated seat, under the shade of a tree.

The assembly was numerous; a croud [sic] of negro lords surrounding their king; and his guards, composed of about fifty men, armed with bows and arrows, the sabre at their side, and the zagaye [spear] in their hand, stood at some distance; the English with muskets on their shoulders, remained opposite his black majesty.

Snellgrave presented the king some European trifles. As he was ending the harangue, he heard groans, at some distance, that made him shudder; and turning round, perceived a little negro tied by the leg to a stake, stuck in the ground: two other negroes, of an hideous aspect, that stood by the side of a hole dug in the earth, armed with hatchets, and drest in an uncouth manner, seemed to guard the child; who looked at them weeping, with his hands in a supplicating posture.

The king, observing the emotion which this strange spectacle evidently caused in Snellgrave, assured him that he had nothing to fear from the two negroes, whom he looked up to with much surprise. "It is 'only,' (said he, with great gravity,) a child whom we are going to sacrifice to the god Egho for the prosperity of the kingdom."

This intelligence made Snellgrave tremble with horror; the English were only twelve men in all; the court and guard of the African prince, were altogether about an hundred; but compassion and humanity would not suffer Snellgrave to consider all he had to fear from the number and ferocity of the barbarians. . . . "Let us save this wretched child, my lads," said he, turning to his sailors, "come, follow me."

So saying, he ran to the little negro; and the English, all animated by the same feelings, as hastily followed. The negroes, at seeing this, yelled dismally, and fell tumultuously upon the English; Snellgrave, presented his pistol, and seeing the king draw back, demanded to be heard.

The king, with a single word calmed the fury of the negroes . . . while Snellgrave . . . explained the motive of his conduct, and ended by entreating the king to sell him the victim. The proposition was accepted; and Snellgrave was determined not to dispute about price. Luckily, however, the negro monarch wanted neither gold nor silver, was ignorant of pearls and diamonds, and thinking he would be sure to ask enough, demanded a necklace of blue glass beads, which was instantly given to him.

Snellgrave then flew to the innocent little creature . . . and drew his cutlass to divide the cord by which it was bound. The affrighted child thought Snellgrave was going to kill him, and gave a shriek of terror: but Snellgrave took him in his arms . . . and pressed him to his bosom. As soon as the child's fears were removed, he smiled, and caressed his deliverer: who, filled with delightful sensations, . . . returned to his ship.

When he came on board, he saw the young negress whom he had bought in the morning; she was ill, and sat weeping beside the surgeon; who, not able to persuade her to eat, obliged her to remain in the open air, for fear she should faint again.

The moment Snellgrave . . . passed by her, she turned her head, and perceiving the little negro in the arms of a sailor, shrieked, rose and ran to the child, who knew its mother, called to her, and held out its arms.

She clasped her infant to her bosom. . . . Every fatal resolution she had formed, her loss of liberty, the dreadful ills she had suffered, the projects of despair, all were forgotten. . . . She was a mother, and had found her lost child.

She learned, . . . from the interpreter, every circumstance of Snellgrave's behaviour; then, still holding her infant in her arms, she ran and threw herself at her benefactor's feet. "Now it is, said she, that I am truly your slave; this night was to have delivered me from bondage: but you have given me more than life; you have given me back my son: you are become my father; henceforth be assured of my obedience. . . . This infant is a dear and certain pledge."

The woman spoke with all the warmth, and energy of impassioned gratitude. . . . Snellgrave, . . . could not receive a sweeter reward for his humanity; which however was productive of other good efforts.

He had more than three hundred negroes on board, to whom the young woman related her adventure; this having heard, after expressing their admiration by redoubled plaudits, they promised unbounded submission; and in effect, Snellgrave, during the rest of the voyage, found in them all the respect and obedience a father could receive from his children.

Source: Eliza Leslie, *The Young Ladies' Mentor, or, Extracts in Prose and Verse for the Promotion of Virtue and Morality* (Philadelphia: Thomas S. Manning, 1803), 51–55.

4. Tapping Reeve, Excerpts from *The Law of Baron and Femme*, 1816

Recognized as the leading instructor in law in the early republic, Tapping Reeve (1744–1823) first published his *Law of Baron and Femme* in 1816. Reeve's reputation flourished, with his Litchfield, Connecticut, office becoming a major center of legal education. This work demonstrates that, in this transitional period, laws built upon older notions of women had begun to erode, although unevenly. Although coverture was no longer understood as absolute, Reeve nonetheless laid out how women's lack of autonomy remained an important legal concept. Although Reeve died in 1823, subsequent revisions of his volume in 1846, 1867, and then again in 1888 documented the changes in women's legal standing in the United States, and the long-standing impact of his original work.

*   *   *

The husband, by marriage, acquires an absolute title to all the personal property of the wife, which she had in possession at the time of the marriage; such as money, goods or chattels personal of any kind. These, by the marriage, become his property, as completely as the property which he purchases with his money; and such property can never again belong to the wife, upon the happening of any event, unless it be given to her by his will; and in case of the death of the husband, this property does not return to the wife, but vests in his executors. . . .

We will now inquire what advantages the wife may gain, eventually by marriage, in point of property, during the coverture. She gains nothing during his life; but upon the death of her husband intestate, she is entitled to one third part of his personal property, which remains after paying the debts due from the estate of the husband, if he left any issue; but if he left no issue, she is entitled to one half of the residuum of the personal estate, after the debts are paid. . . . There is one species of personal property in which she acquires a different interest from that which she may acquire in his other property, which is termed her *paraphernalia*. This is of two kinds: the first consists of her beds and clothing, suitable to her condition in life; the second consists of her ornaments and trinkets, such as her bracelets, jewels, her watch, rich laces, and the like. As to the former, they cannot, with propriety, be considered as his estate, for they are not liable, upon the principles of the common law, without any aid from any statute, to the payment of his debts, and never ought to be inventoried as part of his estate: neither can they be devised from her by will. As to the second kind, these cannot be devised from her by the husband, though he may take them from her, and dispose of them during the coverture: On the death of the husband, they vest in the wife, liable, indeed, to be taken by the executor of the husband, for the payment of his debts, provided that there are not sufficient assets beside to discharge his debts. . . .

By the death of the husband, the wife becomes entitled, during her life, to one third part of the real estate of inheritance (Dower) of which the husband was seised during the coverture. This estate is termed *dower*. Of this, the husband cannot deprive her by will; nor can he, by any conveyance, unless her consent be manifested, by joining with him in the conveyance. . . .

Although the husband is . . . entitled to all the property which the wife acquires during the coverture; yet, if damages be claimed for an injury to her person or reputation during coverture, those damages belong to her, and she must be joined with the husband in the suit. When damages for such an injury are collected, they belong to the husband. . . . From such injury, two actions may arise; as in the case of a battery of the wife, the husband and wife can bring an action to recover for the injury done to her, and the husband may bring an action in his own name, to recover damages which he sustained, by reason of the battery, which is termed an action of trespass *per quod consortium amisit*, in which he will recover for the loss of the company of his wife, if that have been the case, for the loss of her service, and also for expense which has arisen by reason of the battery. The husband may, in an action for a battery on himself, in the same declaration, demand damages for a battery to his wife *per quod consortium amisit*. The husband is also entitled to all the property which the wife acquires by her labour, service, or act, during coverture.

If any man should carry away the wife of another man, it is a trespass, for which a recovery of damages may be had by the husband.

The husband is entitled to an action for criminal conversation with his wife. In form, this is an action of trespass, *vi et armis*; but in substance, it is an action on the case for the seduction of the wife, the alienation of her affections from the husband, and exposing him to shame, ridicule, and the hazard of maintaining a spurious issue. A rigid adherence to a maxim, that has not the least foundation in common sense, that a wife has no will, occasioned the form of the writ to be that of trespass *vi et armis*, proceeding upon the ground that a wife was destitute of a will, and therefore could not have consented to commit adultery, but it must have been altogether a matter of violence.

Although this maxim has given form to the action brought in this case, which considers the defendant as a ruffian, who accomplishes his purposes by brutal violence, and not as an unprincipled seducer, who, by art and intrigue, commits this greatest of all injuries; yet, in the proceedings thereon, and the acknowledged causes for damages, common sense has prevailed. . . .

If the character of the wife were debased before the criminal conversation, the damages would be much less than if she had, before the seduction, maintained a fair reputation for chastity. . . .

I apprehend it will be found difficult to ascertain, with exactness, what power the husband has over the person of his wife. According to the ideas once entertained upon this subject, in the country from which our ancestors emigrated, the husband seems to have had the same right over the person of his wife, that he had over the person of his apprentice; to chastise her moderately or confine her; a right still claimed and enforced in that country, among the lower ranks of society.

In Connecticut, it is not to be denied, that there are to be found brutal husbands who abuse their wives; but the right of chastising a wife is not claimed by any man; neither is any such right recognized by our law. . . .

Children or servants are punishable for crimes which they commit in obedience to the commands of their parents or masters, or by their coercion; but a wife is, in many cases, privileged from punishment, for offences against the laws of society; provided she commits the offence by the coercion of the husband. His command to commit the offence, is in law deemed coercion. When it is committed by her in his company, if he joins in committing it, or also encourages, or in any way approves thereof, the law presumes, that whatever the wife does, is done by the husband's coercion. This is the law, not only as it respects inferior misdesmeanors, but also capital. To this rule there are two exceptions, viz. treason and the keeping of a brothel. The former is supposed to be an offence so dangerous to society, that even the coercion of a husband is no excuse. The latter is an offence of which the wife is supposed to have the principal management. . . .

It is a general rule that a wife cannot so contract, as to bind herself; her contracts are said to be void in law. The principles on which this doctrine is founded are two: 1st. The right of the husband to the person of his wife. This is a right guarded by the law with the utmost solicitude; if she could bind herself by her contracts, she would be liable to be arrested, taken in execution, and confined in a prison; and then the husband would be deprived of the company of his wife, which the law will not suffer. 2d. The law considers the wife to be in the power of the husband; it would not, therefore, be reasonable that she should be bound by any contract which she makes during the coverture, as it might be the effect of coercion. On the first ground she is privileged for the sake of her husband; on the last, for her own sake.

Source: Tapping Reeve, The Law of Baron and Femme, of Parent and Child, of Guardian and Ward, of Master and Servant, and of the Powers of Courts of Chancery, with an Essay on the Terms Heir, Heirs, and Heirs of the Body (New Haven, Conn.: Oliver Steele, 1816), 18, 35–38, 63–66, 73–74.

5. Cherokee Women's Petitions, 1817, 1818, and 1831

In 1817 and 1818, Cherokee women unsuccessfully petitioned their National Council not to accede to a request for the cession of land within their tribal domains in Georgia, Tennessee, and Alabama. Traditionally, Cherokee women had enjoyed access to power and leadership within their society, with kinship reckoned in matrilineal clans—that is, through women's family lines—and women's agricultural productivity valued as a counterpart to men's hunting. Now, however, they failed to slow Euro-American inroads into Cherokee territory and customs. Nancy Ward (1738–1822), whose special message is included in the first petition below, was a "Beloved Woman" who sat in tribal council with Cherokee men to deliberate on the tribe's collective future. The U.S. government and state governments, however, negotiated only with male tribal leaders. While some Cherokee bands left eastern lands in the wake of treaties concluded in 1817 and 1819, others continued to resist displacement, as evidenced in the 1831 petition below. Eventually, all Cherokees were removed to the West as a result of the Treaty of New Echota, with their subsequent forced migration on the Trail of Tears, 1838–1839.

*   *   *

Petition of the Cherokee Women's Council, May 2, 1817

The Cherokee ladys now being present at the meeting of the chiefs and warriors in council have thought it their duty as mothers to address their beloved chiefs and warriors now assembled.

Our beloved children and head men of the Cherokee Nation, we address you warriors in council. We have raised all of you on the land which we now have, which God gave us to inhabit and raise provisions. We know that our

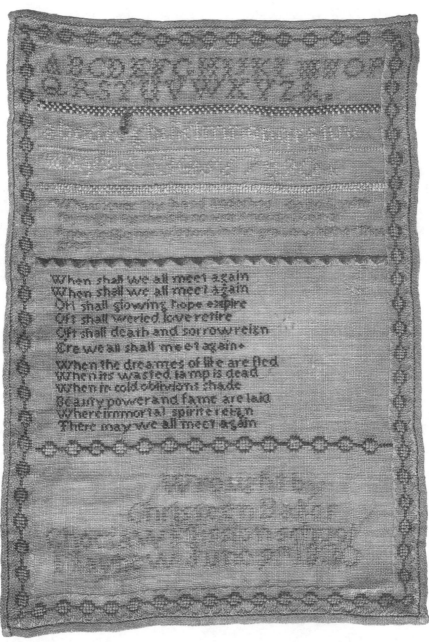

Choctaw Mission School Sampler by Christeen Baker, Mayhew, Mississippi, June 9, 1830. This sampler, with its silk embroidery threads on linen, illustrates the transmission of Euro-American women's culture through schools for Native American girls. (Source: Courtesy of Colonial Williamsburg Foundation)

country has once been extensive, but by repeated sales has become circumscribed to a small track, and [we] never have thought it our duty to interfere in the disposition of it till now. If a father or mother was to sell all their lands which they had to depend on, which their children had to raise their living on, which would be indeed bad & to be removed to another country. We do not wish to go to an unknown country which we have understood some of our children wish to go over the Mississippi, but this act of our children would be like destroying your mothers.

Your mothers, your sisters ask and beg of you not to part with any more of our land. We say ours. You are our descendants; take pity on our request. But keep it for our growing children, for it was the good will of our creator to place us here, and you know our father, the great president, will not allow his white children to take our country away. Only keep your hands off of paper talks for its our own country. For [if] it was not, they would not ask you to put your hands to paper, for it would be impossible to remove us all. For as soon as one child is raised, we have others in our arms, for such is our situation & will consider our circumstance.

Therefore, children, don't part with any more of our lands but continue on it & enlarge your farms. Cultivate and raise corn & cotton and your mothers and sisters will make clothing for you which our father the president has recommended to us all. We don't charge any body for selling any lands, but we have heard such intentions of our children. But your talks become true at last; it was our desire to forwarn you all not to part with our lands.

Nancy Ward to her children: Warriors to take pity and listen to the talks of your sisters. Although I am very old yet cannot but pity the situation in which you will here of their minds. I have great many grand children which [I] wish them to do well on our land.

Source: Susan Oliver, Cerritos College, transcribed from "Presidential Papers Microfilm: Andrew Jackson," series 1, reel 22 (Washington, D.C.: Cerritos College, 1961), www.cerritos.edu/soliver/Student%20Activites/Trail%20of%20Tears/web/cherokee%20women.htm.

*   *   *

Petition of the Cherokee Women's Council, June 30, 1818
Beloved Children,

We have called a meeting among ourselves to consult on the different points now before the council, relating to our national affairs. We have heard with painful feelings that the bounds of the land we now possess are to be drawn into very narrow limits. The land was given to us by the Great Spirit above as our common right, to raise our children upon, & to make support for our rising generations. We therefore humbly petition our beloved children, the head men & warriors, to hold out to the last in support of our common rights, as the Cherokee nation have been the first settlers of this land; we therefore claim the right of the soil.

We well remember that our country was formerly very extensive, but by repeated sales it has become circumscribed to the very narrow limits we have at present. Our Father the President advised us to become farmers, to manufacture our own clothes, & to have our children instructed. To this advice we have attended in every thing as far as we were able. Now the thought of being compelled to remove the other side of the Mississippi is dreadful to us, because it appears to us that we, by this removal, shall be brought to a savage state again, for we have, by the endeavor of our Father the President, become too much enlightened to throw aside the privileges of a civilized life.

We therefore unanimously join in our meeting to hold our country in common as hitherto.

Some of our children have become Christians. We have missionary schools among us. We have hard [sic] the gospel in our nation. We have become civilized & enlightened, & are in hopes that in a few years our nation will be prepared for instruction in other branches of sciences & arts, which are both useful & necessary in civilized society.

There are some white men among us who have been raised in this country from their youth, are connected with us by marriage, & have considerable families, who are very active in encouraging the emigration of our nation. These ought to be our truest friends but prove our worst enemies. They seem to be only concerned how to increase their riches, but do not care what becomes of our Nation, nor even of their own wives and children.

Source: Susan Oliver, Cerritos College, transcribed from "Papers of the American Board of Commissioners for Foreign Missions" (Cambridge, Mass.: Houghton Library, Harvard University), www.cerritos.edu/soliver/Student%20Activites/Trail%20of%20Tears/web/cherokee%20women.htm.

*   *   *

Petition, October 17, 1821 [1831?]
To the Committee and Council,

We the females, residing in Salecluoree and Pine Log, believing that the present difficulties and embarrassments under which this nation is placed demands a full expression of the mind of every individual, on the subject of emigrating to Arkansas, would take upon ourselves to address you. Although it is not common for our sex to take part in public measures, we nevertheless feel justified in expressing our sentiments on any subject where our interest is as much at stake as any other part of the community.

We believe the present plan of the General Government to effect our removal West of the Mississippi, and thus obtain our lands for the use of the State of Georgia, to be highly oppressive, cruel and unjust. And we sincerely hope there is no consideration which can induce our citizens to forsake the land of our fathers of which they have been in possession from time immemorial, and thus compel us, against our will, to undergo the toils and difficulties of removing with our helpless families hundreds of miles to unhealthy and unproductive country. We hope therefore the Committee and Council will take into deep consideration our deplorable situation, and do everything in their power to avert such a state of things. And we trust by a prudent course their transactions with the General Government will enlist in our behalf the sympathies of the good people of the United States.

Source: Susan Oliver, transcribed from *Cherokee Phoenix*, November 12, 1831, www.cerritos.edu/soliver/Student%20Activites/Trail%20of%20Tears/web/cherokee%20women.htm.

6. Lydia Maria Child, Excerpts from *The American Frugal Housewife*, 1830

Author, abolitionist, and reformer Lydia Maria Child (1802–1880) began her career as a novelist, anonymously authoring *Hobomok: A Tale of Early Times*, which appeared in print in 1824. The story of a romance between a white New England woman and a Native American man, the book introduced themes of cross-race relationships to which she would return many times. Child immediately followed with other fiction, including tales for children. *The Frugal Housewife* appeared in 1829 and was reprinted soon thereafter as *The American Frugal Housewife* to emphasize its distinctly American stance. It was part of Child's prolific body of advice books for girls and mothers. But by 1833, Child had embraced radical antislavery, and she became better known for her works arguing for black emancipation and her service as an editor for the *National Anti-Slavery Standard*.

This excerpt from the opening pages of *The American Frugal Housewife* illustrates the integral ties between unpaid work within the household and the family finances, connections that included both economy and ideology. Also presented is a typical section in which Child used stories said to have been drawn from real life. Aimed at the middling ranks of society, Child's work powerfully presents domesticity as woman's "calling," one for which she should be trained.

*   *   *

DEDICATED TO THOSE WHO ARE NOT ASHAMED OF ECONOMY.
A fat kitchen maketh a lean will.—FRANKLIN . . .

The true economy of housekeeping is simply the art of gathering up all the fragments, so that nothing be lost. I mean fragments of *time*, as well as *materials*. Nothing should be thrown away so long as it is possible to make any use of it, however trifling that use may be; and whatever be the size of a family, every member should be employed either in earning or saving money.

"Time is money." For this reason, cheap as stockings are, it is good economy to knit them. Cotton and woollen yarn are both cheap; hose that are knit wear twice as long as woven ones; and they can be done at odd minutes of time, which would not be otherwise employed. Where there are children, or aged people, it is sufficient to recommend knitting, that it is an *employment*.

In this point of view, patchwork is good economy. It is indeed a foolish waste of time to tear cloth into bits for the sake of arranging it anew in fantastic figures; but a large family may be kept out of idleness, and a few shillings saved, by thus using scraps of gowns, curtains, &c.

In the country, where grain is raised, it is a good plan to teach children to prepare and braid straw for their own bonnets, and their brothers' hats.

Where turkeys and geese are kept, handsome feather fans may as well be made by the younger members of a family, as to be bought. The sooner children are taught to turn their faculties to some account, the better for them and for their parents.

In this country, we are apt to let children romp away their existence, till they get to be thirteen or fourteen. This is not well. It is not well for the purses and patience of parents; and it has a still worse effect on the morals and habits of the children. *Begin early* is the great maxim for everything in education. A child of six years old can be made useful; and should be taught to consider every day lost in which some little thing has not been done to assist others.

Children can very early be taught to take all the care of their own clothes.

They can knit garters, suspenders, and stockings; they can make patchwork and braid straw; they can make mats for the table, and mats for the floor; they can weed the garden, and pick cranberries from the meadow, to be carried to market.

Provided brothers and sisters go together, and are not allowed to go with bad children, it is a great deal better for the boys and girls on a farm to be picking blackberries at six cents a quart, than to be wearing out their clothes in useless play. They enjoy themselves just as well; and they are earning something to buy clothes, at the same time they are tearing them.

It is wise to keep an exact account of all you expend—even of a paper of pins. This answers two purposes; it makes you more careful in spending money, and it enables your husband to judge precisely whether his family live within his income. No false pride, or foolish ambition to appear as well as others, should ever induce a person to live one cent beyond the income of which he is certain. If you have two dollars a day, let nothing but sickness induce you to spend more than nine shillings; if you have one dollar a day, do not spend but seventy-five cents; if you have half a dollar a day, be satisfied to spend forty cents.

To associate with influential and genteel people with an appearance of equality, unquestionably has its advantages; particularly where there is a family of sons and daughters just coming upon the theatre of life; but, like all other external advantages, these have their proper price, and may be bought too dearly. They who never reserve a cent of their income, with which to meet any unforeseen calamity, "pay too dear for the whistle," whatever temporary benefits they may derive from society. Self-denial, in proportion to the narrowness of your income, will eventually be the happiest and most respectable course for you and yours. If you are prosperous, perseverance and industry will not fail to place you in such a situation as your ambition covets; and if you are not prosperous, it will be well for your children that they have not been educated to higher hopes than they will ever realize.

If you are about to furnish a house, do not spend all your money, be it much or little. Do not let the beauty of this thing, and the cheapness of that, tempt you to buy unnecessary articles. Doctor Franklin's maxim was a wise one, "Nothing is cheap that we do not want." . . . Begin humbly. As riches increase, it is easy and pleasant to increase in hospitality and splendour; but it is always painful and inconvenient to decrease. . . . Neatness, tastefulness, and good sense, may be shown in the management of a small household, and the arrangement of a little furniture, as well as upon a larger scale; and these qualities are always praised, and always treated with respect and attention. The consideration which many purchase by living beyond their income, and of course living upon others, is not worth the trouble it costs. The glare there is about this false and wicked parade is deceptive; it does not in fact procure a man valuable friends, or extensive influence. More than that, it is wrong—morally wrong, so far as the individual is concerned; and injurious beyond calculation to the interests of our country. To what are the increasing beggary and discouraged exertions of the present period owing? . . . The root of the whole matter is the extravagance of all classes of people. We never shall be prosperous till we make pride and vanity yield to the dictates of honesty and prudence! We never shall be free from embarrassment until we cease to be ashamed of industry and economy. Let women do their share towards reformation—Let their fathers and husbands see them happy without finery; and if their husbands and fathers have (as is often the case) a foolish pride in seeing them decorated, let them gently and gradually check this feeling, by showing that they have better and surer means of commanding respect—Let them prove, by the exertion of ingenuity and economy, that neatness, good taste, and gentility, are attainable without great expense. . . .

The information conveyed is of a common kind; but it is such as the majority of young housekeepers do not possess, and such as they cannot obtain from cookery books. Books of this kind have usually been written for the wealthy: I have written for the poor. . . .

The other day, I heard a mechanic say, "I have a wife and two little children; we live in a very small house; but, to save my life, I cannot spend less than twelve hundred a year." Another replied, "You are not economical; I spend but eight hundred." I thought to myself,—"Neither of you pick up your twine and paper." A third one, who was present, was silent; but after they were gone, he said, "I keep house, and comfortably too, with a wife and children, for six hundred a year; but I suppose they would have thought me mean, if I had told them so." I did not think him mean; it merely occurred to me that his wife and children were in the habit of picking up paper and twine. . . .

Yet it was but lately that I visited a family, not of "moderate fortune," but of no fortune at all; one of those people who live "nobody knows how;" and I found a young girl, about sixteen, practising [sic] on the piano, while an elderly lady beside her was darning her stockings. I was told (for the mother was proud of bringing up her child so genteelly) that the daughter had almost forgotten how to sew, and that a woman was hired into the house to do her mending! "But why," said I, "have you suffered your daughter to be ignorant of so useful an employment? If she is poor, the knowledge will be necessary to her; if she is rich, it is the easiest thing in the world to lay it aside, if she chooses; she will merely be a better judge whether her work is well done by others." "That is true," replied the mother; "and I always meant she should learn; but she never has seemed to have any time. When she was eight years old, she could put a shirt together pretty well; but since that, her music, and her dancing, and her school, have taken up her whole time. I did mean she should learn some domestic habits this winter; but she has so many visiters [sic], and is obliged to go out so much, that I suppose I must give it up. I don't like to say too much about it; for, poor girl! she does so love company, and she does so hate anything like care and confinement! *Now* is her time to enjoy herself, you know. Let her take all the comfort she can, while she is single!" "But," said I, "you wish her to marry some time or other; and, in all probability, she will marry. When will she learn how to perform the duties, which are necessary and important to every mistress of a family?" "Oh, she will learn them when she is obliged to," answered the injudicious mother; "at all events, I am determined she shall enjoy herself while she is young."

And this is the way I have often heard mothers talk! Yet, could parents foresee the almost inevitable consequences of such a system, I believe the weakest and vainest would abandon the false and dangerous theory. What a lesson is taught a girl in that sentence, "*Let her enjoy herself all she can, while she is single!*" Instead of representing domestic life as the gathering place of the deepest and purest affections; as the sphere of woman's *enjoyments* as well as of her *duties*; as, indeed, the whole world to her; that one pernicious sentence teaches a girl to consider matrimony desirable because "a good match" is a triumph of vanity, and it is deemed respectable to be "well settled in the world;" but that it is a necessary sacrifice of her freedom and her gayety. And then how many affectionate dispositions have been trained into heartlessness, by being taught that the indulgence of indolence and vanity were necessary to their happiness; and that to have this indulgence, they *must* marry money! But who that marries for money, in this land of precarious fortunes, can tell how soon they will lose the glittering temptation, to which they have been willing to sacrifice so much? And even if riches last as long as life, the evil is not remedied. Education has given a wrong end and aim to their whole existence; they have been taught to look for happiness where it never can be found, viz. in the absence of all occupation, or the unsatisfactory and ruinous excitement of fashionable competition.

The difficulty is, education does not usually point the female heart to its only true resting-place. That dear English word "*home*," is not half so powerful a talisman as "*the world*." Instead of the salutary truth, that happiness is *in* duty, they are taught to consider the two things totally distinct; and that whoever seeks one, must sacrifice the other.

The fact is, our girls have no *home education*. When quite young, they are sent to schools where no feminine employments, no domestic habits, can be learned; and there they continue till they "come out" into the world. . . .

The bride is awakened from her delightful dream, in which carpets, vases, sofas, white gloves, and pearl earrings, are oddly jumbled up with her lover's looks and promises. Perhaps she would be surprised if she knew exactly how *much* of the fascination of being engaged was owing to the aforesaid inanimate concern. Be that as it will, she is awakened by the unpleasant conviction that cares devolve upon her. And what effect does this produce upon her character? Do the holy and tender influences of domestic love render self-denial and exertion a bliss? No! They would have done so, had she been *properly educated*; but now she gives way to unavailing fretfulness and repining; and her husband is at first pained, and finally disgusted, by hearing, "I never knew what care was when I lived in my father's house." "If I were to live my life over again, I would remain single as long as I could, without the risk of being an old maid." How injudicious, how short-sighted is the policy, which thus mars the whole happiness of life, in order to make a few brief years more gay and brilliant! I have known many instances of domestic ruin and discord produced by this mistaken indulgence of mothers. *I never knew but one, where the victim had moral courage enough to change all her early habits.*

Source: Lydia Maria Child, *The American Frugal Housewife*, 2nd ed. (Boston: Carter and Hendee, 1830), 1, 3–8, 99–103.

7. Alexis de Tocqueville, Excerpts from *Democracy in America*, Volume II, 1840

The conservative French aristocrat Alexis de Tocqueville (1805–1851) visited the United States in 1831–1832 to escape from the tumult that accompanied the overthrow of the restored Bourbon kings. Nominally on a tour of American penitentiaries, Tocqueville pondered the impact of what he called the "providential fact" of democracy on society and culture. In the two volumes published as *Democracy in America* in 1835 and 1840, he reflected on how Americans had created social stability in the absence of an inherited aristocracy and old world traditions. In several chapters in the second volume, Tocqueville explored the particular ways in which American political and social culture shaped the lives and status of women in a Protestant and postpatriarchal culture quite different from his native France. His description deftly presents the paradoxes of domesticity in the early republic.

*   *   *

Chapter IX: Education of Young Women in the United States

No free communities ever existed without morals; and . . . morals are the work of woman. Consequently, whatever affects the condition of women, their habits and their opinions, has great political importance in my eyes.

Amongst almost all Protestant nations young women are far more the mistresses of their own actions than they are in Catholic countries. This independence is still greater in Protestant countries like England, which have retained or acquired the right of self-government; the spirit of freedom is then infused into the domestic circle by political habits and by religious opinions. In the United States the doctrines of Protestantism are combined with great political freedom and a most democratic state of society; and no-where are young women surrendered so early or so completely to their own guidance.

Long before an American girl arrives at the age of marriage, her eman-cipation from maternal control begins; she has scarcely ceased to be a child when she already thinks for herself, speaks with freedom, and acts on her own impulse. The great scene of the world is constantly open to her view; far from seeking concealment, it is every day disclosed to her more completely, and she is taught to survey it with a firm and calm gaze. Thus the vices and dangers of society are early revealed to her; as she sees them clearly, she views them without illusions, and braves them without fear; for she is full of reliance on her own strength, and her reliance seems to be shared by all who are about her.

An American girl scarcely ever displays that virginal bloom in the midst of young desires, or that innocent and ingenuous grace which usually attends the European woman in the transition from girlhood to youth. It is rarely that an American woman at any age displays childish timidity or ignorance. Like the young women of Europe, she seeks to please, but she knows precisely the cost of pleasing. If she does not abandon herself to evil, at least she knows that it exists; and she is remarkable rather for purity of manners than for chastity of mind.

I have been frequently surprised, and almost frightened, at the singular address and happy boldness with which young women in America contrive to manage their thoughts and their language, amid all the difficulties of stimulating conversation; . . . even amid the independence of early youth, an American woman is always mistress of herself: she indulges in all permitted pleasures, without yielding herself up to any of them; and her reason never allows the reins of self-guidance to drop. . . .

The Americans . . . have found out that in a democracy the indepen-dence of individuals cannot fail to be very great, youth premature, tastes ill-restrained, customs fleeting, public opinion often unsettled and power-less, paternal authority weak, and marital authority contested. Under these circumstances, believing that they had little chance of repressing in woman the most vehement passions of the human heart, they held that the surer way was to teach her the art of combating those passions for herself. As they could not prevent her virtue from being exposed to frequent danger, they determined that she should know how best to defend it; and more reliance was placed on the free vigor of her will, than on safeguards which have been shaken or overthrown. . . . As it is neither possible nor desirable to keep a young woman in perpetual or complete ignorance, they hasten to give her a precocious knowledge on all subjects. Far from hiding the corruptions of the world from her, they prefer that she should see them at once and train herself to shun them; and they hold it of more importance to protect her conduct than to be over-scrupulous of her innocence. . . .

An education of this kind is not without danger . . . it tends to invigorate the judgment at the expense of the imagination, and to make cold and virtu-ous women instead of affectionate wives and agreeable companions to man. Society may be more tranquil and better regulated, but domestic life has often fewer charms. . . . [A] democratic education is indispensable, to protect women from the dangers with which democratic institutions and manners surround them.

Chapter X: The Young Woman in the Character of a Wife
In America the independence of woman is irrevocably lost in the bonds of matrimony: if an unmarried woman is less constrained there than elsewhere, a wife is subjected to stricter obligations. The former makes her father's house an abode of freedom and of pleasure; the latter lives in the home of her hus-band as if it were a cloister. . . .

Religious peoples and trading nations entertain peculiarly serious notions of marriage: the former consider the regularity of woman's life as the best pledge and most certain sign of the purity of her morals; the latter regard it as the highest security for the order and prosperity of the household. The Americans are at the same time a puritanical people and a commercial na-tion: their religious opinions, as well as their trading habits, consequently lead them to require much abnegation on the part of woman, and a constant sacrifice of her pleasures to her duties . . . the inexorable opinion of the public carefully circumscribes woman within the narrow circle of domestic interest and duties, and forbids her to step beyond it.

Upon her entrance into the world a young American woman finds these notions firmly established; she sees the rules which are derived from them;

she is not slow to perceive that she cannot depart for an instant from the established usages of her contemporaries, without putting in jeopardy her peace of mind, her honor, nay even her social existence . . . she finds the energy required for such an act of submission in the firmness of her understanding and in the virile habits which her education has given her. . . .

No American woman falls into the toils of matrimony as into a snare held out to her simplicity and ignorance. She has been taught beforehand what is expected of her, and voluntarily and freely does she enter upon this engagement. She supports her new condition with courage, because she chose it. As in America paternal discipline is very relaxed and the conjugal tie very strict, a young woman does not contract the latter without considerable circumspection and apprehension. . . . Thus American women do not marry until their understandings are exercised and ripened; whereas in other countries most women generally only begin to exercise and to ripen their understandings after marriage.

. . . When the time for choosing a husband is arrived, that cold and stern reasoning power which has been educated and invigorated by the free observation of the world, teaches an American woman that a spirit of levity and independence in the bonds of marriage is a constant subject of annoyance, not of pleasure; it tells her that the amusements of the girl cannot become the recreations of the wife, and that the sources of a married woman's happiness are in the home of her husband. . . .

The same strength of purpose which the young wives of America display, in bending themselves at once and without repining to the austere duties of their new condition, is no less manifest in all the great trials of their lives. In no country in the world are private fortunes more precarious than in the United States. It is not uncommon for the same man, in the course of his life, to rise and sink again through all the grades which lead from opulence to poverty. American women support these vicissitudes with calm and unquenchable energy: it would seem that their desires contract, as easily as they expand, with their fortunes. . . .

Chapter XI: That the Equality of Conditions Contributes to the Maintenance of Good Morals in America

. . . Equality of conditions does not of itself engender regularity of morals, but it unquestionably facilitates and increases it.

Among aristocratic nations birth and fortune frequently make two such different beings of man and woman, that they can never be united to each other. Their passions draw them together, but the condition of society, and the notions suggested by it, prevent them from contracting a permanent and ostensible tie. The necessary consequence is a great number of transient and clandestine connexions. . . .

This is not so much the case when the equality of conditions has swept away all the imaginary, or the real, barriers which separated man from woman. No girl then believes that she cannot become the wife of the man who loves her; and this renders all breaches of morality before marriage very uncommon: for, whatever be the credulity of the passions, a woman will hardly be able to persuade herself that she is beloved, when her lover is perfectly free to marry her and does not.

The same cause operates, though more indirectly, on married life. Nothing better serves to justify an illicit passion, either to the minds of those who have conceived it or to the world which looks on, than compulsory or accidental marriages.

In a country in which a woman is always free to exercise her power of choosing, and in which education has prepared her to choose rightly, public opinion is inexorable to her faults. The rigour of the Americans arises in part from this cause. They consider marriages as a covenant which is often onerous, but every condition of which the parties are strictly bound to fulfil, because they knew all those conditions beforehand, and were perfectly free not to have contracted them.

The very circumstances which render matrimonial fidelity more obligatory also render it more easy. . . .

Almost all men in democracies are engaged in public or professional life; and on the other hand the limited extent of common incomes obliges a wife to confine herself to the house, in order to watch in person and very closely over the details of domestic economy. All these distinct and compulsory occupations are so many natural barriers, which, by keeping the two sexes asunder, render the solicitations of the one less frequent and less ardent—the resistance of the other more easy.

Not indeed that the equality of conditions can ever succeed in making men chaste, but it may impart a less dangerous character to their breaches of morality. As no one has then either sufficient time or opportunity to assail a virtue armed in self-defence, there will be at the same time a great number of courtezans and a great number of virtuous women. This state of things causes lamentable cases of individual hardship, but it does not prevent the body of society from being strong and alert; it does not destroy family ties, or enervate the morals of the nation. Society is endangered not by the great profligacy of a few, but by laxity of morals among all. In the eyes of a legislator, prostitution is less to be dreaded than intrigue.

Chapter XII: How the Americans Understand the Equality of the Sexes
. . . The social changes which bring nearer to the same level the father and son, the master and servant, and superiors and inferiors generally speaking, will raise woman and make her more and more the equal of man. . . .

There are people in Europe who, confounding together the different characteristics of the sexes, would make of man and woman beings not only equal but alike. They would give to both the same functions, impose on both the same duties, and grant to both the same rights: they would mix them in all things—their occupations, their pleasures, their business. It may readily be conceived, that by thus attempting to make one sex equal to the other, both are degraded; and from so preposterous a medley of the works of nature, nothing could ever result but weak men and disorderly women.

It is not thus that the Americans understand that species of democratic equality which may be established between the sexes. They admit, that as nature has appointed such wide differences between the physical and moral constitution of man and woman, her manifest design was to give a distinct employment to their various faculties; and they hold that improvement does not consist in making beings so dissimilar do pretty nearly the same things, but in getting each of them to fulfill their respective tasks in the best possible manner. The Americans have applied to the sexes the great principle of political economy which governs the manufactures of our age, by carefully dividing the duties of man from those of woman, in order that the great work of society may be the better carried on.

In no country has such constant care been taken as in America to trace two clearly distinct lines of action for the two sexes, and to make them keep pace one with the other, but in two pathways which are always different. American women never manage the outward concerns of the family, or conduct a business, or take a part in political life; nor are they, on the other hand, ever compelled to perform the rough labor of the fields, or to make any of those laborious exertions which demand the exertion of physical strength. No families are so poor as to form an exception to this rule. If on the one hand an American woman cannot escape from the quiet circle of domestic employments, on the other hand she is never forced to go beyond it. Hence it is that the women of America, who often exhibit a masculine strength of understanding and a manly energy, generally preserve great delicacy of personal appearance and always retain the manners of women, although they sometimes show that they have the hearts and minds of men. . . .

It has often been remarked that in Europe a certain degree of contempt lurks even in the flattery which men lavish upon women: although a European frequently affects to be the slave of woman, it may be seen that he never sincerely thinks her his equal. In the United States men seldom compliment women, but they daily show how much they esteem them. They constantly display an entire confidence in the understanding of a wife, and a profound respect for her freedom; they have decided that her mind is just as fitted as that of a man to discover the plain truth, and her heart as firm to embrace it; and they have never sought to place her virtue, any more than his, under the shelter of prejudice, ignorance, and fear. . . .

The legislators of the United States, who have mitigated almost all the penalties of criminal law, still make rape a capital offence [sic], and no crime is visited with more inexorable severity by public opinion. This may be accounted for; as the Americans can conceive nothing more precious than a woman's honor, and nothing which ought so much to be respected as her independence, they hold that no punishment is too severe for the man who deprives her of them against her will. . . .

As for myself, I do not hesitate to avow that, although the women of the United States are confined within the narrow circle of domestic life, and their situation is in some respects one of extreme dependence, I have nowhere seen woman occupying a loftier position; and if I were asked, now that I am drawing to the close of this work, in which I have spoken of so many important things done by the Americans, to what the singular prosperity and growing strength of that people ought mainly to be attributed, I should reply—to the superiority of their women.

Source: Alexis de Tocqueville, *Democracy in America, Volume II*, trans. Henry Reeve, book III, chaps. IX–XII (New York: Langley, 1840), 209–27.

8. Catharine Beecher, Excerpts from A *Treatise on Domestic Economy*, 1841

Catharine Beecher (1800–1878) was the eldest child of Lyman Beecher, a legendary preacher who spread the message of the Second Great Awakening throughout New England and the Old Northwest. Like her father, she took seriously issues of vocation and calling, which for Catharine manifested themselves in her commitment to teaching and writing for women about how they could best pursue their domestic mission. A *Treatise on Domestic Economy* offered instruction that mixed moral and practical advice. In this selection, Beecher presents the "problem" of domestic service as an issue that the emergent market economy has brought into the home, where it can be solved by enlightened ladies, for the benefit of the "neglected children" in her employ. The book held a position of popularity such that it was republished almost unchanged for more than thirty years, even when the class problem posed by

native-born Yankee domestics had been complicated by ethnic clashes between New Englanders and their Irish immigrant houseworkers.

*   *   *

Chapter XVIII: On the Care of Domestics

There is no point, where the women of this Country need more wisdom,
patience, principle, and self-control, than in relation to those whom they
employ in domestic service. The subject is attended with many difficulties,
which powerfully influence the happiness of families; and the following suggestions are offered, to aid in securing right opinions and practice.

One consideration, which it would be well to bear in mind, on this subject, is, that a large portion of the peculiar trials, which American women
suffer from this source, are the necessary evils connected with our most valuable civil blessings . . . while we rejoice at a state of society, which so much
raises the condition and advantages of our sex, the evils involved should be
regarded as more than repaid, by the compensating benefits. If we cannot secure the cringing, submissive, well-trained, servants of aristocratic lands, let
us be consoled that we thus escape from the untold miseries and oppression,
which always attend that state of society.

Instead, then, of complaining that we cannot have our own peculiar advantages, and those of other nations, too, or imagining how much better off
we should be, if things were different from what they are, it is much wiser and
more Christianlike to strive cheerfully to conform to actual circumstances;
and, after remedying all that we can control, patiently to submit to what is
beyond our power. If domestics are found to be incompetent, unstable, and
unconfirmed to their station, it is Perfect Wisdom which appoints these trials, to teach us patience, fortitude, and self-control; and, if the discipline is
met, in a proper spirit, it will prove a blessing, rather than an evil.

But, to judge correctly in regard to some of the evils involved in the state
of domestic service, in this Country, we should endeavor to conceive ourselves placed in the situation of those, of whom complaint is made, that we
may not expect, from them, any more than it would seem right should be
exacted from us, in similar circumstances.

It is sometimes urged, against domestics, that they exact exorbitant wages.
But what is the rule of rectitude, on this subject? Is it not the universal law
of labor and of trade, that an article is to be valued, according to its scarcity
and the demand? When wheat is scarce, the farmer raises his price; and when
a mechanic offers services, difficult to be obtained, he makes a corresponding
increase of price. And why is it not right, for domestics to act according to a

rule, allowed to be correct in reference to all other trades and professions? It is a fact, that really good domestic service must continue to increase in value, just in proportion as this Country waxes rich and prosperous; thus making the proportion of those, who wish to hire labor, relatively greater, and the number of those, willing to go to service, less.

Money enables the rich to gain many advantages, which those of more limited circumstances cannot secure. One of these, is, securing good domestics, by offering high wages; and this, as the scarcity of this class increases, will serve constantly to raise the price of service. It is right for domestics to charge the market value, and this value is always decided by the scarcity of the article and the amount of demand. Right views of this subject, will sometimes serve to diminish hard feelings towards those, who would otherwise be wrongfully regarded as unreasonable and exacting.

Another complaint against domestics, is, that of instability and discontent, leading to perpetual change. But in reference to this, let a mother or daughter conceive of their own circumstances as so changed, that the daughter must go out to service. Suppose a place is engaged, and it is then found that she must sleep in a comfortless garret; and that, when a new domestic comes, perhaps a coarse and dirty foreigner, she must share her bed with her. Another place is offered, where she can have a comfortable room, and an agreeable room-mate; in such a case, would not both mother and daughter think it right to change?

Or, suppose, on trial, it was found that the lady of the house was fretful, or exacting, and hard to please; or, that her children were so ungoverned, as to be perpetual vexations; or, that the work was so heavy, that no time was allowed for relaxation and the care of a wardrobe;—and another place offers, where these evils can be escaped: would not mother and daughter here think it right to change? And is it not right for domestics, as well as their employers, to seek places, where they can be most comfortable?

In some cases, this instability and love of change would be remedied, if employers would take more pains to make a residence with them agreeable; and to attach domestics to the family, by feelings of gratitude and affection. There are ladies, even where well-qualified domestics are most rare, who seldom find any trouble in keeping good and steady ones. And the reason is, that their domestics know they cannot better their condition, by any change within reach. It is not merely by giving them comfortable rooms, and good food, and presents, and privileges that the attachment of domestics is secured; it is by the manifestation of a friendly and benevolent interest in their comfort and improvement. This is exhibited, in bearing patiently with their faults; in kindly teaching them how to improve; in showing them how to make and take proper care of their clothes; in guarding their health; in teaching them to read, if necessary, and supplying them with proper books; and, in short, by endeavoring, so far as may be, to supply the place of a parent. . . .

Another subject of complaint, in regard to domestics, is, their pride, insubordination, and spirit not conformed to their condition. They are not willing to be called *servants*; in some places, they claim a seat, at meals, with the family; they imitate a style of dress unbecoming their condition; and their manners and address are rude and disrespectful. That these evils are very common, among this class of persons, cannot be denied; the only question is, how can they best be met and remedied.

In regard to the common feeling among domestics, which is pained and offended by being called "servants," there is need of some consideration and allowance. It should be remembered, that, in this Country, children, from their earliest years, are trained to abhor slavery, in reference to themselves, as the greatest of all possible shame and degradation. They are perpetually hearing orations, songs, and compositions of all sorts, which set forth the honor and dignity of freemen, and heap scorn and contempt on all who would be so mean as to be slaves. Now the term servant, and the duties it involves, are, in the minds of many persons, nearly the same as those of slave. And there are few minds, entirely free from associations which make servitude a degradation. It is not always pride, then, which makes this term so offensive. It is a consequence of that noble and generous spirit of freedom, which every American draws from his mother's breast, and which ought to be respected, rather than despised. In order to be respected, by others, we must respect ourselves; and sometimes the ruder classes of society make claims, deemed forward and offensive, when, with their views, such a position seems indispensable to preserve a proper self-respect.

Where an excessive sensibility on this subject exists, and forward and disrespectful manners result from it, the best remedy is, a kind attempt to give correct views, such as better-educated minds are best able to attain. It should be shown to them, that, in this Country, labor has ceased to be degrading, in any class; that, in all classes, different grades of subordination must exist; and that it is no more degrading, for a domestic to regard the heads of a family as superiors in station, and treat them with becoming respect, than it is for children to do the same, or for men to treat their rulers with respect and deference. They should be taught, that domestics use a different entrance to the house, and sit at a distinct table, not because they are inferior beings, but because this is the best method of securing neatness, order, and convenience. They can be shown, if it is attempted in a proper spirit and manner, that these very regulations really tend to their own ease and comfort, as well as to that of the family. . . .

Every woman, who has the care of domestics, should cultivate a habit of regarding them with that sympathy and forbearance, which she would wish for herself or her daughters, if deprived of parents, fortune, and home. The fewer advantages they have enjoyed, and the greater difficulties of temper or of habit they have to contend with, the more claims they have on compassionate forbearance. They ought ever to be looked upon, not as the mere ministers to our comfort and convenience, but as the humbler and more neglected children of our Heavenly Father, whom He has sent to claim our sympathy and aid.

Source: Catharine Beecher, *A Treatise on Domestic Economy, For the Use of Young Ladies at Home, and at School*, 3rd ed. (Boston: Marsh, Capen, Lyon, and Webb, 1841; New York: Harper, 1845), 205–13. Harper edition was used for this document.

9. Letters by Amy Galusha, A Lowell Mill Girl, 1849–1851

Amy M. Galusha (1825–1869) left the home of her parents, the Reverend William and Polly Galusha, in rural Berkshire, Vermont, to work in the mills at Lowell, Massachusetts, sometime before her twenty-fourth birthday. These letters, written to her parents, to her younger brother Aaron Lealand ("LeLe"; born 1832) and her younger sister Arvilla (born 1838), span three years, and touch on working conditions, boarding house culture, politics, religion, gender, and aspirations. They clearly outline the sexual division of labor in the mills, and the different prospects for men and women as well as the continuing importance of family ties, concerns for morality, and the ever present threat of illness. Amy Galusha never married and continued to work in the mills until shortly before her early death.

*   *   *

Aaron L. Galusha West Berkshire, VT
Lowell, April 3, 1849
Dear Brother,
I do not know but you will blame me for not answering youre kind letter sooner but I think you will excuse me when I tell you the reason which is this: I have been very sick with the vere Loyd [varioloid]. I do not know as you will know what that is so I will tell you: it is the same as the small pox only it does not go quite so hard on account of being evaxionated. I was

at the Hospital one week and I was sick enough I can tell you my face was swolen so that if you had seen me you would not have known me from Adam but I am getting pretty smart again. I am not sorry that I have had it now it is over for I shall not fear the small pox any more but I had a pretty hard time. I think I shall go to work again next week. I expect my sickness will cost me about 15 dollers time and all which is quite a sum as low as wages are now.

You wanted I should write about mens wages in the mill. mens wages are good but boys wages very low. I do not think it will be best for you to try to work in the mill. you will have to work a good many years before you will be a capable overseer and none but such can get good wages. if you go into the mill now you will have to be very steady and I know that youre disposition will not admit of youre being confined from 5 in the morning till 7 at night in a noisey factory and luging around a great basket of bobbins—you would soon get tired of that fun I will promise you and then you must put up with a great many things which you never had to put up with before. you would probably get scolded sometimes and that you know that you would not bear very patiently which would make it all the worse for you. you would soom get weary and discontented and then you would not be much better off for what you had done. a boy canot get along so easy in the mill with their work as the girls do with theirs for it is harder to learn it. the girls have nothing to do but tend the work after it is all fixed and set to going. the men have to keep the looms and machinery in order and put in the webs [——] and fix them all in order for weaving before the girls have anything to do with it which makes the mens work more trying and more particular a great deal than the girls. when I come home I will tell you all about it more than I can write. I should be very glad to have you here whare I can see you but I know in all reason Lele it will not be for your best interest.

I think the best thing that you can do will be to go into some country town and learn a good trade get into some respectable shop and be steady and industrious and do what you think is perfectly right. take youre bible keep it by you where you can get at it handy read a portion of it every day and fol-low its precepts every day be considerate in everything. if any one asks you to do a thing stop and think if it is right you can easely tell whether a thing is right or wrong by stopping to to [sic] think. if you think it is wrong tell them at once that it is not right and that you will not do it and let that be the last of it. do not stop to argue the point at all for they may be better skilled in argument then you are and by that I means you may weaken a strong point. if you think it is wrong say so and that will be enough be independent. do not be persuaded by any one however smart or rich or influential to do a wrong action. you have a good mind enough for anybody if you will be guided by that. do not let the evil spirit get the uper hand at any time if you can't decide upon any question yourself go to someone that you know to be good for advise do not associate with any whose character is the least doubtful of either sex especialy the oposite.

Lealand for heavens sake let no fancy get the uper hands of reason. do not be too ardent an admirer of outside apearances. if you are attracted by a beautiful form or face stop and consider watch the actions and words with a jealous eye. see if retiring modesty reigns there. . . . Leland I think of you a great deal and tremble for youre welfare for many a boy has been ruined when young by keeping bad company but my sheet (is almost full or I might say quite full. you must answer my letter as soon as you receive it. . . .)

Amy L. Galusha

(dear Lele be kind to pa an ma. do not do any thing to greive or hurt their feelings for you do not know how much they feel for youre welfare. Lele the world is cold pitiless and miserliy. what I have suffered no one knows but I have lived to find a calm a blessed calm in a land of strangers. I know that youre feelings are tender like as mine were and capable of believing the insinuations of heartless wretches who will deceive you and then expose every little word and action and egreavate it to the highest pitch. put no confidence in any one however friendly they may appear until you have thoroughly proved them) (give my love to [——] enquiring friends. give my love to Aunt I and L and J and all uncle Bens folks) (you must not show this letter to any body except ma or pa. it is written from the fountain of an overflowing and affectionate heart and must not be exposed to the scorn of an unfeeling world)

*   *   *

[on cover] Rev. William Galusha Berkshire, VT
[Lowell] Dec 15 1850
Dear Mother
I received youre kind letter and Hellens both in the same day and read them with feelings which can better be imagined than described.

I was not at all surprised to learn of youre trouble for I had been warned by dreams and dark forebodings that all was not right at home which was the source of my great weariness. I expected to hear bad news when with a trembling hand and beating heart I broke the seal. But I am thankful that it is as well with you as it is. I feared least Fathers long protracted cough had at length worn out his constitution and nature had sank under the oppression of disease and the grave had claimed him as its prey. but when I leaned that it was you that was the sufferer and from that dreadfull disease to which you have so long been subject the currant of my feelings was turned from dispair to sorrow and grief intermingled with thankfullness for youre recovery. and now my dear Mother I do entreat you to be careful of youre health. do not work too hard. keep Arvilla with you and have her do all she can for you. do not take cold. do not wet youre feet. be still and quiet in the house as much as you can.

I received youre letter of nov 6 but not till after I had mailed mine of Dec 1st. I went to the office myself and in looking over the advertised list I found my own name and got my letter. it had laid thare nearly a month. the reason of my not receiving it through the penny post was that you directed it to Lawrance 19 instead of Tremont. It may seem strange that I do not board on the corporation on which I am working but I have some very warm friends at Mrs Thomas that I want to stay with, those with whom I first became acquainted when I came to Lowell Mrs Peirce is here and sends her love to you. she is one of the kindest old ladies you ever seing. she is a mother to me and I do not know how I should get along without her. We room in the lower back. we have a nice little fire place which keeps us warm as toast we have fire satturday evenings and sunday and other evenings too if we want it.

Well I suppose Christmas is close upon us and I hope it will be welcomed with joy as the birth day of our redeemer you and Father must sing "While Shepherds Watch their flocks by night" and think I am joining you for I shall remember all the good old times that we have had together. I am glad that Father has got reconciled to my staying here for I was afraid he never would be. I shall probably stay another year if I am well. I want you should find out how much it will cost to get an adition built for you but you must get some man to take hold of it for you one that will go ahead and make good calculer. I wish uncle George would do the calculating. he is the best one that I can think of if he has not too many cares of his own for I am confident that Le-aland will never do anything about it. if he cannot keep himself cloathed he certainly cannot think of building houses. I will send you one hundred dollars in one year from the first of next month if I have my health but I do not know as you can get much of a building up for that and perhaps people will not trust me for so large a sum in Berkshire. but if you could get a comfortable house next summer I should be willing to suffer any privation for the sake of ading to youre comfort.

If you can get along for provisions and wood without my help I shall be able to lay up the most of [torn] wages which will amount to something like 9 dollars per month the year round. I shall put it in the bank whare it will gain a little acording to the proffit of their money

. . . I should like very much to be with you all this winter but I must be content to stay with my looms awhile longer. they are the best friends I have here—no not friends for they are poor unconcious things, but very good company nevertheless.

Tell Aunt Milla that I was very much obliged to her for her kind offer of having me come to stay with her this winter but think it best to stay here at present.

Give my love and thanks to Aunt Lucy and all the friends that you may see.

I expect that John French and Rhoda have gone to Lawrince to work. I have not seen them since a fortnite ago to day and they were talking of going then. . . . I cannot write much about the church for I have left off going to meeting because I cannot go without nice cloths and paying for a seat [torn letter] have had a great many very unhappy feelings since but if God makes the path of duty plain to me I will try to walk in it. I never made so great a sacrifice as that in my life. I do not feel happy when I am away from meeting. I am uncomfortable all the time but I hope God will not impute the sin to my charge for it seems to be the only way that I can do. if I had some one to assist it would seem a lighter burden but I am alone and must stand alone in the performance of my duties. I hoped that L would be thoughtful enough to do something to help me but that is out of the question

*   *   *

Lowell, May 9th 1851

Dear Parents

Jane called to see me last week and brought me a letter from you with which I was very much pleased. she did not stay but a few minutes with me for they were in a great hurry; she said you were all well, and that you wanted to have Arvilla come down here; I should like to have arvilla here with me very much, but I am afraid that she would not stand it while she is so young and her health being poor into the bargain. I think that you had better keep her with you a year longer at least, if she could once get through with the task of learning she would do well enough, but that is a very severe trial to a young girl especially in the summer time; it is so different from any thing she has been acustomed to doing that I think it would be rather hard for her.

I think that I shall come home in a year from this spring, and by that time I hope that you will be settled so as not to have to work so hard as you have done. I want to see you have a good little house to live in and not have to be crowded as you have been. I have got about over my cold that I had when I wrote to Lele and my health is pretty good. . . .

I should like to step in and see you how you get along some days; I hope the carrs will be so much pleasenter riding in them than in the thrilling old stage. but I do not know as it is of much use to ever think of going home so long before hand. I should be very glad to come this summer if I could but I supose I cannot. I donot love to write for I cannot think of any things to write about, I had rather work in the mill a week than to write a letter. you must not blame me for not writing oftener and better for I do as well as I can and that is very bad. I am getting to be rather dull lately. my mind is engrossed with evry kind of a thing but the right things. I wish I could take that pleasure in reading and writing that I did when I was at home, but I cannot and never shall again. . . .

I have been thinking of going to Rhode Island to see cousin Benedicts folks but donot know as it is best, I believe I must go to Boston this summer for I have never been there yet and I have very grate curiosity to see it, but perhaps I shall not;

O I want to tell you that the Whigs have lost Mass slick enough. we have a democrat governor and all the rest are democrat or freesoil. I supose you have heard of the fuss that they have had in Boston about the fugitives. a great many people think that the manufacturing business will have to be given up entirly by the north on acount of the southern market being soo poor. the southern traders have all left Boston and gone to New York on acount of the fuss about slaves.

Mrs Peirce went home three or four weeks ago her foot was the worst looking sore that ever I saw, she did not dare to stay aney longer, I told her of Sands Sarsaparilla, but she has no faith in patent medicine of aney kind, and would not try it. Mrs Thomas and her family are all well I believe. Rhoda has not been very well this winter. she does not work in the mill now. she lives down to Lawrence. Jane looked so natural I almost imagined myself at home when I saw her, it makes me real home sick to see aney body from the vicinity of home so that I donot care about seeing them unless they can stay long enough to see me and tell me about matter and things. I was sorry that you sent me all the sugar you had for I get along very well. I have enough to eat and that is good enough for me.

I am very sorry that it hurts you to write, for youre writing looks as well as ever it did and I donot see but youre composition is as good as ever. I am very glad to here that you have such good friends. youre flour was much cheaper that it can be got here I hope that God will take care of you and that is all that I can do for you. I am glad that Fathers health is as good as it is, and hope he will not be any worse off but I fear you will boath work so hard while you are building that you will be sick. I wish that it was done with; I hope that you will have a good sabath school but do not want that you should join it if it is a going to be an injury to youre health. give my best respects to Maryette Levins and tell her that I should be glad to recieve a letter from her she is a good girl I always knew. give my love to all enquiring friends

Amy M Galusha

This letter is written so bad that I am ashamed to send it.

Source: Center for Lowell History, University of Massachusetts at Lowell, Lowell National Historical Park, Galusha Family Collection, Letters 001, 004, and 128, http://library.uml.edu/clh/All/Gal.htm.

Phase 2: Companionate Co-laborers

10. Salem Female Charitable Society Constitution, 1804

Characteristic of the organizations brought together by women in the early years of the republic, the Salem Female Charitable Society began to aid women and female children in 1801; with an official act of incorporation in 1804, this benevolent group empowered its members to act in a broader world on behalf of sex-specific objectives. It clearly promulgated an ethos that demanded class deference and gratitude, mandating an unapologetically vocational education for the female orphans in its care. Note that its members demonstrated their familiarity with the rules of procedure generally followed in legislative bodies and voluntary societies, and their knowledge of the limits to the control married women could exert over property or finances.

*   *   *

Commonwealth of Massachusetts

In the year of our Lord one thousand eight hundred and four. An Act to incorporate Lucretia Osgood and others, into a Society, by the name of the *Salem Female Charitable Society*.

Whereas a number of Ladies of the town of *Salem*, have associated for the charitable purpose of relieving, instructing and educating in a manner suitable to their condition and situation in life, poor and destitute female children; and of assisting aged and infirm widows, who, through misfortunes,

have fallen into poverty and distress; and to carry their association into effect, have petitioned to be incorporated:

SECTION 1. *Be it enacted by the Senate and the House of Representatives,
in General Court assembled, and by the authority of the same,* That the said
Lucretia Osgood and her associates, together with such others as may become
subscribers to the same institution in the manner hereafter proved, be, and
they hereby are incorporated into a society, by the name of the *Salem Female
Charitable Society,* and by that name shall be a corporation forever; with
power to have a common seal; to make contracts relative to the objects of
their institution; to sue and be sued; to establish bye-laws and orders for the
regulation of said society, and the preservation and application of the funds
thereof, provided the same be not repugnant to the Constitution or Laws of
the Commonwealth; to take, hold and possess any estate, real or personal, by
subscriptions, gift, grant, purchase, devise or otherwise, free from taxes, and
the same to improve, lease, exchange or sell, and convey, for the sole benefit
of said institution. . . .

SECT. 2. *Be it further enacted,* That every married woman, belonging to
said society, who shall, with the consent of her husband, receive any of the
money or other property of said society, shall thereby render her said husband
accountable therefore to said society; and every woman, whether sole or married, who shall subscribe and pay the funds of said society the sum of *three
dollars* annually, shall by such subscriptions and payment, become a member
of said society, liable, however to be removed, whenever she shall refuse or
neglect to pay her said annual subscription.

SECT. 3. *Be it further enacted,* That the said society shall meet in *Salem,*
on the first Wednesday of May, annually, for the purpose of electing, by bal-
lot, from their members, a first and second directress, a treasurer, a secretary,
and a board of not less than six, nor more than twelve, managers; all which
officers shall hold said offices for one year. . . . Upon any urgent occasion,
the first or second directress, or in their absence, the secretary, or whenever
requested in writing by fifty of the members of said society, any five of the
mangers may appoint a special meeting of said society, to be notified in the
same manner as at annual meetings. . . .

SECT. 4. *Be it further enacted,* That the treasurer of said society shall always, after the first Wednesday of May next, be a single woman of the age
of twenty-one years upwards; and shall give bond and sufficient surety to account annually, or oftener if required by aid society, or the board . . . for all
money and other property. . . .

SECT 5. *Be it further enacted,* That the board of managers . . . shall have
the management and application of the subscriptions, funds and estate of the
society, solely for the purpose of this institution; . . . they shall likewise have

authority at discretion to take under the care and direction of their society, such poor and destitute children, as they may judge suitable objects of charity, to enjoy the benefits of the institution, and also to accept a surrender in writing, by the father, or where there is no father, by the mother of any female child or children: and to bind out in virtuous families, until the age of 18 years, or marriage within that age, any such children thus surrendered, or any female children or children who, being destitute of parents within this Commonwealth, shall have been relieved and supported by said society; *Provided,* that any parent, whose child or children, during the absence of the said parent out of this Commonwealth, shall have received relief and support, or been bound out as aforesaid, shall have liberty, at his or her return, to receive such child or children upon paying to the treasurer of said society, the expence incurred in her or their relief and support as aforesaid. . . .

SECT. 6. *Be it further enacted,* That any writ or process, against said corporation, may be served by the officer's leaving an attested copy thereof with the treasurer of said society, or at her usual place of residence, thirty days before the return day thereof; . . . .

SECT. 8. *And be it further enacted,* That Lucretia Osgood shall continue first directress; Elizabeth White, second directress; Abigail Mason Dabney, treasurer; Elizabeth Gardner, secretary; Lydia Nichols, Eunice Richardson, Abigail Lawrence, Catharine G. Prescott, Margaret Murphy, Lucia Gardner, Lois Pulling, and Sarah Dunlap, managers, until the first Wednesday of May next, and until a new election be made as aforesaid; . . . .

STATEMENT OF THE SOCIETY FOR THE FOURTH YEAR,
Which commenced on April Fourth, 1804
FOURTEEN Children have been received to the protection of the Society.

Five of them are placed at service

The Receipts for the present year amount to 901 dls. 96 ½ cts. The Disbursements to 889 dls. 98 cts.

DONATIONS

By a Lady, one piece of Handkerchiefs

Presented by a Lady, 16 yeards India Calico

A case, containing nine Drawers for the Children, presented by Mrs. Murphy.

Presented by MRS. ELIZABETH HARLOW, of Duxbury, *Twenty Dollars*

*   *   *

FIFTY SEVEN Dollars were distributed among twenty seven aged Widows, on the 15th NOV. 1804.

TWENTY-SIX subscribers are added to the list for the present year. The whole number of subscribers is two hundred.

OCT. 3d, 1804. —Agreeable to the Direction of the Board, a subscription Paper was drafted, and addressed to the Gentlemen of Salem, for the purpose of raising a sufficient sum to purchase a House for the reception of the children patronised by this society. From their liberality they have received Six Hundred nineteen Dollars; which the Board of Managers acknowledge with gratitude.

RULES AND REGULATIONS
OF THE
SALEM FEMALE CHARITABLE SOCIETY

THE DESIGN Is to raise funds for the benefit of Female Orphans, or Children from three to ten years of ages, whose parents are not capable of supporting them; and to board them with some capable, discreet Woman, who shall teach them reading, writing, plain needle work, and all kinds of domestic business, until old enough to be placed in reputable families.

THE DONATIONS To be vested in some productive Stock. The interest shall be appropriated for the relief of aged and infirm Widows, "who by misfortunes have fallen into poverty and distress."

. . . [The] Board shall manage the affairs of the Society, and see that the Children are well treated, decently clothed, and instructed at the expence of the Society. They shall have the intire direction of the children; and when they are of proper age to be put out, shall choose suitable places for them. . . .

A COMMITTEE, consisting of two Managers, shall be chosen every quarter; whose duty it shall be to pay the board of the Children, provide their necessary clothing, inspect their improvement, and at each monthly meeting present their bills to the Directress; who shall give an order on the Treasurer for payment.

RELIEF Shall not be granted to any applicants till they have been visited at their dwellings by one of the Managers; and particular inquiry is made into their character and circumstances.—*Immorality* excludes from the patronage of this Society.

PERSONS Wishing relief from this Society, must apply to one of the Managers, who shall represent their case at the meeting.

MEMBERS Of the Society pay three dollars annually; and none shall be admitted Members for a less sum. . . . Twenty-five Subscribers in any town adjacent to Salem, may be entitled to offer a Child;—and may expect it will be supported by the Society, for the time they continue their subscription annually.

No child will be admitted to the protection of the Society until its parents or relatives have relinquished all claim to it whatever. A list of Children proposed to admission, shall be kept by the Secretary. Priority of application will have the preference, unless in the opinion of the managers at a regular meeting, the circumstances of a particular child shall require immediate relief. The children, at a suitable age, shall be placed in good families until the age of eighteen, "or marriage within that age."

Any child, whose infirmities render her unfit to go into a family as a domestic, shall be apprenticed to a mantua-maker or milliner, &c. at the age of fourteen. When any persons wish to take a child from the patronage of the Society, they must apply to one of the Managers, who shall inform the Board at their next meeting, that the Secretary may register her name. Preference will be given to subscribers. One suit of clothes only shall be furnished a child at her departure from the Asylum. Should any child, patronized by the Society, be claimed by her connections, she shall not be returned to them until all expences incurred on her account are reimbursed.

*   *   *

Rules for the Governess
She shall conduct the children, every Sabbath-day, to public worship, except prevented by sickness. She must endeavor to impress their minds with a becoming sense of God and Religion; and of the great importance of a modest and virtuous behavior. She shall be particularly careful to bring them up in habits of industry. She shall instruct them in reading, writing, plain needlework, and all kinds of domestic business; and shall . . . endeavor so to educate them as to make them good and useful members of Society. They shall not make visits or see their connections, except in the presence of the Governess, unless by order of the Board of Direction.—They shall all be dressed alike, in neat and decent apparel. The Governess shall see that, their faces and hands are washed, and hair combed every morning; and shall take great pains to establish habits of order and cleanliness among them. . . .

Source: Salem Female Charitable Society, Report of the Salem Female Charitable Society (Salem, Mass.: R. Carlton, 1804).

11. African Dorcas Association, 1828

The African Dorcas Association was a black women's charitable group focused on providing clothes for children who attended classes sponsored by the privately financed New York African Free Schools. Founded in 1828, the group was organized by the men of the New York Manumission Society and supervised by a committee of black ministers. Despite the prominent role of men in the organization, a dedicated group of African American women ran the society with skill and tenacity, meeting weekly to sew and collect clothes for schoolchildren. Many protestant churches in the early republic sponsored such societies, named after the biblical Dorcas who sewed for the poor of her village and, after her death, was awakened and raised by Saint Peter. The African Dorcas Association was one of dozens of groups that encouraged women to practice mutual cooperation in support of the education and "uplift" of the race. These groups also encouraged women to adopt a self-sacrificing spirit and avoid too much aggrandizement. The articles below are all from the *Freedom's Journal*, an African American newspaper based in New York City.

*   *   *

Notice

AT a large meeting of Females of Colour, Ministers of the different coloured Churches in this city, and Members of the Manumission Society, convened at the Society's School Room, Mulberry street, on Wednesday evening the 23d January, to take into consideration the subject of forming a FRAGMENT SOCIETY; the Rev. PETER WILLIAM'S was called to the Chair, and JNO. B. RUSSWURM, appointed Secretary.

The object of the meeting having been stated by the Chairman, and the following Constitution (prepared expressly by Mr. Andrews, for the new Society) read by the Secretary; the meeting was addressed by Messrs. Andrews, Hatch, Hale, and Todd, all highly approving the contemplated object, and urging the immediate formation of a Society to carry its benevolent plans into operation. . . .

Constitution:

1st. That, whereas, an unusual number of children belonging to the African Free Schools under the care of the Manumission Society, from various causes, absent themselves from school, and, as we have reason to believe, that such absence in numerous instances, is owing to want of suitable clothing; WE, whose names are hereunto subscribed, do agree to form ourselves into an association for the purpose of procuring donations in clothing, &c. both for males and females of the said schools, to furnish them to such children as may need supply.

2d. That this Association be called, THE AFRICAN DORCAS ASSOCIATION; and that its objects shall be to afford relief in clothing, hats, and shoes, as far as our means may enable us, to such children as regularly attend the schools belonging to the Manumission Society, and to such others as a committee to be appointed, as advisers, may from time, recommend.

3d. That a committee, consisting of the Minister of each African Church in this city, shall be considered an advising committee. They shall be requested to perform the following duties.

1st. To arrange all our stated meetings, and keep all necessary records and minutes in books to be provided by this Association for that purpose.

2d. They shall be authorized to receive all donations either in money or clothing, for distribution, accounting therefor to the Treasurer of the Association every three months.

3d. They shall provide a suitable place of deposit of clothing, and for our stated meetings, giving due notice of the latter in the respective Churches. They shall be authorized to make By-Laws for their own government, as experience may dictate.

4th. The stated meetings of this Association shall be semi-annually, that is, in September and March, on such day as the advising committee shall agree on.

5th. All contributions of money, shall, after defraying incidental expenses of the Association, be expended for hats, shoes, &c. for distribution, and no money shall at any time be expended in any other way than to provide hats, shoes, and clothing, except according to the provision made by this article.

6th. Twenty-one members of this Association, to be annually chosen in March, from a ticket of nomination, agreed upon by the advising committee, shall form a Board of Managers, who shall at their first meeting in every year, appoint a First Manager to preside at their meetings and at the meetings of the Association, or she shall have power to appoint any one of the advising committee to preside in her place, at such meeting. The Board of Managers shall also appoint one of their number, Treasurer, for one year, at this same meeting, who shall have charge of the cash concerns of the Association, and shall be assisted in the performance of her duties by any of the advising committee, whom they may appoint.

7th. All clothing for distribution shall be properly adjusted, repaired, made up or altered, under the superintendance of this Board, and all distributions shall be under their direction, conformably with the second article.

8th. We individually consider it a great blessing for our children, and those of our friends of Colour, to enjoy the advantages of a good education, and that it is our duty to use every proper means in our power, to promote a regular attendance at school, so that the rising generation amongst us, may freely participate in the good which their and our benefactors are so liberally tendering them.

9th. Every person, on becoming a member of this Association, shall pay into the hands of the Treasurer, or to any one of the advising committee, twelve and an half cents, and twenty-five cents, at every semi-annual meeting.

10th. Every Female of Colour of a good moral character complying or agreeing to comply with the requirements of the 9th article, shall be considered a member of this Association.

It was also agreed, that until the contemplated meeting in March next, the affairs of this Association, shall be nominated by the Ministers, present, and that they be requested to enter upon that duty forthwith.

Agreed also, that in conformity with the 3d article of the Constitution, the following named persons, be, and hereby acknowledged by this Association as their Advising Committee, that is to say—

William Miller, Christopher Rush, Samuel Todd, William Quinn, Peter Williams, Benjamin Paul, Samuel E. Cornish.

Source: "Notice," *Freedom's Journal*, February 1, 1828.

*   *   *

Dorcas Association

Mr. Editor:—To be a friend to the poor is one of the greatest characteristics of the christian religion, and is highly honourable to human nature. We have always opportunities of exercising our benevolence for "the poor ye have always with you," says Christ. My object in reminding you of these truths, is to reach through your valuable paper, the ears and feelings of those who have something to spare for the needy.

Your readers generally know that the children of our colour have opportunities for gaining useful knowledge without respect to the condition of their parents; whether rich or poor, in an institution in this city, which is believed to be equal at least, to any establishment of the kind among whites, in this country: I mean the African Free Schools.

Many of the children who have the advantages of these seminaries, have not suitable nor comfortable clothing to attend school in, and are therefore, for a great part of the year deprived those opportunities of learning, which might prove to them invaluable blessings. I wish by this means to call the attention of our more prosperous brethren and sisters to this subject, and hope, when they are informed how useful the [sic] might be, that they will help the needy in their distress. I am informed that about a year ago, a considerable number of our female friends, formed themselves into a Society, under the title of the African Dorcas Association; for the purpose of making up garments for the children belonging to the schools males and females, and to receive for this purpose such donations in materials, garments, hats, shoes, & as may be sent to them.

I have been present on a Wednesday afternoon, (the regular time of meeting) when a large committee of our own colour had assembled at the African School in Mulberry St. to cut and fit garments for destitute children. It was an interesting sight; they will have a rich reward. This society has already done much good; but requires aid from those who are able to bestow something to promote its humane object. I have no doubt that many of our white friends would contribute largely (and some have already) if they but knew of an institution such as is here noticed. The inclement season is just commencing; no time should be lost in giving publicity of the existence of a society which does so much honour to our colour.

Articles of clothing, materials, & I understand may be left at the School room in Mulberry St., at P.S. Titus' 457 Pearl St. or at Mahlon Day's 376 Pearl St.

Blessed is he that considereth the poor: the Lord will deliver him in time of trouble. Psalm 41.I.

CATO.

Source: "Dorcas Association," letter to editor, *Freedom's Journal*, November 21, 1828.

*   *   *

Our Dorcas Society

We are glad to learn, that the members of this highly useful society, have commenced their labours this season, with a determination to perform every thing in their power to enable the poor children of our coloured brethren to attend their winter's school. In so large a city as this, we must always expect that there will be hundreds of destitute little ones; and though, we cannot procure suitable clothing for all, we are in duty bound to do all in our power—as the widow did, when she cast her mite into the treasury. We do not hold to benevolent societies, like the Dorcas, meeting year after year, to raise funds in order to make somewhat of a shew when they begin now is the time for action, if we are really anxious of doing any thing for the benefit of the rising generation—when charitable individuals and societies are doing all in their power, that we should second them by contributing our mite, if

never so small. The folly of a society waiting for funds before going into operation, reminds us of the simplicity of the youth, who waited on the banks
of the river, for the subsiding of the current, in order that he might cross
over. Now is the time, while we are blessed with health and strength, that
we should come forward and assist those who are so happy as to precede us,
in this noble work of charity.

While upon this subject, we would invite the attention of our female
readers, in other cities to the formation of societies of a similar nature. What
good has been effected by our Dorcas society is incalculable; for what shall
we compare with the advantage to the young of attending a well regulated
school? The members of the society deserve our commendation for the business like manner in which they conduct their affairs; they have no annual
processions; they have no blazing banners; pharisee like to proclaim to the
world the nature of their work. Their march has been slow but steady: and
we trust, many of the members will yet have the happiness to witness the
beneficial effects of their labours on the rising generation.

Source: "Our Dorcas Society," *Freedom's Journal*, January 9, 1829.

*   *   *

Dorcas Association

It is a fact which ought to be publicly known, not for the purposes of *osten-
tation*, but as in inducement to others to persevere in any good work, that
the DORCAS ASSOCIATION have during the present season of cold,
distributed among the destitute scholars of the public African Schools of
this city, 168 articles of clothing, and have thus fitted up 64 boys & girls, so
as to appear at school, in decent and comfortable apparel. This has been accomplished by the labours of a few benevolent females, (not exceeding 15 or
20) in their sewing meetings, held at the house of Mrs. Margaret A. Francis,
in Leonard street, every Wednesday evening.

In the prosecution of this truly charitable work, they have in the appro-
bation of their consciences, and the many expressions of gratitude, which
they have witnessed from the children they have clothed, and also from the
parents of those children, enjoyed so rich a reward, that their zeal for it appears to be greatly increased. They have found, that there is no pleasure like
the pleasure of doing good, and are determined to persevere. How pleasant,
and how profitable must it be to our females to spend their leisure evenings,
in clothing and making comfortable, & thus keeping in school (where they
may learn wisdom and virtue) many little children, who would be otherwise

running the streets at this inclement season, suffering for the want of clothing, and learning nothing but wickedness! May they and their labours' be ever favoured with the blessings of HEAVEN.

Source: "Dorcas Association," *Freedom's Journal*, February 7, 1829.

12. Female Moral Reform Society Report, 1835

The organizations known as "Female Moral Reform Societies" grew out of the evangelical fervor of the Second Great Awakening that stimulated activities to help human beings to prepare for the millennium by renouncing sin and embracing salvation. Female moral reform focused on eliminating sexual transgressions, especially those in which women were victimized or stigmatized, while their male partners evaded censure. Targeting prostitution and seduction, women organized to demand an end to the sexual double standard and the protection of women. At its height, the movement boasted membership of over fifty thousand women in more than six hundred local organizations. Yet, its critics—including other evangelical reformers—questioned the propriety of such public action by women as well as the sexual knowledge they acquired in the service of their cause. Although critical to a generation of women activists, female moral reform fell into decline by midcentury. This first report from the New York society clarifies goals and purposes, underscoring a gendered militancy that characterized the organizers.

*   *   *

Report at the First Annual Meeting of the New York Female Moral Reform Society, May 15, 1835

The Board of Managers of the *Female Moral Reform Society of the City of New York*, in presenting their First Annual Report, feel that some account of the origin and present state of efforts in the cause of Moral Reform, may not be unacceptable to the public.

The first society in this city for the suppression of licentiousness, of which we have any definite knowledge, was organized in 1830, and styled "The Magdalen Society." This society embraced some of the most wealthy and respectable inhabitants of the city. Its efforts were mainly directed to the reformation of abandoned females, and for this purpose an asylum was opened on Bowery Hill, for such as appeared willing to return to a virtuous life. Its first report, published in 1831, and giving some account of the existing state of morals in the city, called forth many bitter feelings and much opposition. Not long after its publication the society ceased its operations and was dissolved. There was one individual, however, connected with the society, the Rev. J. R. McDowall, who felt that he could not retire from the field. For a long time he continued to labor alone. His "Magdalen Facts," published in 1832, awakened a deep interest in many minds in the cause of Magdalen Reform. To sustain him in his self-denying labors societies were formed in 1832 among the ladies of the Laight-street and Spring-street congregations. It was soon felt however, that some more extended efforts were necessary to the advancement of the cause; a meeting of ladies from different churches was therefore called, which resulted in the formation of the N. Y. Female Benevolent Society. This society soon took under its charge the females who had been received into the family of Mr. McDowall, and the latter devoted himself to the publication of his Journal, which a short time previous he had commenced. Here again Mr. McDowall stood alone, unsustained by any society, and laboring entirely on his own responsibility, until the American Seventh Commandment Society came into existence in the winter of 1833. By this time the feelings of many benevolent ladies were deeply enlisted in the cause; and while some connected with the Female Benevolent Society were endeavoring to reclaim the vicious, others felt that a preventive influence might be exerted by united efforts to change the tone of public sentiment in relation to the sin of licentiousness, to one more in accordance with the Bible. They accordingly formed a society in May 1834, called the Female Moral Reform Society of the City of New York, auxiliary to the American Seventh Commandment Society.

Our Object.

The great object of the society was the diffusion of light as to the causes, the extent, and the evils of licentiousness in our land; to warn the young of their danger; to show *all* their duty in relation to this vice, and to persuade them to do it, with the hope that a barrier might be raised to stop the progress of the evil, and the Redeemer's kingdom thereby be extended. The members of the society did not enter on this work because they supposed it easy of accomplishment, or because they thought that *females* were peculiarly fitted to labor in this cause. They felt that if ever there was a cause that imperiously demanded the strength and energies of *men*, it was this. But they had seen *all* the men (except those connected with the Seventh Commandment Society) who had entered this field, retire from it disheartened, *save one*, whom they felt themselves solemnly called upon to rise up and sustain in his self-denying and persevering efforts. When the husbands and fathers and sons will come up to this work with the noble spirit they evince in other labors of Christian philanthropy, the wives and mothers and daughters will gladly retire from their present prominent station in the cause of Moral Reform, and become, as they were designed to be, the efficient helpers of the stronger sex.

What the Society Has Done.

Immediately after the organization of the society, the Board issued a circular addressed to the females of every religious denomination in the United States, inviting their cooperation in this great work. To this call not a few of the virtuous daughters of America have nobly responded. Thirty-one auxiliaries have been reported, all the members of which have pledged themselves not to countenance the man who is licentious, and twenty of these auxiliaries have reported as connected with them 1444 members. . . . In the fall, the Board . . . sought advice from the executive committee of the Seventh Commandment Society, and upon their recommendation, Resolved to employ missionaries to labor among the abandoned of the city, and to provide a suitable place for the reception of females wishing to reform. Two missionaries were accordingly engaged, and a house taken. . . . By these movements new interest was excited, and a fresh impulse was given to the cause; its friends were stirred up to prayer and the wicked began to tremble.

Effects of Missionary Labor.

The hope of doing good by these missionary operations lay not so much in the expectation of reclaiming profligate females, as in disturbing the licentious in their evil practices; in preventing those who wish to appear virtuous from committing sins which they would be ashamed to have exposed; and in obtaining such information as to the causes, extent and consequences of this evil, as to enable us to warn the virtuous of their danger, and thus exert an influence to prevent our land from becoming a mass of pollution. This hope has not been disappointed. The Board have carefully watched the result of these missionary operations, and they have seen enough to be induced to continue them and to aim at extending them, till this and the other principal cities in the United States are supplied with missionaries, acting on a systematic and efficient plan, believing that when this is accomplished, multitudes would be deterred from visiting haunts of iniquity by the fear of exposure, and that consternation and confusion would reign among the shameless. It is believed that God has stamped with his seal the operations of the past winter, for he has appeared, in more than one instance, both in judgment and in mercy, to verify the declarations of his word. In one portion of the city to which missionary efforts were principally directed, many of the guilty inhabitants would hide themselves on the approach of the missionaries, and some broke up their houses, and *professed* to give up their business but perhaps left, only

to find another place, where they might carry on their wretched calling un-
disturbed by the messengers of God. One man who had been faithfully told
of his guilt and warned of the coming judgment if he persisted in his course
of sin, after a few days died a sudden and awful death. Several similar deaths
in the same neighborhood, about the same time, caused the guilty to tremble,
and many of them to say, *They believed God was coming in judgment to punish
them for their sins.*

Hope of Reclaiming the Abandoned.

Efforts to reclaim the abandoned females are incidentally and necessarily
connected with these missionary operations. It was the last command of our
Savior to preach the gospel to every creature; and while our missionaries
have been laboring to do this from house to house, and through the streets
and lanes of the city, several females, professing a wish to forsake their sins,
have been thrown into their hands and provided for in the society's house.

The Board wish to have their sentiments on this point fully understood.
While they consider the reformation of abandoned females to be an important object, and while they *hope* that many will be reformed, they conceive
that even the *reformation of thousands* would contribute but very little towards checking the tide of licentiousness that is rapidly increasing in our
country. This may easily be shown by drawing a familiar illustration from
the temperance reform. Suppose the main efforts in the cause of temperance
had been directed to reclaim those who had given themselves up to beastly
drunkenness. What *would* have been done compared with what *has* been
done? Distilleries might now have stood in stately grandeur; the maker and
the vender of ardent spirits could still fatten on the tears of wretched wives
and starving children; polite Christians could still tip the glass, and drink
the health of ministers, and all could have shed tears of sympathy over the
wide spread evil, and could have eased their consciences by aiding in the
benevolent effort to reclaim the drunkard; and all this without fear that the
objects of their charity would have diminished in number, for the drunkard-
making machinery would still be in operation to supply the place of those
who might be reformed. Just so in the cause of Moral Reform. We have not
only reason and analogy, but experience and facts to show, that while Christians were engaged in efforts to reclaim abandoned females the machinery of
Satan would still be at work to ruin the innocent. The base seducer would
be caressed by the virtuous, and at the same time stab to the heart those
who smiled upon him. Multitudes of the male sex could gratify their passions
without fear of exposure, contracting and entailing disease and death. The
conduct of unfaithful husbands would be covered up, and if perchance their

virtuous wives should suffer in consequence, not a word would be said. . . .
The impure, unmolested, would circulate their obscene books, prints, &c.
while all cried Hush, and this work of manufacturing for hell would be carried on with increasing energy.

To carry this illustration farther: there is quite as little hope in reforming
"strange women," as in reforming drunkards. Indeed, they are intimately
connected, for a "strange woman" is almost always a drunkard. It is well
known that licentiousness has a most debasing influence on the mind. Many
of the poor creatures who are its victims acknowledge that they are going to
hell, and weep and tremble when compelled to look at the fact, but like the
drunkard, whose mind is under the influence of beastly bodily appetites, they
seem not to have the power to break the chains that bind them to their sins.
Very few of those that *might* be reclaimed, *can* be induced to enter a Magdalen asylum, while the great majority of those who are willing to seek a refuge
there, are sunk so low in vice, as to warrant but little hope of their reformation. They will readily yield to temptation, and the force of habit, and return
like the "dog to his vomit, or the sow that was washed to her wallowing in
the mire." Those who are not so debased, flatter themselves with the hope
of a voluntary return to virtue at some convenient season, while they go on
sinning as it were, "with a cart rope, and drinking in iniquity like water."
The Board have been led to these conclusions from witnessing the results of
their own, as well as other operations, to reclaim abandoned females. During
the last six months, 30 females have been received into the society's house;
of these, 3 have gone to service, 4 have been sent to the asylum of the N.Y.
Female Benevolent society, and one who was previously reclaimed, and had
entered to obtain a home, being in ill health, having partially recovered, is
now taking care of herself. The others after staying some a longer and some
a shorter time have returned to their sins. . . .

Advocate of Moral Reform.
    . . . The Board feel that the principal hope of the cause of Moral Reform
is in the power of the press in communicating to the world light, as to the
sin, the causes, and the consequences of the evil of licentiousness. Indeed it
was one primary object in the organization of the society, to give support to
McDowall's Journal, the only publication that had ever dared to speak out,
and take a bold and decided stand against this giant sin. . . .

Licentious Men.
    One great object to be effected in the work of Moral Reform is, the for-
mation of a public sentiment, that will place the licentious *man* on a level

with the licentious woman. The crime is as great, and we venture to say in a majority of cases greater, in the male than in the female. We see no reason why either should be exempt from merited disgrace. When men are guilty of this sin, let them lose their character as women do, and much of this abominable vice would be done away at once. This change in public sentiment we humbly conceive it is in the power of virtuous females to effect; and the way to effect it is, to *induce virtuous females to look down on licentious men as virtuous men now look down on licentious women.* Let virtuous women band together to keep such men at a distance and the work is done. Until they will do this, they must expect to see their daughters ruined and covered with infamy, while the base villain who has done this work, is regarded as a *gentleman*, received into respectable society, and thus encouraged to go on in his deeds of villainy. . . . O, if woman would stand for her rights, and insist upon it that the licentious man should be put down on a level with his guilty paramour, what good to the human race and to the cause of Christ would be the result. . . .

Warning to the Country.

The Board have ascertained that there are annually brought into the larger cities from the country, a large number of young women under various pretences, but really for the purpose of supplying the market of sin. Some are brought in under the promise of marriage; and here, friendless and destitute, their seducers abandon them to infamy to hide their own guilt. Others, in coming to the city, are committed by their anxious mothers, to some *gentleman* for protection, but who gives them the protection the vulture does the dove. And others on visits to their friends are drawn into *her* doors, whose "house is the way to hell, going down to the chambers of death." Our operations are bringing to light more and more of the secrets of this abominable traffic, carried on in all its departments almost as regular as the trade in dry goods. To every anxious mother and every virtuous daughter throughout the land, we would raise the loud note of alarm, and cry, Beware of unprincipled men in the garb of *gentlemen*. . . .

. . . The field of usefulness in the cause of Moral Reform is opening wider and wider every day. It remains for the Christian community to say whether it shall be occupied. We earnestly invite to our aid in the difficult and self-denying work, the influences of the minister of the gospel, and the virtuous of every class; and we doubt not, if we labor prayerfully and diligently, that God will succeed us in our labors, and permit us to see the triumph of virtue over vice, AND TO HIM BE ALL THE GLORY.

Source: Female Moral Reform Society of the City of New York, *Report at the First Annual Meeting of the New York Female Moral Reform Society, May 15, 1835* (New York: William Newell, 1835), www.teachushistory.org/second-great-awakening-age-reform/resources/report-female-moral-reform-society.

13. Maria Sturges, Address to Christian Females in Slaveholding States, 1836

As the corresponding secretary for a Female Anti-Slavery Society in central Ohio, Maria Sturges (1799–1843) put her name to the address printed by abolitionist editor Gamaliel Bailey in his paper, *The Philanthropist*, in Cincinnati. The appeal of the Muskingum antislavery sisters to their sex in the South appeared six months before Angelina Grimké (1805–1879) published her more famous *Appeal to the Christian Women of the South*. In fact, dozens of female abolitionists across the North wrote "appeals" and "addresses" to southern women, usually arguing that all women had a Christian duty to use their influence to help end slavery.

*   *   *

Address to Christian Females in the Slaveholding States, from the Female Anti-Slavery Society of Muskingum County, Ohio

Christian Sisters: Our proximity to the slave-holding section of our country, and the interest we feel in *you*, as members of the household of Christ, render us greatly solicitous, to obtain the co-operation of your sympathy, and efforts in behalf of the suffering slave. We have therefore felt it our duty, to spread out before you some of the motives which have actuated us, (and to which we trust your hearts will not be insensible) in espousing the cause of immediate emancipation.

If we are truly what we profess to be—however widely we may differ in many of our views and usages, we must be actuated by the same spirit; that spirit is love—love to man, love to God, manifesting itself in every possible form for the good of our fellows, and the glory of our Redeemer's kingdom. In the exercise of this spirit we hope to address you; a spirit which we would fain hope will be reciprocated, and enable you to judge charitably of our intentions, and to shield us from any reproach, by which the enemies of the cross of Christ may seek to bring Christianity itself into contempt.

You may perhaps be ready to ask, what possible good can we hope to accomplish, by addressing those who themselves have no direct control over the continuance or abolition of slavery—matters which belong so exclusively to your husbands and fathers to exempt you from all responsibility in regard to them? We reply, asking with all kindness, are you exempt from all responsibility? We grant, that so far as mere forms of business and legislation are concerned, it is not within your province. But do you exert *no* influence? Are you really such ciphers in the domestic circle, and in society, that your opinions have no weight? Are your principles and feelings so entirely disregarded?

Different as are the modifications which society assumes where slavery exists, we cannot for a moment admit, that its influence has been such as to render woman the *toy*, rather than the rational companion of man; but however small may be the influence of *some*, with man, have not *all* influence with God? Is not his throne of grace always accessible, and can you not plead there in behalf of the heart-stricken captives in your midst, with fervency and importunity that shall be blessed of him to their final deliverance?

The most civilized and intellectual heathen nations, seem to have well understood the power of female influence, when they deified a woman as goddess both of *wisdom* and *war*—and though some of your orators have indulged in no very gallant raillery against our sex, on the floor of Congress, we are not thence to infer, that, our sisters of the south are plunged into the barbarism of remote antiquity, or sunk in Asiatic imbecility and voluptuousness. Indeed we cannot forget, that we are inhabitants of free America, enjoying the light of the 19th century under the glorious gospel of the Son of God—one of the distinguished features of which, is, the *restoration* of woman to that moral and intellectual standing for which she was originally designed, when God pronounced her an help *meet* for man—that is every way suited to his rank and dignity in creation.

We address you as women, therefore, whose influence through all the ramifications of society cannot but be felt; as those whose power, in giving tone to public morals, in forming the principles and moulding [sic] the character of the rising generation, cannot be questioned,—and we would beseech you to exert that influence on the side of justice and mercy. As christian women; a fearful responsibility rests upon us all, to do every thing in our power to remove this great evil from the church of Christ, where it has so long found refuge and protection.

That it is wrong to hold property in man, we conceive to be evident, from the fact, that God created him in his own image, destined him to immortality, and constituted him lord of creation,—a distinct species from all that moved upon the face of the earth. This order of things are found no where reversed in the word of God. Some, indeed, in the dispensation of his providence, are "hewers of wood and drawers of water"—this, however, by no means involves forfeiture of these heaven-chartered rights, with which their Creator endowed them—and whosoever deprives his fellow of these, and reduces him to the condition of property—a thing, to be bought and sold, and used as the brutes that perish, is guilty of rebellion against God, and exposes himself to the just judgment of insulted Deity.

We believe, too, that it is utterly at variance with that great law of love "as ye would that men should do unto you, do ye even so unto them"—and directly opposed to those pure and benevolent principles, which actuated the Redeemer in his mission to this fallen world. He left his throne of blessedness, and suffered all that the envy, malice, and hatred of a wicked world could inflict, that he might procure pardon for the *guilty*. Can it be the same spirit which forges chains and fetters for the *innocent*—accused of no crime save that of having "a skin not colored like our own?" Is there a plague-spot on the soul—an incubus on the intellect? Who hath made us discerners of the heart and of the mind? An inspired Apostle hath said, "if any man hath not the spirit of Christ he is none of his."

Nor is it more compatible with that other and paring command of our ascending Redeemer, "go ye into all the world and preach the gospel to every creature." For many years, the attention of Christendom has been directed to the duty of fulfilling this command; and doubtless, your own charities have assisted in erecting the standard of the cross in every far-off shore and sea-girt isle. While we are thus compassing the earth with our missionary efforts, is there not one class of our fellow-travellers [sic] to eternity, within our borders, who are by law rendered nearly or quite inaccessible to all missionary or christian operations? What is it, that in a land professedly Christian, has erected this impious barrier between the soul and its God? What is it that absolutely forbids immortal being searching the Scriptures as God commands? Is it not SLAVERY? Do not mistake our meaning. We speak now of the system, not of individual practice. *You* perhaps, are honestly laboring, so far as you think circumstances will admit, for the spiritual welfare of your slaves; (verily it is a mighty responsibility,) and we trust we do duly appreciate that moral courage which animates such as refuse to fall in with a corrupted public sentiment, and stand unappalled by cruel statutes:—Nevertheless, these *exceptions* to the rule, these kind efforts, form no argument in favor of the system, as it is, and ever must be. For are there not thousands of slaves beyond the reach of all religious influence, who never have heard of Jesus as the Saviour of sinners? and hundreds of thousands, who have never been taught, or permitted to read the book of God's love?

Nor, is it any palliation, to say that many persons in the free states are entirely ignorant of the first principles of religion. If there be such, and we admit there are—it is not because the missionary is shut out by legal enact-ments—there is no law to exclude the word of God from the humblest cot-tage of the poorest poor—on them, and not on our free institutions, rests, the guilt. And now we ask if slavery, viewed in all its bearings on the spiritual welfare of its victims, (to say nothing of their physical sufferings) is, or can be, in accordance with the *word* or *will* of God? Indeed, we ourselves cannot avoid the conclusion, that slavery is not only in itself a sin, but that sins of every name and character cluster in its train.

Will you not then, dear sisters, be induced to examine this subject, if you have not already done so, in the light of God's holy word? Settle it, first, in your own minds, that slaveholding is a SIN, and like all other sins, ought to be immediately abandoned. Should such an investigation however, fail to convince you of your own individual guilt, do you not see, that however mild and compassionate your own course may be, you are nevertheless sanctioning a system, which is polluting the land with crime, and filling it with tears and groans of an afflicted and heart-broken people.

In what way emancipation shall be effected, we cannot pretend to say. We know that it rests with the slaveholders themselves, and through them, with the legislatures of the several states, to accomplish so desirable an object. But this much we believe, that whenever the moral sense of the community on this subject shall be rectified, the path of duty will be both plain and practicable.

The limits of a newspaper address, do not admit of any detail on this point. Could you be induced to look into our anti-slavery publications, treasonable and incendiary as they are represented, you would, we doubt not, find many of those difficulties removed, which at first view embarrass and discourage you. We pray you, let not prejudice prevent you from acquainting yourselves with our real sentiments.

In conclusion we would say—dear sisters, harden not your hearts against those miserable out-casts, your slaves,—each of whom is endowed with an immortal soul—unspeakably precious—and like ourselves,—they are placed on probation and eternity.

Many of them, at least, as you know, are made to suffer in cruel and hopeless bondage—borne down beneath the burden of life—their earthly comforts few, and at the disposal arbitrary masters, arrogating to themselves supreme control, not only over *their* persons, but over every other creature in whom their affections center; and above all, immuring their souls in darkness deep and midnight, upon which no day-star of life is permitted to dawn—no beam of hope to enter, that they may be cheered on their journey to that other land of which they vaguely dream.

How can we expect to escape judgment, as a nation, or enjoy prosperity as the people of God, if we forbear to cry aloud against the oppression under which our brethren groan? So sure as a righteous Judge sitteth on the throne of the universe, so surely will he avenge the wrongs which we vainly attempt to justify. When he maketh inquisition for blood, shall not judgment begin at the house of God?

Let us therefore labor together in this righteous cause, as those who must give account. The time is coming, when we, with those poor afflicted ones, shall stand before the judgment-seat of Christ. At that awful crisis, how shall we look upon those who have perished through our abuse, or neglect, and expect justification through that blood which was poured forth for *all?*

May God give us grace to discern and do his will, is the constant prayer of your sisters in the gospel.

By order of the board,

Mrs. H. Sturges, *Cor. Secretary.*

Source: Maria Sturges, "Address to Christian Females in the Slaveholding States, from the Female Anti-Slavery Society of Muskingum County, Ohio," *Philanthropist,* March 25, 1836.

14. Fathers and Rulers Petition, 1836

The "Fathers and Rulers" petition, as it became known, was the most common petition used by female antislavery societies in the 1830s. Distributed to female antislavery groups and reprinted locally for circulation, thousands of women signed this petition, which asked Congress to abolish slavery in the District of Columbia. It adopted a deferential attitude and relied on common assumptions about woman's sympathetic nature. Although authorship is usually attributed to abolitionist Theodore Dwight Weld (1803–1895), it was more likely written by the Putnam, Ohio, women who were the first to promote the petition in 1836. Women's abolition petitions precipitated the congressional crisis known as the "Gag Rule," when representatives sought to block the introduction of these documents into their sessions.

*   *   *

Fathers, and Rulers of our country:—
Constrained not only by our sympathy with the suffering, but also by a true regard for the honor and welfare of our beloved country, we beg leave to lay before you this our humble memorial, in behalf of that oppressed and deeply injured class of native Americans, who reside within the limits of

your exclusive jurisdiction. We should poorly estimate the virtues which ought ever to distinguish your honorable body, could we anticipate any other than a favorable hearing when our appeal is to men, to philanthropists, to patriots, to the legislators and guardians of a Christian people. We should be less than women, if the nameless wrongs of which the slaves, of our sex, are made the defenceless victims, did not fill us with horror, and constrain us, in earnestness and agony of spirit, to pray for their deliverance. By day and by night, their woes and injuries rise up before us, throwing shades of mournful contrast over all the joys of domestic life, and filling our hearts with sadness at the recollection of those whose hearths are desolate.

Nor do we forget, in the contemplation of their other sufferings, the intellectual and moral degradation to which they are doomed! how the soul formed for companionship with Angels, is despoiled and brutified and consigned to ignorance, pollution and ruin.

Surely then, as the Representatives of a people professedly Christian, you will bear with us, when we say with Jefferson, "we tremble for our country when we remember that God is just, and that his justice cannot sleep forever"; and, when—in obedience to a divine command, "we *remember* those who are in bonds as bound with them." Impelled by these sentiments, we solemnly purpose, the grace of God assisting, to importune High Heaven with prayer, and our National Legislature with appeals, until this Christian people abjure, forever, a traffic in the souls of men, and the groans of the oppressed no longer ascend to God from the dust where now they welter.

We do not ask your honorable body to transcend your Constitutional powers, by legislating on the subject of slavery within the boundaries of the slave-holding states—but we do conjure you, to abolish slavery in the District of Columbia, where you exercise "exclusive jurisdiction." In the name of humanity, justice, equal rights, and impartial law, our country's weal, her honor, and her cherished hopes, we earnestly implore for this our humble petition, your favorable regard. If, both in Christian and Heathen lands, kings have revoked their edicts at the intercession of woman, and Tyrants have relented when she appeared a suppliant for mercy, surely we may hope that the legislators of a free, enlightened and christian people, will not regard our prayer as "abominable, malicious and unrighteous," when the only boon we crave is the deliverance of the fettered and the down trodden from the bondage under which they groan.

And as in duty bound your petitioners will ever pray.

Source: "Petition of the Ladies Resident in the State of Ohio," *Philanthropist*, June 24, 1836.

15. Controversy over Abolitionist Lectures by the Grimké Sisters, 1837

In June 1837, the Massachusetts Congregational Clergy as an official body reacted to the divisive impact of debates over slavery taking place in its churches and the related issue of the antislavery lecturing undertaken by Sarah (1792–1873) and Angelina (1805–1879) Grimké in these churches. From a prominent slaveholding family in South Carolina, Angelina had followed her sister Sarah to Philadelphia in 1829, where, seven years later, she made public their abolitionist sentiments in her *Appeal to the Christian Women of the South*. In early 1837, Angelina began to speak in support of immediate emancipation in the New York area; in May, the sisters began a tour of Massachusetts that provoked the clergy's hostility, documented below. The following year, Sarah Grimké defended their public speaking in her *Letters on the Equality of the Sexes and the Condition of Women*.

*   *   *

General Association of Massachusetts, June 28, 1837

Brethren and Friends,

Having assembled to consult upon the interests of religion within this commonwealth, we would now, as Pastors and Teachers, in accordance with the custom of this Association, address you on some of the subjects which at the present time appear to us to have an important bearing upon the cause of Christ. . . .

We invite your attention to the dangers which at present seem to threaten the female character with wide spread and permanent injury. The appropriate duties and influence of women, are clearly stated in the New Testament. Those duties and that influence are unobtrusive and private, but the sources of mighty power. When the mild, dependent, softening influence of woman upon the sternness of man's opinions is fully exercised, society feels the effects of it in a thousand forms. The power of woman is in her dependence, flowing from the consciousness of that weakness which God has given her for her protection and which keeps her in those departments of life that form the character of individuals and of the nation.

There are social influences which females use in promoting piety and the great objects of christian benevolence, which we cannot too highly commend. We appreciate the unostentatious prayers and efforts of woman, in advancing the cause of religion at home and abroad:—in Sabbath schools, in leading religious inquirers to their pastor for instruction, and in all such associated effort as becomes the modesty of her sex; and earnestly hope that she may abound more and more in these labours of piety and love. But when she assumes the place and tone of a man as a public reformer, our care and protection of her seem unnecessary, we put ourselves in self defence against her, she yields the power which God has given her for protection, and her character becomes unnatural.

If the vine, whose strength and beauty is to lean upon the trellis work and half conceal its clusters, thinks to assume the independence and the over-shadowing nature of the elm, it will not only cease to bear fruit, but fall in shame and dishonour into the dust.

We cannot, therefore, but regret the mistaken conduct of those who encourage females to bear an obtrusive and ostentatious part in measures of reform, and countenance any of that sex who so far forget themselves as to itinerate in the character of public lecturers and teachers.

We especially deplore the intimate acquaintance and promiscuous con-versation of females with regard to things "which ought not to be named"; by which that modesty and delicacy which is the charm of domestic life, and which constitute the true influence of women in society are consumed, and the way opened, as we apprehend, for degeneracy and ruin. . . .

Source: General Association of Massachusetts, *Minutes of the General Association of Massachusetts at their meeting at North Brookfield, June 28, 1837; with the Narrative of the State of Religion, and the Pastoral Letter* (Boston: Crocker and Brewster, 1837).

*   *   *

Sarah Grimké, to Mary S. Parker, President of the Boston Female Anti-Slavery Society, Haverhill, 7th Mo. 1837

Dear Friend,

When I last addressed thee, I had not seen the pastoral Letter of the General Association. It has since fallen into my hands, and I must . . . make some re-marks on this extraordinary document. I am persuaded that when the minds of men and women become emancipated from the thralldom of superstition and "traditions of men," the sentiments contained in the Pastoral Letter will be recurred to with as much astonishment as the opinions of Cotton Mather and other distinguished men of his day, upon the subject of witchcraft; nor will it be deemed less wonderful, that a body of divines would gravely as-semble and endeavor to prove that woman has no right to "open her mouth for the dumb," than it now is that judges would have sat on the trials of witches, and solemnly condemned nineteen persons and one dog to death for witchcraft.

But to the letter. It says, "We invite your attention to the dangers which at present seem to threaten the FEMALE CHARACTER with wide-spread and permanent injury." I rejoice that they have called the attention of my sex to this subject, because I believe if woman investigates it, she will soon discover that danger is impending, though from a totally different source from which the Association apprehends,—danger from those who, having long held the reins of usurped authority, are unwilling to permit us to fill that sphere which God created us to move in, and who have entered into league to crush the immortal mind of woman. I rejoice, because I am persuaded that the rights of woman, like the rights of slaves, need only be examined to be understood and asserted, even by some of those, who are now endeavoring to smother the irrepressible desire for mental and spiritual freedom which glows in the breast of many, who hardly dare to speak their sentiments.

"The appropriate duties and influence of women are clearly stated in the New Testament. Those duties are unobtrusive and private, but the source of mighty power. When the mild, dependent, softening influence of woman upon the sternness of man's opinions is fully exercised, society feels the effects of it in a thousand ways." No one can desire more earnestly than I do, that woman may move exactly in the sphere which her Creator has assigned to her; and I believe her having been displaced from that sphere has introduced confusion into the world. It is, therefore, of vast importance to herself and to all the rational creation, that she should ascertain what are her duties and her privileges as a responsible and immortal being. The New Testament has been referred to, and I am willing to abide by its decisions, but must enter my protest against the false translation of some passages by the MEN who did that work, and against the perverted interpretation by the MEN who undertook to write commentaries thereon. I am inclined to think, when we are admitted to the honor of studying Greek and Hebrew, we shall produce some various readings of the Bible a little different from those we now have.

The Lord Jesus defines the duties of his followers in his Sermon on the Mount. He lays down grand principles by which they should be governed, without any references to sex or conditions.—"Ye are the light of the world. A city that is set on a hill cannot be hid. Neither do men light a candle and put it under a bushel, but on a candlestick, and it giveth light unto all that are in the house. Let your light so shine before men, that they may see your good works, and glorify your Father which is in Heaven" [Matthew 5:14–16]. I follow him through all his precepts, and find him giving the same directions to woman as to men, never even referring to the distinction now so strenuously insisted upon between masculine and feminine virtues: this is one of the anti-Christian "traditions of men" which are taught instead of the "commandments of God." Men and women were CREATED EQUAL; they are both moral and accountable beings, and whatever is right for man to do, is right for woman. . . .

The General Association say, that "when woman assumes the place and tone of man as a public performer, our care and protection of her seem unnecessary; we put ourselves in self-defense against her, and her character becomes unnatural." Here again the unscriptural notion is held up, that there is a distinction between the duties of men and women as moral beings; that what is virtue in man, is vice in woman; and women who dare to obey the command of Jehovah, "Cry aloud, spare not, lift up thy voice like a trumpet, and show my people their transgression" [Isaiah 58:1], are threatened with having the protection of the brethren withdrawn. If this is all they do, we shall not even know the time when our chastisement is inflicted; our trust is in the Lord Jehovah, and in him is everlasting strength. The motto of woman, when she is engaged in the great work of public reformation should be,—"The Lord is my light and my salvation; whom shall I fear? The Lord is the strength of my life; of whom shall I be afraid?" [Psalm 27:1]. She must feel, if she feels rightly, that she is fulfilling one of the important duties laid upon her as an accountable being, and that her character, instead of being "unnatural," is in exact accordance with the will of Him to whom, and to no other, she is responsible for the talents and the gifts confided to her. As to the pretty simile, introduced into the "Pastoral Letter," "If the vine whose strength and beauty is to lean upon the trellis work, and half conceal its clusters, thinks to assume the independence and the overshadowing nature of the elm," &c. I shall only remark that it might well suit the poet's fancy. . . . Ah! how many of my sex feel in the dominion, thus unrighteously exercised over them, under the gentle appellation of protection, that what they have leaned upon has proved a broken reed at best, and oft a spear.

Thine in the bonds of womanhood,
Sarah M. Grimké

Source: Sarah M. Grimké, *Letters on the Equality of the Sexes* (Boston: Isaac Knapp, 1838), 14–22.

16. Mary Lyon's Plans for the Mount Holyoke Female Seminary, 1837

When Mary Lyon (1797–1849) penned her prospectus for the Mount Holyoke Female Seminary, she had already been teaching for more than two decades. Born into a struggling farm family in Massachusetts, Lyon followed the pattern of many rural young women, alternating between periods of teaching and continued schooling of her own. Committed to raising the academic quality of female education and educators, Lyon planned an institution that would serve American women and professionalize teaching. Opening in 1837, the Mount Holyoke Female Seminary soon achieved recognition as a leading institution.

*   *   *

This institution is established at South Hadley, Mass. It is to be principally devoted to the preparing of female teachers. At the same time, it will qualify ladies for other spheres of usefulness. The design is to give a solid, extensive, and well-balanced English education, connected with that general improvement, that moral culture, and those enlarged views of duty, which will prepare ladies to be *educators* of children and youth, rather than to fit them to be mere teachers, as the term has been technically applied. Such an education is needed by every female who takes the charge of a school, and sustains the responsibility of guiding the whole course and of forming the entire character of those committed to her care. And when she has done with the business of teaching in a regular school, she will not give up her profession; she will still need the same well-balanced education at the head of her own family, and in guiding her own household.

1. This institution professes to be founded on the high principle of enlarged Christian benevolence. In its plans, and in its appeals, it seeks no support from local or private interest. It is designed entirely for the public good, and the trustees would adopt no measures, not in accordance with this design. . . .
2. The institution is placed on a firm legal basis. An Act of Incorporation has been obtained with a Board of Trustees. . . .
3. The institution is designed to be permanent. The permanency of an institution may be considered as consisting of two particulars—first, its perpetual vitality, and second, its continual prosperity and usefulness. The first is to be secured in the same manner, that the principle of perpetual life in our higher institutions for young men, has been so effectually preserved. A fund is to be committed to an independent, self-perpetuating board of trustees, known to the churches as faithful, responsible men—not as a proprietary investment, but as a free offering, leaving them no way for an honorable retreat from their trust, and binding them with solemn responsibilities to hundreds and thousands

of donors, who have committed their sacred charities to their conscientious fidelity.

The usefulness of this institution, like all others, must depend on its character. This may be very great for a time, where there is no principle of perpetual life, as is the case with some of our most distinguished female seminaries. Amidst all their prosperity they have no solid foundation, and in themselves no sure principle of continued existence. . . . In view of the many changes which are ever breaking in upon the continued services of those to whose care these institutions are committed, every reflecting mind must regard it as of the very first importance, to secure to them [continual prosperity].

4. The general course of study, and the general character of the instruction, will be like those of the Ipswich Female Seminary. The successful labors of many who have been educated there, and the powerful influence which they have been able to exert over the school, the family, and the neighborhood, prove, that the intellectual discipline and moral culture of that Seminary are of no inferior order—and the continual applications for teachers, not only from our most important schools in New England, but from almost all the States and territories in the Union, show the estimation in which it is held by the community.

5. The institution is to be entirely for an older class of young ladies. The general system for family arrangements, for social improvement, for the division of time, for organizing and regulating the school, and the requirements for entrance, will be adapted throughout to young ladies of adult age, and of mature character. Any provision in an institution like this for younger misses, must be a public loss far greater than the individual good. Their exclusion from the institution will produce a state of society among the members, exceedingly pleasant and profitable to those whose great desire is to be prepared to use all their talents in behalf of the cause of education, and of the Redeemer's kingdom; and it will secure for their improvement the entire labors of the teachers, without an interruption from the care and government of pupils too immature to take care of themselves.

6. Every member of the school will board in the establishment. All the teachers and pupils, without exception, will constitute one family. This will give great unity and regularity to the system. It will furnish aids to improvement, which are peculiarly adapted to adult young ladies, and are greatly needed by them in developing and maturing all their talents for usefulness, and which it is difficult to secure to them in any other manner.

7. This institution is designed to furnish the best facilities for education, at a very moderate expense. The way by which these two advantages are to be secured in the same seminary, has been extensively adopted in our higher institutions for young men. How moderate are the charges in our colleges, compared with the real expense of the privileges. But these two advantages are not found thus united in any large female seminary in the land, and probably never will be united, unless it be by the power of disinterested benevolence on an extensive scale.

The present effort in behalf of this institution is to raise a fund for the erection of buildings for the school, including a large seminary-hall, recitation-rooms, a library and reading-room, chemical-room, etc., and accommodations for all the domestic work, and all the family arrangements, and private chambers for the teachers and pupils, together with the furniture for the whole, and also library and apparatus for the school. The charges to the pupils for board and instruction will be placed at cost, without rent for buildings or furniture. . . .

8. The principle of entire equality among the pupils is to be adopted. The charges will be the same to all without reference to their means. Whatever of favor in this respect they receive, will come to them not as an individual charity, demanding individual gratitude, but through the medium of a public institution, founded by the liberality of the Christian community, not for their sakes as individuals, but for the sake of the children and youth of our country. . . . It comes to them as a high and valuable testimonial of the estimate in which are held the services of female teachers, and though it imposes on them a debt of gratitude, it will be a debt which shall ennoble and elevate the soul—one, which can never be cancelled by gold and silver, but which demands a far richer return, even the consecration of time, talents, and acquisitions to the cause of Christ.

9. The young ladies are to take a part in the domestic work of the family. This also is to be on the principle of equality. All are to take a part—not as a servile labor, for which they are to receive a small weekly remuneration, but as a gratuitous service to the institution of which they are members, designed for its improvement and elevation. . . . The arrangements for boarding all the pupils in the establishment, will give to it an independence with regard to private families in the neighborhood, without which it would be difficult, if not impossible, to secure its perpetual prosperity. . . .

The other object of this arrangement is to promote the health, the improvement, and the happiness of the pupils—their health, by its furnishing them with a little daily exercise of the best kind—their improvement, by its tending to preserve their interest in domestic pursuits—and their happiness, by its relieving them from that servile dependence on common domestics, to which young ladies, as mere boarders in a large establishment, are often subject, to their great inconvenience. . . .

The vast importance of supplying our country with well-qualified female teachers, is felt and acknowledged by many. The number of teachers must be greatly increased, and the standard of their education raised. They must have more benevolence and self-denying zeal, and more enlarged views of the great end of education. Many of the most candid and discriminating fully believe, that all other means without this, will be insufficient to save our nation from threatening destruction. And is it not evident, that we cannot depend principally on the other sex for teachers? . . . Will those men who can resist the urgent claims of the ministry, and the pressing calls from the missionary field, cheerfully settle down as teachers in the more self-denying and less lucrative stations, while they are met on every hand by many a fair promise of competence and wealth, rendered more flattering by the increasing wants of a rising family?

It is not to be understood, that we would supply the country with female teachers who shall devote their lives to the business as a profession. In the first place, this is not necessary to furnish good teachers. Females, thoroughly prepared for their work, and devoting to it the whole uninterrupted energies of their minds and souls, are often very successful, though they continue to teach but for a short time. In the second place, it would not have the best effect on the usefulness of other females. What class of men or women among us, are suffering so much from idle and vacant hours, and from time half improved, and from days busily occupied without any important end, as our adult unmarried females? . . . What period more needs some great and noble object of pursuit, calling forth all the talents, and the best energies of the soul? . . . Without this wide and increasing field of usefulness for females, that would be a dark providence, which, by means of manufacturing establishments, has taken from families so much domestic labor, which had its influence in forming the character of our maternal ancestors. But "providence meets providence." And when we behold the opening and increasing field of usefulness and beneficence in this department, and listen to its urgent claims on the time and talents of females, can we not discover the hand of One, wiser than Solomon, in all the labor-saving machinery of the present day?

The demand for female teachers is very great and urgent, while the materials are abundant. . . . But what has been the public voice of the church to
female teachers? Has it not been, "We need not your services, ... We can
save our country, and convert the world without your aid?" This delusive
voice has been heard, and its power has long been operating on the community. It has gone out from New England, and extended over the land. . . .
Mothers too . . . believe, that the selection of teachers for their children is a
subject of inferior importance. At first, they become willing to commit them
to the guidance of those, whom we would not send to a foreign land to teach
the ignorant heathen. At length, we find them cheerfully giving them up to
Roman Catholic schools, fearing not their secret and sure influence, though
they would tremble at the thought, that the Pope of Rome may yet set his
foot on the neck of this great nation, and on the necks of their children and
children's children. . . .

This enterprise was commenced nearly three years ago. The work has
ever since been going regularly, though slowly, forward. The first edifice is
now erecting. It is 94 feet by 50, and four stories besides the basement. It
will furnish good accommodations for the school and the family, and private
chambers for the teachers and for eighty young ladies. It is to be ready for the
reception of scholars early next autumn. . . .

This institution now presents its claims to the Christian community.
It asks for aid, not for its own sake alone—nor merely for the sake of the
many hundreds and thousands of teachers, which it may send forth to bless
the world—but it asks, as the representative of the great cause of raising up
female teachers by benevolent effort.

1. *We appeal to men in moderate pecuniary circumstances.* This class of
   individuals have ever taken a prominent part in establishing all the
   branches of the great benevolent operations, which are promising so
   much good to this dark and wicked world. . . .
2. *We appeal to men of wealth.* This class of men sustain responsibilities
   peculiar to themselves. When any enterprise is struggling for a standing
   among the benevolent operations of the day, to them is often given the
   high privilege of settling the claim and of affixing the final seal. . . .
3. *We appeal to aged men.* A few of the fathers in Israel, whose heads are
   whitening for the grave, still remain. . . . Some have trembled on observing indications, that all was not right. . . . And is it not even so? The
   females have been passed by. . . .
4. *We appeal to young men.* If it is a privilege to increase the velocity of
   the various wheels of benevolence put in motion by our fathers, how

much greater the privilege to give the first impulse to one of the most important. . . . We look for aid to young men, who are strong, and on whose strength, the church, under God, is beginning to rely.

5. *We appeal to ministers of the gospel.* . . . They have given a precious and interesting pledge, that as they have done for the education of young men, so they are ready to do for females, according to their ability, and even beyond their ability. . . .

6. *We appeal to females themselves.* Females have manifested their interest in this cause in a most decisive manner. . . . The hearts of those deeply enlisted in this cause have been greatly cheered by the intelligent interest and active labors of many ladies. . . .

7. *Finally, we appeal to the intelligent of all classes.* We come to those, who can appreciate this object—to those, in whose view the education of the female for her appropriate sphere of usefulness is no dream of the fancy, and the supplying of our country with well-qualified female teachers, is no game of chance. We come to those, who believe, that in this thing, "whatsoever we sow, that shall we also reap."

Source: Mary Lyon, "General View of the Principles and Designs of the Mount Holyoke Female Seminary," 1837, in *Mary Lyon: Documents and Writings*, ed. James Hartley, 161–79 (South Hadley, Mass.: Doorlight Publications, 2008).

17. Jane Elizabeth Hitchcock Jones, "Anti-Slavery Sewing Circles," 1847

The author of this article, Jane Elizabeth Hitchcock Jones (1813–1896), was a coeditor of the *Anti-Slavery Bugle* and an experienced abolitionist lecturer. Here, she instructed women on how to organize antislavery sewing societies and explained the major tenets of the Garrisonian faction of antislavery. A minority among abolitionists, particularly in the West, Garrisonians promoted several unpopular and controversial policies including having the North secede from the Union (disunionism) and blaming the church for the continuation of slavery. The Garrisonians also discouraged antislavery groups from focusing on aid to fugitives (the "Canada Mission" mentioned below) and black education because they were not direct attacks on slavery. Jones hoped to spark the engagement of women through these gender-specific antislavery groups specifically designed to promote radical abolitionist ideas.

*   *   *

Within a few months past I have been repeatedly solicited to assist in the formation of Anti-Slavery Sewing Circles, by drafting Constitutions and conferring with those who were desirous to aid the cause of liberty in this way. As a matter of convenience to myself, and also to those who may choose to use it, I subjoin the following Constitution, which may be made to suit different localities or otherwise altered as shall be deemed advisable.
J. ELIZABETH JONES

CONSTITUTION OF THE_____ANTI-SLAVERY SEWING CIRCLE

We, the undersigned, being desirous to aid the anti-slavery cause by contributing of our means and labor for the support and promulgation of correct views in relation to this subject, do hereby agree to form ourselves into a Sewing Circle and adopt the following

CONSTITUTION

ART. 1st.—This association shall be called the Anti-Slavery Sewing Circle of _____

ART. 2d.—Its object shall be to furnish by manufacture and otherwise, suitable articles by whose sale a fund may be created to aid in the dissemination of anti-slavery light and truth.

ART. 3d.—The funds of this association shall be appropriated to the support of the Western Anti-Slavery Society, or by decision of the majority to any branch of the anti-slavery reform in accordance with the objects of said Society.

ART. 4th—The officers of this association shall be a President, Treasurer, Secretary, and three Managers.

ART. 5th—The President shall preside at all the business meetings of this Circle, and perform the duties usually pertaining to that office.

ART. 6th.—The Treasurer shall receive and hold the funds of this Association, subject to the order of the Managers, or a majority of the Circle.

ART. 7th.—The Secretary shall keep a record of the proceedings of all the business meetings of this Circle.

ART. 8th.—The Managers shall see that sufficient work is provided for those in attendance—shall receive on deposit all articles belonging to this Circle—shall dispose of them, as opportunity offers, at private sale—shall superintend such Fairs as the Association may decide to hold, and have a general oversight of all matters pertaining thereto.

ART. 9th—The President shall direct the Secretary to call a business
meeting at such time and place as may be agreed upon by herself and
two for the Managers.

ART. 10th.—This Constitution may be amended at any business meeting
by a vote of the majority of the members present, notice of proposed
amendment having been given in the call for said meeting.

ART. 11th.—Any person agreeing to, and signing this Constitution, may
become a member of the Circle.

There may be some who are desirous to labor for the anti-slavery cause, but
who, from their recent conversion, know but little about the character and
design of the Western A. S. Society, and would therefore, very naturally, feel
backward in placing their funds at its disposal, as suggested in the 3d article.
To such let me say, the Western Society advocates the Disunion doctrine—it
has taken the only ground consistent abolitionists can occupy—its object is
to effect a peaceable abolition of slavery, by enforcing through its agents and
publications the duty of all who love the cause of freedom, to secede from
churches, political parties, and governments that are pro-slavery, believing that
to be the only means by which we can wash our hands in innocency [sic] and
benefit the bondman. It occupies the position you will occupy if you apply
anti-slavery principles to all the existing institution of our land. It advocates
no political action—proposes no measures in which woman may not as fully
engage as man, and seeks only to regenerate public sentiment by the preaching of truth.

As the doctrine it advocates is unpopular, so is there more need for all
who endorse it, to labor faithfully for its growth, and much may be done by
the formation of Sewing Circles. A good beginning has already been made.
The Western Society has received aid, and the *Anti-Slavery Bugle* is much indebted to these associations. . . . There are not less than fifty towns in Western Pennsylvania, Ohio, and Indiana, who could by Sewing Circles raise on
an average $20 a year; this would create a fund of $1000, which would enable
the Society to send out many more agents—scatter more publications, and
thus diffuse much light on the question of slavery. I saw by a late number of
the *True Wesleyan* that the women in several towns on the Western Reserve,
had recently sent articles for the support of the Canada Mission, amounting
to nearly $300. This is a benevolent object. It is well to do what we can to
benefit and improve those whom we have helped to degrade. Obligations
of this nature rest upon us that will take a whole life time to discharge. But
while the Canada Mission commends itself to the philanthropic, an effort in
its behalf is not the first work an abolitionist has to perform. There are those

in a far worse condition than the emancipated bondman on the free soil of Canada. Those are being consumed in the fires of slavery—these have escaped from its devouring flames. Those drag the chain of the captive—these have cast aside their fetters and stand up in the dignity of men. Those are unprotected and defenceless, the prey of the marauder, the victims of legalized piracy—these have the power of the British Government pledged to their defence. Shall not our first and most vigorous effort then, be in behalf of those who are in the worst condition?

It is not anti-slavery work to colonize the negro, or to aid and educate him after he is colonized; but it is the duty of the abolitionist to labor to regenerate public sentiment so that the bondman may have his freedom on the soil where he now dwells—so that the lights of science may shine upon him in his native clime. Let us labor faithfully in the cause of emancipation till the last yoke be broken—till the last fetter falls from the limbs of the last slave; and then we will go to work in right good earnest to enlighten, to elevate our common brother. But now, if we use the money which was raised for anti-slavery purposes, to clothe and educate the few who have escaped, we do it at the expense of the many who are still groaning in the prisonhouse. Every dollar raised for the anti-slavery cause, and diverted from its legitimate purpose, prolongs the day of the slave's deliverance. Benevolent associations may raise money for the support of Missions; but *anti-slavery* societies should use their funds for *anti-slavery* purposes.

Assisting fugitives in their flight is also a work of benevolence and of mercy, such a one as every abolitionist will engage in. Heaven forbid that any of us should ever refuse to divide our last loaf with the half-starved victim of oppression as he comes to our door and begs for food and shelter. But in doing this let us remember, that although we may thereby greatly benefit the individual whom, we succor, yet the place he has vacated may soon be filled by another, and perchance by one who would not otherwise be doomed to slavery.

I trust the women who read the A. S. Bugle will allow me to urge upon them all, the necessity of individual and associated action in behalf of the slave. It may be deemed arrogant by some, and extravagant by others yet I venture to assert, that the women of the nominally free States might abolish slavery if they would. When the women of Great Britain petitioned the English Parliament on this subject its members said,—"Here are the names of our mothers, our sisters, our wives—now we must yield." So let the women of the North bear a bold and decided testimony against slavery—let them give it no countenance either in Church or in State, in the social circle or at the domestic fireside, and their fathers and brothers, their husbands and sons would soon yield to this influence and withdraw their support from the system; and when that is done slavery *must* fall. Shall we not then exert ourselves to the utmost to bring this moral influence to bear upon those who are using their political ecclesiastical power to perpetuate this blighting curse?

We have a system in our midst which robs mothers of their children, should not mothers labor earnestly for its overthrow? We have a system which robs wives of their husbands, should not wives be zealous to destroy it?—We have an institution that degrades and brutalizes woman, sells her for gold, destroys the virtuous emotions of her nature, should not woman ever be hostile to it, and strive to save her sex from so sad a fate?

> Shall we behold, unheeding,
> Life's holiest feelings crushed?
> When woman's heart is bleeding,
> Shall woman's voice be hushed?
>
> Oh no! by every blessing
> That Heaven to thee may lend—
> Remember their oppression.
> Forget not, sister, friend.

Source: Jane Elizabeth Hitchcock Jones, "Anti-Slavery Sewing Circles," *Anti-Slavery Bugle*, January 22, 1847.

18. "World's" Temperance Conventions, 1853

Debates over the participation of women in reform wracked not only anti-slavery but temperance as well. These documents follow the controversy that emerged in New York City in May 1853 when Unitarian clergyman Thomas Wentworth Higginson (1823–1911) advocated the inclusion of women in the self-styled "World's Temperance Convention." After the rebuff to him, to Susan B. Anthony (1820–1906), to Abby Kelley Foster (1811–1887), and to others, many woman's rights supporters withdrew from the meeting to reconvene in September in a "Whole World's Temperance Convention," pointedly including women in the proceedings. At the latter gathering, speakers, including Antoinette Brown (1825–1921), the first woman ordained in a regular Protestant denomination, and Lucy Stone (1818–1893), antislavery and woman's rights speaker (and Brown's future sister-in-law), connected women's issues and temperance issues.

*   *   *

World's Temperance Convention

Agreeably to a call previously, a number of the friends of Temperance met yesterday morning in the Lecture Room of the Brick Church, with a view to adopt the necessary preliminaries to hold a grand World's Convention in the City of New York. . . .

Rev. John Marsh, of New York, moved that all gentlemen present, who were friends of Temperance, be admitted as delegates.

Dr. Trall, of New York, stated that there were delegates present from the Women's State Temperance Society, and moved that the word "ladies" be inserted in the motion offered by Mr. Marsh, which was carried unanimously.

The motion as amended was then adopted, and the names of the gentlemen and ladies present were collected by the Secretaries, and enrolled by States. Those holding credentials also handed them in to the Secretaries.

[Twelve men] were appointed a Business Committee.

Mr. Higginson, of Massachusetts, one of the above-named Committee, rose and said—That as women were very properly acting as delegates in the Convention, they should be represented on the Committee, and moved that Miss Susan B. Anthony, of Rochester, be admitted a member of the above named Committee.

Dr. Hewett hereupon arose and said, that in certain parts of the country women had received a good deal of celebrity and notoriety. He did not mean to disparage them; but it was quite sufficient for his purpose merely to state that he was not prepared to give to women that prominent place in arranging the affairs of mankind. . . .

Mr. Higginson was proceeding to reply, when he was interrupted by cries of "Out of order . . ." Mrs. Lydia F. Fowler, of New York [handed in names and credentials for women delegates]. Their unexpected presence created quite a sensation. . . .

Mr. Higginson [said:] He thought that in a World's Convention woman should be represented, otherwise it would be only a Semi-World's Convention. The ladies present have done good work in the cause in this city, through the State of New York, and in the Assembly. He felt they were entitled to have an equal voice in the proceedings. . . .

The committee who had been appointed to examine the credentials of Delegates, . . . returned from their deliberations, and presented their report. The Chairman reported that the committee were unanimous in favor of not receiving the "Women Delegations." This gave rise to a second debate, more exciting by far than the first, and brought Mr. Higginson again to the floor. He said . . . I certainly never . . . considered that women were to be excluded from this meeting. . . . It is the question as to whether this is to be considered a meeting of the friends of temperance. Are these women not the friends of temperance? Are they not advocates of temperance? Then why exclude them? . . .

The question, on the original motion, that the report [excluding women delegates] be adopted, was then put and carried—ayes 34, noes 21. . . .

Rev. [T.] W. Higginson, Dr. R. T. Trall, Abby K. Foster, Susan B. Anthony, Lucy Stone, Lydia F. Fowler, Emily Clark, Mary C. Vaughan, E. L. Baldwin and others of the minority then withdrew. . . .

*   *   *

Call: Whole World's Temperance Convention

Whereas, In response to a call for a preliminary meeting of the friends of Temperance in North America, to make arrangements for a World's Temperance Convention in the City of New York, during the World's Fair, a meeting assembled in that City, on the 12th of May, 1853, which assumed the power to exclude several regularly elected Delegates because they were Women;

And Whereas A portion of the members of that meeting retired from it, regarding it as false both to the letter and spirit of the call;

The undersigned, consisting in part of such seceding Delegates, hereby invite all those in favor of a World's Temperance Convention, *which shall be true to its name*, to meet in the City of New York on Thursday and Friday, the 1st and 2d of September next, to consider the present needs of the Temperance Reform.

[followed by many names]

*   *   *

Whole World's Temperature Convention

The convention met at 10 o'clock Thursday morning, at Metropolitan Hall, about 1,000 persons being present, representing different sections of the United States, Canada and England. . . .

Rev. T. W. Higginson, of Massachusetts, moved the temporary organization of the Convention. . . . Miss Susan B. Anthony of Rochester, was unanimously elected temporary Secretary of the Convention. . . .

Rev. T. W. Higginson, the Chairman, was received with applause. He said:

I need hardly say I deem it a high honor to preside over a Convention like this. . . . Let it be understood, once for all, what this Convention is; this is not a Woman's Rights Convention—it is simply a Convention in which Woman is not wronged—and that is enough. [Applause] It is what it aims to be, in spirit, if not in numbers—a whole World's Convention; it claims to be so, and it rightly claims it, because its spirit is what ought to be the spirit of the whole world in carrying on a Temperance movement; a spirit which knows no limitation of sect or sex—a spirit which knows no limitation of station or color—which knows no limitation except that between those who earnestly desire to prosecute the Temperance movement and that of those who would stand in its way, perhaps because "they know not what they do." . . . I am glad to see that it is a Convention composed of a due and satisfactory proportion of women as well as men; . . . we must have women here to take part in our delib-erations. It was said by some, after we came out from the preliminary meeting which led to the call for this World's Convention, "How could you, who love the Temperance cause, risk it by coming out from that meeting, one-sided though it be?" Our answer is—because we did not desire to risk the Temper-ance cause by staying in [applause]; because we knew that staying in was to risk it, by cutting off one-half the human race, whose energies and whose feelings, hearts, heads, and hands, must co-operate in this great movement. We thought that an attempt to carry on the Temperance movement, without a full and equal co-operation of women, would be like the boy who tried to row himself in a boat with but one oar. He reasoned that if one side went forward, the other would also; so the consequence was he kept rowing round and about in the East River, for a whole day, without making any progress. [Laughter] . . .

The President . . . introduced Rev. Miss Antoinette L. Brown, the Pastor of an Orthodox Congregational Church at South Butler, N. Y., who was enthusiastically received. She said:

. . . The Whole World's Temperance Convention,—room on its broad plat-form for everybody! . . . Here is Woman invited to speak into the great ear-trumpet of the world, that all may hear. No wonder that the Woman's Rights Convention should be called directly hereafter. . . . But I am reminded that in this Temperance gathering teetotalism is to be discussed in its length and breadth—nothing else and nothing more; not a word about Woman and her rights. . . . Say . . . not a breath . . . about a woman's owing service or labor to her intemperate husband, and his right to take her earnings. . . . Do not let it be known that the father has the whole custody of the children, although a drunkard, and that he may take them away from the mother and appren-tice them as a security for his own grog-bill; and that he may, in his last will and testament, give them over to the rum-seller for the whole term of their minority. Not a word about all this. Why, this belongs to Woman's Rights, and what has it to do with the temperance cause? It may be that this is after all a distinction without a difference; for we always find the degradation of women connected with the rum-traffic. . . .

A few words in regard to Temperance. The rattlesnake is the father of rattlesnakes,—the crocodile begets crocodiles; and so the drunkard is the parent of drunkards. "Can the Ethiopian change his skin, or the leopard his spots?" Then, can the child of the drunkard, that caricature of humanity—half madman and half brute—go untamed? There is One who can give him a new heart, and a high and holy purpose of soul. But is there any one to give him a new physical organization?—is there any balm in Gilead to soothe his heavy pulses, full of the drunkard's blood, that courses with scorching labor through his entire system? Who is there to caution him against plucking the forbidden fruits of self-indulgence? God help thee poor child of the drunkard! temptation lying at every point along this road of life, Alas! then, how great the struggle that awaits thee, lying in the presence of inebriated humanity almost strangled by the serpents that are come to devour thee while thou art yet in thy cradle! . . . Poor child, with that worn little face smothered with dirt and filth. Fit emblem of your life is the little mole that lives under ground. There is sunshine in the sky, but you will never look upward. . . . God of justice, must there be every year thousands of such children born in our land? Here is another child, with baby smiles and baby tears crossing each other down its face, gushing up from its little heart-fountain, struggling each for the mastery. If God would only take her to Heaven now, she would become one of the happiest of angel cherubs; but the fevered effect of the wine-cup delirium descends though her face, and the angels will weep over her, and remorse will pluck out the smiles, while she is yet a child. Her bright young head will grow grey in early womanhood, they will lay it down in an early grave—the earth will not be moistened by a single tear—no flowers will grow over her; or if they do, the old sexton will cut them down, muttering as he passes by. We should grow weary in reading the destinies of children such as these—types of human depravity and human sin. They are the children of intemperance, but they are heirs of the same inheritance, and so, as surely as the cup of temptation is not taken from them, will they thus miserably perish. Has the law nothing to answer for in all this? . . .

Miss Lucy Stone then presented herself, and, when the plaudits which greeted her had subsided, said:

. . . We are met here as a Whole World's Temperance Convention. . . . Our country has been laboring under this evil for a long time . . . men and women impelled by the danger, rose up together and in a general effort to rid the community of the curse of intoxicating drinks. They tried to legislate it out of use. The fifteen-gallon law, and the twenty-eight gallon law, and one and another similar efforts of legislative action failed; men, women, and children went to work to cope with the destroyer. They went still farther. The mother, seated by her fireside, took the little boy and taught him the Temperance songs, which were sung in the Cold Water Armies, with their beautiful banners; and they went up and down the streets singing their beautiful Cold Water songs; and the young men and young women formed Total Abstinence Societies—the women pledging themselves not to marry the man who might be in the habit of using intoxicating drinks, and the men knowing that it was dangerous to wed the women who did. Old men and women were cheered by the encouragement which they received from the progress of the cause, and the middle-aged joined heartily in the glorious rejoicing, till finally it was a stigma upon the character of an individual to indulge in intoxicating liquor, and those who did drink labelled the jug with some other name, and it became a common expression that those who drank did it behind the doors, and disguised their breaths by sugar-plums or peppermints that nobody should detect them. With success, the efforts of the people relaxed, and men resumed their cups; then came the new effort the Maine Liquor Law—and in it we have a sign of a healthy public sentiment, and there is a falling off in the use of intoxicating drinks. We are all glad of it.

I only desire to propose some thoughts in which I can hope for the co-operation of the sons and daughters of Temperance, old and young, that we may hedge in still more closely the bounds which lead to the drunkard's grave. . . . To remedy the evil of domestic suffering arising out of intemperance, I propose that we shall create a public sentiment which shall make it utterly impossible for any man or woman who is a drunkard, ever to sustain any marriage or parental relation. God has planted deeply in the human soul a love of those social ties that bind us to life. We are happier and better for the ties of parent and child, brother and sister, husband and wife, and God has written all this in the human soul. Now, I would say to the man who goes to the wine cup, or where temptation of any kind should come to induce him to taste it, and from tasting it to learn so as to love it, and, by loving it, to throw away manhood, and all that is noble in life, for the pleasure of the wine cup,—I would say to this man take it, and you alone shall incur the odium that attaches to the drunkard, and never know the relation of husband or of father. Drink the intoxicating cup, and you poison your whole being, and enfeeble your mind, and as a drunken man or woman, you shall not be entitled to the marriage relation. And I would say to the man or woman who is a drunkard, and who has a husband or wife, you shall forfeit the marriage relation that others should not have their prospects in life blighted by the acts of the drunkard. Public sentiment should say that the wife, the husband, or the child, whose nearest interests were affected by the intemperance of either, should be allowed to separate from the one who caused the misery. . . . There is not a father or mother here present who would not rather their child should die than be united to a drunkard, their hearts and arms would be open to receive her, and when the drunkard or the man who is tempted to be a drunkard, knows that the wife of his love can be no longer his, if he does not reform, and when he knows that if he indulges he must forever forego the enjoyment of social life, he will lay down the tempting cup, and pause before he commits the crime. He will think before he passes that threshold. . . .

Mr. Greeley having been loudly called for, now came forward. . . . He wanted to see men carrying their temperance to the ballot-box.

Source: The Whole World's Temperance Convention Held at Metropolitan Hall in the City of New York on Thursday and Friday, Sept. 1st and 2d. 1853 (New York: Fowlers and Wells Publishers, 1853).

19. "Linda Brent" (Harriet Jacobs), Excerpts from *Incidents in the Life of a Slave Girl Written by Herself,* 1861

Born a slave in Edenton, North Carolina, Harriet Jacobs (1813–1897) was somewhat sheltered by a loving mother and, after her death in 1819, by her grandmother, a freedwoman, and by a sympathetic mistress who taught her to read. Yet, after her kind owner died too, she experienced sexual exploitation and gender-specific abuses as she came of age. Sexually pursued by her new owner whom she calls here Mr. Flint, Jacobs, who called herself Linda Brent for this book, instead developed a relationship with an unmarried white man she names Mr. Sands for this account. Jacobs ultimately escaped from slavery first after hiding for seven years in her grandmother's attic, and then by flight to the North. In 1856, she began writing the autobiography that was published under the pseudonym Linda Brent in 1861. Some critics were offended by Jacobs's frank discussion of the sexual exploitation of enslaved women, although Jacobs skillfully demonstrates how powerless women might deploy their sexuality in order to bargain for minor advantages and momentary autonomy.

*   *   *

Chapter IX: Sketches of Neighboring Slaveholders

No pen can give an adequate description of the all-pervading corruption produced by slavery. The slave girl is reared in an atmosphere of licentiousness and fear. The lash and the foul talk of her master and his sons are her teachers. When she is fourteen or fifteen, her owner, or his sons, or the overseer, or perhaps all of them, begin to bribe her with presents. If these fail to accomplish their purpose, she is whipped or starved into submission to their will. She may have had religious principles inculcated by some pious mother or grandmother, or some good mistress; she may have a lover, whose good opinion and peace of mind are dear to her heart; or the profligate men who have power over her may be exceedingly odious to her. But resistance is hopeless. . . .

The slaveholder's sons are, of course, vitiated, even while boys, by the unclean influences everywhere around them. Nor do the master's daughters always escape. Severe retributions sometimes come upon him for the wrongs he does to the daughters of the slaves. The white daughters early hear their parents quarrelling about some female slave. Their curiosity is excited, and they soon learn the cause. They are attended by the young slave girls whom their father has corrupted; and they hear such talk as should never meet youthful ears, or any other ears. They know that the women slaves are subject to their father's authority in all things. . . .

You may believe what I say; for I write only that whereof I know. I was twenty-one years in that cage of obscene birds. I can testify, from my own experience and observation, that slavery is a curse to the whites as well as to the blacks. It makes the white fathers cruel and sensual; the sons violent and licentious; it contaminates the daughters, and makes the wives wretched. And as for the colored race, it needs an abler pen than mine to describe the extremity of their sufferings, the depth of their degradation. . . .

Chapter X: A Perilous Passage in the Slave Girl's Life

And now, reader, I come to a period in my unhappy life, which I would gladly forget if I could. The remembrance fills me with sorrow and shame. It pains me to tell you of it; but I have promised to tell you the truth, and I will do it honestly, let it cost me what it may. I will not try to screen myself behind the plea of compulsion from a master; for it was not so. Neither can I plead ignorance or thoughtlessness. For years, my master had done his utmost to pollute my mind with foul images, and to destroy the pure principles inculcated by my grandmother, and the good mistress of my childhood. The influences of slavery had had the same effect on me that they had on other young girls; they had made me prematurely knowing, concerning the evil ways of the world. I knew what I did, and I did it with deliberate calculation.

But, O, ye happy women, whose purity has been sheltered from childhood, who have been free to choose the objects of your affection, whose homes are protected by law, do not judge the poor desolate slave girl too severely! If slavery had been abolished, I, also, could have married the man of my choice; I could have had a home shielded by the laws; and I should have been spared the painful task of confessing what I am now about to relate; but all my prospects had been blighted by slavery. I wanted to keep myself pure; and, under the most adverse circumstances, I tried hard to preserve my self-respect; but I was struggling alone in the powerful grasp of the demon Slavery; and the monster proved too strong for me. I felt as if I was forsaken by God and man; as if all my efforts must be frustrated; and I became reckless in my despair.

. . . Dr. Flint's persecutions and his wife's jealousy had given rise to some gossip in the neighborhood . . . a white unmarried gentleman had obtained some knowledge of the circumstances in which I was placed. He knew my grandmother, and often spoke to me in the street. He became interested for me, and asked questions about my master, which I answered in part. He expressed a great deal of sympathy, and a wish to aid me. He constantly sought opportunities to see me, and wrote to me frequently. I was a poor slave girl, only fifteen years old.

So much attention from a superior person was, of course, flattering; for human nature is the same in all. I also felt grateful for his sympathy, and encouraged by his kind words. It seemed to me a great thing to have such a friend. By degrees, a more tender feeling crept into my heart. He was an educated and eloquent gentleman; too eloquent, alas, for the poor slave girl who trusted in him. Of course I saw whither all this was tending. I knew the impassable gulf between us; but to be an object of interest to a man who is not married, and who is not her master, is agreeable to the pride and feelings of a slave, if her miserable situation has left her any pride or sentiment. It seems less degrading to give one's self, than to submit to compulsion. There is something akin to freedom in having a lover who has no control over you, except that which he gains by kindness and attachment. A master may treat you as rudely as he pleases, and you dare not speak; moreover, the wrong does not seem so great with an unmarried man, as with one who has a wife to be made unhappy. There may be sophistry in all this; but the condition of a slave confuses all principles of morality, and, in fact, renders the practice of them impossible.

When I found that my master had actually begun to build the lonely cottage [to which he had threatened to take her], other feelings mixed with those I have described. Revenge, and calculations of interest, were added to flattered vanity and sincere gratitude for kindness. I knew nothing would enrage Dr. Flint so much as to know that I favored another; and it was something to triumph over my tyrant even in that small way. I thought he would revenge himself by selling me, and I was sure my friend, Mr. Sands, would buy me. He was a man of more generosity and feeling than my master, and I thought my freedom could be easily obtained from him.

The crisis of my fate now came so near that I was desperate. I shuddered to think of being the mother of children that should be owned by my old tyrant. I knew that as soon as a new fancy took him, his victims were sold far off to get rid of them; especially if they had children. I had seen several women sold, with babies at the breast. He never allowed his offspring by slaves to remain long in sight of himself and his wife. Of a man who was not my master I could ask to have my children well supported; and in this case, I felt confident I should obtain the boon. I also felt quite sure that they would be made free. With all these thoughts revolving in my mind, and seeing no other way of escaping the doom I so much dreaded, I made a headlong plunge. Pity me, and pardon me, O virtuous reader! You never knew what it is to be a slave; to be entirely unprotected by law or custom; to have the laws reduce you to the condition of a chattel, entirely subject to the will of another. You never exhausted your ingenuity in avoiding the snares, and eluding the power of a hated tyrant; you never shuddered at the sound of his footsteps, and trembled within hearing of his voice. I know I did wrong. No one can feel it more sensibly than I do. The painful and humiliating memory will haunt me to my dying day. Still, in looking back, calmly, on the events of my life, I feel that the slave woman ought not to be judged by the same standard as others.

The months passed on. I had many unhappy hours. I secretly mourned over the sorrow I was bringing on my grandmother, who had so tried to shield me from harm. I knew that I was the greatest comfort of her old age, and that it was a source of pride to her that I had not degraded myself, like most of the slaves. I wanted to confess to her that I was no longer worthy of her love; but I could not utter the dreaded words.

As for Dr. Flint, I had a feeling of satisfaction and triumph in the thought of telling him. From time to time he told me of his intended arrangements, and I was silent. At last, he came and told me the cottage was completed, and ordered me to go to it. I told him I would never enter it. He said, "I have heard enough of such talk as that. You shall go, if you are carried by force; and you shall remain there."

I replied, "I will never go there. In a few months I shall be a mother."

He stood and looked at me in dumb amazement, and left the house without a word. I thought I should be happy in my triumph over him. But now that the truth was out, and my relatives would hear of it, I felt wretched. Humble as were their circumstances, they had pride in my good character. Now, how could I look them in the face? My self-respect was gone! I had resolved that I would be virtuous, though I was a slave. I had said, "Let the storm beat! I will brave it till I die." And now, how humiliated I felt!

I went to my grandmother. My lips moved to make confession, but the words stuck in my throat. I sat down in the shade of a tree at her door and began to sew. I think she saw something unusual was the matter with me. The mother of slaves is very watchful. She knows there is no security for her children. After they have entered their teens she lives in daily expectation of trouble. . . . Presently, in came my mistress, like a mad woman, and accused me concerning her husband. My grandmother, whose suspicions had been previously awakened, believed what she said. She exclaimed, "O Linda! has it come to this? I had rather see you dead than to see you as you now are. You are a disgrace to your dead mother." She tore from my fingers my mother's wedding ring and her silver thimble. "Go away!" she exclaimed, "and never come to my house, again." Her reproaches fell so hot and heavy, that they left me no chance to answer. Bitter tears, such as the eyes never shed but once, were my only answer. I rose from my seat, but fell back again, sobbing. She did not speak to me; but the tears were running down her furrowed cheeks, and they scorched me like fire. She had always been so kind to me! So kind! How I longed to throw myself at her feet, and tell her all the truth! But she had ordered me to go, and never to come there again. After a few minutes, I mustered strength, and started to obey her. With what feelings did I now close that little gate, which I used to open with such an eager hand in my childhood! It closed upon me with a sound I never heard before.

Chapter XI: The New Tie to Life
When my babe was born, they said it was premature. It weighed only four pounds; but God let it live. I heard the doctor say I could not survive till morning. I had often prayed for death; but now I did not want to die, unless my child could die too. Many weeks passed before I was able to leave my bed. I was a mere wreck of my former self. For a year there was scarcely a day when I was free from chills and fever. My babe also was sickly. His little limbs were often racked with pain. Dr. Flint continued his visits, to look after my health; and he did not fail to remind me that my child was an addition to his stock of slaves. . . .

As the months passed on, my boy improved in health. When he was a year old, they called him beautiful. The little vine was taking deep root in my existence, though its clinging fondness excited a mixture of love and pain. When I was most sorely oppressed I found a solace in his smiles. I loved to watch his infant slumbers; but always there was a dark cloud over my enjoyment. I could never forget that he was a slave. Sometimes I wished that he might die in infancy. God tried me. My darling became very ill. The bright eyes grew dull, and the little feet and hands were so icy cold that I thought death had already touched them. I had prayed for his death, but never so earnestly as I now prayed for his life; and my prayer was heard. Alas, what mockery it is for a slave mother to try to pray back her dying child to life! Death is better than slavery. It was a sad thought that I had no name to give my child. His father caressed him and treated him kindly, whenever he had a chance to see him. He was not unwilling that he should bear his name; but he had no legal claim to it; and if I had bestowed it upon him, my master would have regarded it as a new crime, a new piece of insolence, and would, perhaps, revenge it on the boy. O, the serpent of Slavery has many and poisonous fangs! . . .

Chapter XIV: Another Link to Life

I had not returned to my master's house since the birth of my child. The old man raved to have me thus removed from his immediate power; but his wife vowed, by all that was good and great, she would kill me if I came back; and he did not doubt her word. Sometimes he would stay away for a season. Then he would come and renew the old threadbare discourse about his forbearance and my ingratitude. He labored, most unnecessarily, to convince me that I had lowered myself. The venomous old reprobate had no need of descanting on that theme. I felt humiliated enough. My unconscious babe was the ever-present witness of my shame. I listened with silent contempt when he talked about my having forfeited his good opinion; but I shed bitter tears that I was no longer worthy of being respected by the good and pure. Alas! slavery still held me in its poisonous grasp. There was no chance for me to be respectable. There was no prospect of being able to lead a better life. . . .

When Dr. Flint learned that I was again to be a mother, he was exasperated beyond measure. He rushed from the house, and returned with a pair of shears. I had a fine head of hair; and he often railed about my pride of arranging it nicely. He cut every hair close to my head, storming and swearing all the time. I replied to some of his abuse, and he struck me. Some months before, he had pitched me down stairs in a fit of passion; and the injury I received was so serious that I was unable to turn myself in bed for many days. He then said, "Linda, I swear by God I will never raise my hand against you again"; but I knew that he would forget his promise. . . .

When they told me my new-born babe was a girl, my heart was heavier than it had ever been before. Slavery is terrible for men; but it is far more terrible for women. Superadded to the burden common to all, they have wrongs, and sufferings, and mortifications peculiarly their own.

Source: "Linda Brent" [Harriet Jacobs], *Incidents in the Life of a Slave Girl, Written by Herself*, ed. Lydia Maria Child (Boston: privately printed, 1861).

Phase 3: Passionate Partisans

20. Mary Davis Letter in Support of Abolition and the Liberty Party, 1847

Liberty Party supporter and Peoria, Illinois, abolitionist Mary Davis (1800–1874) emphatically advocated women's partisan activity in this letter to the Chicago-based antislavery newspaper, *Western Citizen*. She argued not only that women were needed to save the nation from the destructive influence of slavery but also that women were required to become active in politics for their own interests.

*   *   *

Mr. Editor:—I saw in the Citizen of the 3d inst., a communication from Mrs. Blanchard, of Galesburgh, containing an account of the female meeting at Farmington. I rejoiced to see it—to know that one so well qualified as Mrs. B. has adopted that method of arousing to efficient action the women of Illinois. True, we may be derided by these who regard woman as designed by Providence to fill a subordinate sphere in life—who contend that the domestic circle alone is appropriate to her. But we must not be deterred from the performance of duty by any of these things. Woman has influence, and directing that influence in the proper channel, she can affect mighty things. I cannot but feel that the time has arrived when the co-operation of our sex is greatly needed. The apathy apparently existing in the anti-slavery ranks at the present time, is a loud call upon us to be more active and efficient in doing in the cause of humanity whatsoever our hands findeth to do. We must consent to be ridiculed and derided, and determine to permit our thoughts to stray beyond the narrow limits of the family circle, and of the present hour. *We have* an interest in the welfare of our country—we are concerned for the honor of our State—we feel deeply interested *for* and greatly sympathize *with* the oppressed millions of the South—and earnestly desire the elevation of the colored population of the free States generally, and especially of Illinois; and to this end we affectionately invite the co-operation of every anti-slavery woman in the State. Sisters! be not startled, but come to the rescue. You can do much if you will only try. Let every mother, wife, and sister, use all the influence she may possess, (and who that sustains these endeared relations but can wield a might influence) in leading those around her to be firm to the principles of freedom. Let the anti-slavery women one and all resolve to do something the present year to advance the cause of humanity, and as one means of doing good to the cause, let us commence without delay to circulate the petition accompanying the letter of Mrs. B., referred to above. As many as choose can cut it out from the Citizen, and to those who do not get that paper, (though I hope that number is small) I would say I have had one hundred copies printed in such a form as to be conveniently attached to a slip of paper. These I will distribute as I have opportunity; and any one can obtain them by calling at Davis's Job Printing Office, in Peoria.

Before concluding this article, I will ask why it is that the Liberty vote has decreased in so large a ratio as the election returns indicate? In our county there were only 71 votes of that party cast, and but *seven* in the city. I rejoice that there are seven men true to their principles under all circumstances, and feel happy in the belief that some, *one* at least of that seven, is not above acknowledging the potency of woman's influence. The cause of the decline at the polls at the recent election in Peoria, was not owing to a decrease in the numbers of the Liberty party, but because many of them voted for their respective favorites belonging to other parties. The papers of Peoria FORGOT to notice the Liberty vote with the exception of the American. I am glad we have *one* paper that *most commonly* possesses a liberal and independent course. I wish I could say ALWAYS does. M. B. D. *Peoria, August 14th.*

Source: Mary B. Davis, "For the Western Citizen," *Western Citizen* (Chicago), August 24, 1847.

21. Resolutions and Declaration of Sentiments Adopted by the Seneca Falls Woman's Rights Convention, 1848

With the claims made in *Declaration of Sentiments and Resolutions* presented at the Seneca Falls convention in upstate New York in July 1848, the American movement for woman's rights entered a distinctive public phase. Cleverly modeled on the Declaration of Independence, the document issued a call for equal citizenship—including the right to vote, equality in the professions, elimination of the sexual "double standard," and the empowerment of women as "public teachers." Credited as the primary author, Elizabeth Cady Stanton gave her first woman's rights lecture at this landmark gathering.

*　　*　　*

Resolutions

WHEREAS, The great precept of nature is conceded to be, that "man shall pursue his own true and substantial happiness." Blackstone in his *Commentaries* remarks, that this law of Nature being coequal with mankind, and dictated by God himself, is of course superior in obligation to any other. It is binding over all the globe, in all countries and at all times; no human laws are of any validity if contrary to this, and such of them as are valid, derive all their force, and all their validity, and all their authority immediately and immediately, from this original; therefore,

- *Resolved,* That such laws as conflict, in any way, with the true and substantial happiness of woman, are contrary to the great precept of nature and of no validity, for this is "superior in obligation to any other."
- *Resolved,* That all laws which prevent woman from occupying such a station in society as her conscience shall dictate, or which place her in a position inferior to that of man, are contrary to the great precept of nature, and therefore of no force or authority.
- *Resolved,* That woman is man's equal was intended to be so by the Creator, and the highest good of the race demands that she should be recognized as such.
- *Resolved,* That the women of this country ought to be enlightened in regard to the laws under which they live, that they may no longer publish their degradation by declaring themselves satisfied with their present position, nor their ignorance, by asserting that they have all the rights they want.
- *Resolved,* That inasmuch as man, while claiming for himself intellectual superiority, does accord to woman moral superiority, it is preeminently his duty to encourage her to speak and teach, as she has an opportunity, in all religious assemblies.
- *Resolved,* That the same amount of virtue, delicacy, and refinement of behavior that is required of woman in the social state, should also be required of man, and the same transgressions should be visited with equal severity on both man and woman.
- *Resolved,* That the objection of indelicacy and impropriety, which is so often brought against women when she addresses a public audience, comes with a very ill-grace from those who encourage, by their attendance, her appearance on the stage, in the concert, or in feats of the circus.
- *Resolved,* That woman has too long rested satisfied in the circumscribed limits which corrupt customs and a perverted application of the Scrip-

tures have marked out for her, and that it is time she should move in the enlarged sphere which her great Creator has assigned her.

- *Resolved,* That it is the duty of the women of this country to secure to themselves their sacred right to the elective franchise.
- *Resolved,* That the equality of human rights results necessarily from the fact of the identity of the race in capabilities and responsibilities.

Resolved, therefore, That, being invested by the Creator with the same capabilities, and the same consciousness of responsibility for their exercise, it is demonstrably the right and duty of woman, equally with man, to promote every righteous cause by every righteous means; and especially in regard to the great subjects of morals and religion, it is self-evidently her right to participate with her brother in teaching them, both in private and in public, by writing and by speaking, by any instrumentalities proper to be used, and in any assemblies proper to be held, and this being a self-evident truth growing out of the divinely implanted principles of human nature, any custom or authority adverse to it, whether modern, or wearing the hoary sanction of antiquity, is to be regarded as a self-evident falsehood, and at war with mankind.

Declaration of Sentiments

When, in the course of human events, it becomes necessary for one portion of the family of man to assume among the people of the earth a position different from that which they have hitherto occupied, but one to which the laws of nature and of nature's God entitle them, a decent respect to the opinions of mankind requires that they should declare the causes that impel them to such a course.

We hold these truths to be self-evident: that all men and women are created equal; that they are endowed by their Creator with certain inalienable rights; that among these are life, liberty, and the pursuit of happiness; that to secure these rights governments are instituted, deriving their just powers from the consent of the governed. Whenever any form of government becomes destructive of these ends, it is the right of those who suffer from it to refuse allegiance to it, and to insist upon the institution of a new government, laying its foundation on such principles, and organizing its powers in such form, as to them shall seem most likely to effect their safety and happiness. Prudence, indeed, will dictate that governments long established should not be changed for light and transient causes; and accordingly all experience hath shown that mankind are more disposed to suffer while evils are sufferable, than to right themselves by abolishing the forms to which they are accustomed. But when a long train of abuses and usurpations, pursuing invariably the same object, evinces a design to reduce them under absolute despotism, it is their duty to throw off such government, and to provide new guards for their future security. Such has been the patient sufferance of the women under this government, and such is now the necessity which constrains them to demand the equal station to which they are entitled.

The history of mankind is a history of repeated injuries and usurpations on the part of man toward woman, having in direct object the establishment of an absolute tyranny over her. To prove this, let facts be submitted to a candid world.

- He has never permitted her to exercise her inalienable right to the elective franchise.
- He has compelled her to submit to laws, in the formation of which she had no voice.
- He has withheld from her rights which are given to the most ignorant and degraded men—both natives and foreigners.
- Having deprived her of this first right of a citizen, the elective franchise, thereby leaving her without representation in the halls of legislation, he has oppressed her on all sides.
- He has made her, if married, in the eye of the law, civilly dead.
- He has taken from her all right in property, even to the wages she earns.
- He has made her, morally, an irresponsible being, as she can commit many crimes with impunity, provided they be done in the presence of her husband. In the covenant of marriage, she is compelled to promise obedience to her husband, he becoming, to all intents and purposes, her master—the law giving him power to deprive her of her liberty, and to administer chastisement.
- He has so framed the laws of divorce, as to what shall be the proper causes, and in case of separation, to whom the guardianship of the children shall be given, as to be wholly regardless of the happiness of women—the law, in all cases, going upon a false supposition of the supremacy of man, and giving all power into his hands.
- After depriving her of all rights as a married woman, if single, and the owner of property, he has taxed her to support a government which recognizes her only when her property can be made profitable to it.
- He has monopolized nearly all the profitable employments, and from those she is permitted to follow, she receives but a scanty remuneration. He closes against her all the avenues to wealth and distinction which

he considers most honorable to himself. As a teacher of theology, medicine, or law, she is not known.

- He has denied her the facilities for obtaining a thorough education, all colleges being closed against her.
- He allows her in church, as well as state, but a subordinate position, claiming apostolic authority for her exclusion from the ministry, and, with some exceptions, from any public participation in the affairs of the church.
- He has created a false public sentiment by giving to the world a different code of morals for men and women, by which moral delinquencies which exclude women from society, are not only tolerated, but deemed of little account in man.
- He has usurped the prerogative of Jehovah himself, claiming it as his right to assign for her a sphere of action, when that belongs to her conscience and to her God.
- He has endeavored, in every way that he could, to destroy her confidence in her own powers, to lessen her self-respect, and to make her willing to lead a dependent and abject life.

Now, in view of this entire disfranchisement of one-half the people of this country, their social and religious degradation—in view of the unjust laws above mentioned, and because women do feel themselves aggrieved, oppressed, and fraudulently deprived of their most sacred rights, we insist that they have immediate admission to all the rights and privileges which belong to them as citizens of the United States.

In entering upon the great work before us, we anticipate no small amount of misconception, misrepresentation, and ridicule; but we shall use every instrumentality, within our power to effect our object. We shall employ agents, circulate tracts, petition the State and National legislatures, and endeavor to enlist the pulpit and the press in our behalf. We hope this Convention will be followed by a series of Conventions embracing every part of the country.

Source: Report of the Woman's Rights Convention, Held at Seneca Falls, N.Y., July 19th and 20th, 1848 (Rochester, N.Y.: John Dick at the North Star Office, 1848).

22. Mary Sheldon's Composition Book Entry: "Women and Politics," 1848

Mary Sheldon (1825–1887) studied at Oberlin College from 1848 to 1852. She joined the Ladies Literary Society, as well as the Ladies Anti-Slavery

Society. The entry below from her "Composition Book" pursues the question of woman's role in partisan politics, a topic of growing interest throughout the 1840s as more women began to appear at Whig and Liberty Party gatherings. Although progressive in its antislavery stance, Oberlin's faculty and administration generally discouraged women from staking political claims. Upon graduating from the literary course in 1852, Sheldon became principal of the ladies department at the Austinburg Academy in Austinburg, Ohio.

*   *   *

What has woman to do with *politics*? What can she do more than occasionally to attend a convention or mass meeting, and wave her handkerchief or hand to cheer the politician?

What more can she do! do you ask as though she would attempt to effect a great object by cheers alone. We will take time to answer this question; and first enquire what are woman's duties. In our country these consist mainly in attending to the duties of the household, a general phrase designed to include all the various arts of cooking & cleaning, smoothing, making, mending etc. all that pertains to the house and by way of recreation fancy needle-work and perhaps a share in the duties of Voluntary Associations sometimes known under the name of Sewing Societies. Besides this on her devolves the onerous task of caring for and instructing children, not only the care of girls until they arrive at age but often the management of boys until they are prepared to leave home for College instruction or the duties of active life. These one would think were sufficient and yet with the assistance of domestics or in a small family much leisure is found for the improvement of the mind, which many with very limited advantages have accomplished to a wonderful extent. How, we ask, could she better employ a portion of this time than in making herself acquainted with the principles of civil government and the economy of our own.

In a republican government such as our own no mother can tell that her son may not be called to important offices[;] no common school teacher can say that she is not moulding the mind of a future president.

Look around on our country. See to what a depth of degradation the great political parties of our nation have sunk. Is it not proverbial that the worst man has the best chance of succeeding in an election? Look again at our halls of legislation. One fourth (I speak within bounds) of the time of the public servants, our senators and representatives is spent in electioneering speeches in listening to or making speeches to advance the interest of one or another set of men and these things increasing annually. Each session seem to be more corrupt than the preceding. If, as Napolean [sic] thought, mothers were to be the salvation of France where else should we look for reform. See our public offices filled with the basest of men—gluttonous, winebibbus, licentious; and what shall effect a reformation if the healthful moral influence of woman be not brought to bear upon these things.

All this can be effected without doing violence to the present usages of society. Let her become acquainted with government and the characters of the leading men of the nation. Let her influence be felt by her friends as on the side of justice and right. Hers it is to frown upon oppression and vice, and especially to instill into the minds of youth a patriotic spirit, a spirit of self sacrifice for the good of the country rather than a spirit of self aggrandisement at its expense. Hers it is to encourage the virtuous and deserving & to strengthen the weak and vasillating mind to do the right.

Source: Mary Sheldon, "Composition Book," 1842–1853, September 20, 1848 (Mary Sheldon's Papers, 1836–1852, box 1, folder 2, Oberlin College Archives), 48–49.

23. Jane Swisshelm Attacks the Compromise of 1850

Jane Swisshelm (1815–1884) was a reformer and abolitionist who began editing her own newspaper, the *Pittsburgh Saturday Visiter*, in 1847, after returning from Louisville, Kentucky, where her husband's business had failed. The *Visiter* initially endorsed the Liberty Party and later the Free Soil Party. Newspapers across the North reprinted Swisshelm's editorials. A strong advocate of the "Higher Law" position, Swisshelm believed that God's law took primacy over all other laws, including the Constitution. The letter below, addressed to Horace Greeley (1811–1872), the editor of the *New York Tribune*, expresses her disgust for the provisions of the then-pending Compromise of 1850 that reinforced slavery, including the Fugitive Slave Act and proposals for popular sovereignty to decide the fate of slavery in the territories. Later in her career, Swisshelm edited progressive newspapers in St. Cloud, Minnesota, clerked at the War Department, and lectured for woman suffrage and prohibition.

*   *   *

There is one thing, Mr. Greeley, that strikes my mind very forcibly: this is the constant and gratuitous glorifications of the Constitution. I have heard four speeches—two Pro-Slavery, on the Democratic side, and two Anti-Slavery on the Whig side; but about one fourth of every one has "our glorious Constitution"—its compromises—its wisdom—its strength and perfection. To me this looks as if the speakers felt that it required praise. The Constitution has been published, I think, and most of their audience have read or can read it! Is it not very strange that they cannot trust it to speak for itself?—or that when they have spoken for it, and no one contradicted, they cannot proceed to something else? They keep such a ding dong about "*supporting* the Constitution." One might imagine it was some miserable, decrepit old creature that was no longer able to totter on crutches, but must needs be held up on every side, and dragged along like a drunken loafer, on his road to the "lock up."

I have some considerable respect for the Constitution and am sorry those who should best understand it, think it so weak as to require such a continual bolstering up, a propping and defending, a blustering, a swaggering, a blowing, a bragging. Strength should bring calmness! The consciousness of integrity should set folks at their ease; and the nervous eagerness with which these gentlemen haste to defend and laud the Constitution, when no one is attacking it, looks as if they thought it very vulnerable. As administered and generally understood there is no doubt but it is so. Those compromises it is said to have made do really require some defence. For instance, in going from Pittsburg to Cincinnati a few days ago there was a woman on board our boat, who had been purchased by a man who had her in charge, for five hundred and fifty dollars—as much as would pay a Congressman's salary sixty-eight days.—She had been sold "for no fault," but because her master was in debt. She had left father, mother, brother, sisters, a husband and three small children, one of them an infant.

> I looked on her face with its haggard grief
> Where "Compromises" were written in brief;
> I counted her tears as they fell amain,
> Saying "Compromises" again and again.
> I thought of a babe at a cabin door,
> Where a mother's shadow shall fall no more—
> I thought of the wisdom of this great land
> Assembled together—a mighty band,
> With armies and navies at its command,
> With thundering cannon and gleaming swords,
> And praying chaplains, and learned boards,
> With their pompous words about Freedom's charms.
> As they tore the babe from its mother's arms,
> The tears might have moved them;—they were but men,—
> But what of the Compromises them?
> I looked on her pallid cheek again—
> On her sunken eyes with their scalding rain,
> And thought of the husband far away,

> She should meet no more at the close of the day;
> Of the hearts all torn and the hearth laid waste;
> And, like David of old, "I said in my haste,"
> Some things that I fain would repeat below
> But the Compromises say plainly, "No."

. . . The case of this poor woman affects me much; and sadness seeks rhyme for expression. It was looking on this poor mother weeping for her children that determined me to come to Washington. I wanted to see what the descendants of our Revolutionary fathers looked like, when in Congress assembled to devise ways and means to extend the area of such deeds of Chivalry. I go now into their great marble wonder, and wander through its magnificent rotundas and halls, its labyrinths of stairs and passages, gaze on its wonders of art, and before me at every turn flits up the shadowy apparition of that sorrow-stricken face. I see the humble form of the servant woman skulking hither and thither as though she would escape to her children. At every turn an impediment prevents! Here there is a cold, dead wall. There in the open passage, stands a group of sentinels! strange-looking sentinels, too—children and pitying men, and beautiful, kind-hearted women.—There were many of them who would scarcely kill a worm, who would weep that a poor bird should be taken from her nestlings: but they will all form themselves into phalanxes, with bristling bayonets and naked swords, to prevent the stricken mother flying to her child!—Why is it so? Why is the voice of Nature and of God suppressed within us, and bidden to be silent? It is that we may hear what the compromisers say: and how honorable gentlemen talk about a few more compromises. You with the rest, Mr. Greeley, indulge "a *generous* spirit of compromise." It is considered very praiseworthy to do so; and no doubt you are a very clever man; but in this matter your generosity does not cost you much. It is very easy for you, or any other Northern gentleman, to make a bow to a Southern gentleman, and in the spirit of the "most generous compromise," agree that he may tear a mother from her babes and set her up on an auction block to get money to buy a race-horse or gold chain, and banish her, forever, from all that she has known or loved. You are nothing the poorer when the deed is done. It is the mother and her children who are called upon to foot the bill; and it not unfrequently costs one of them the last remnant of a life your former generosity had made a scene of suffering and toil.

I am a little thick in the skull, and never could understand nice distinctions in etiquette or ethics. When Mr. Harris of Tenn., rose the other day, and with all his powers of oratory . . . pleaded for "the rights of the South" it just sounded to me as if he had been saying,

Gentlemen, we have a right—a natural and inalienable right, to whip women and sell babies. Our Revolutionary fathers died on the battle-field to establish the glorious principle of woman-whipping and baby-selling. Our immortal Constitution was founded to secure to us the exercise of these inestimable privileges; and I, Sir, I, Mr. Harris of Tenn. do now proclaim myself the valorous champion of American woman-scourging! It is our privilege, Sir. We of the South, here, on the floor of this House, claim the right to sell our children with our sheep and oxen. We, Sir, it is, who can and do, and *w-i-l-l* sell our daughters to infamy, and traffic in the bodies and souls of our brethren—Yea, of our brethren, Sir—of those for whom a common Saviour has shed his blood—of those who with us, are joint heirs of immortality. We, Sir, *we*, will carry them to the shambles, remembering that, inasmuch as we do it unto the least of His brethren, we do it unto Him. We will there *barter* for gold the very Son of God himself! We it is, Sir, who sell upon the auction-block the image of God for handsfull of silver coin! We are the fearless champions who will dissolve this Union—all union between ourselves and the spirit of Freedom abroad in the earth—the favor of Heaven and the approval of all good men, for this our privilege of selling men and whipping women.

I could make nothing else of it, Mr. Greeley. I know these *are* the rights for which the South contends. I know it is quite as common and respectable for a Southern gentleman to horsewhip his washerwoman as to smoke a cigar. I know this, for I have lived there; and all the eloquence . . . about Southern rights and Constitutional compromises resolve themselves to this one point—the right to horsewhip a woman and sell her baby. Every concession you make about guaranties is just that much of a yielding to this clamor.
    JANE G. SWISSHELM.

Source: Jane Swisshelm, "Letters of Mrs. Swisshelm-No. 2," *Farmer's Cabinet*, May 9, 1850.

24. Harriet Beecher Stowe, Excerpts from *Uncle Tom's Cabin*, 1851

Uncle Tom's Cabin was the most popular novel of the nineteenth century. Written by Harriet Beecher Stowe (1811–1896), a younger sister of Catharine Beecher and daughter of the influential preacher Lyman Beecher, it was published in serial form in the antislavery newspaper *National Era* in 1851 and 1852, and as a novel in 1852. It is a sentimental novel that humanizes slavery by emphasizing individuals and relationships. The book follows a Kentucky slave named Tom and the series of events that ensue when his owner is forced by financial hardship to sell some of his slaves. The excerpt below begins with

"I Am Going There," Sheet Music for Uncle Tom's Cabin, Boston. The portrayal of
Eva's deathbed scene on the front of this publication underscores the popularity of
Stowe's book in many formats and for many audiences. (Source: Courtesy of Special
Collections, Oberlin College Library)

a discussion between an Ohio state legislator who has just voted for a fugitive slave law and his abolitionist wife, who is mortified by her husband's willingness to support this law. They are interrupted by the arrival of fugitive slaves at their door. These fugitives have escaped from the same plantation where Tom resided. This excerpt well illustrates the "Higher Law" argument employed by many Republican Party women.

*   *   *

The light of the cheerful fire shone on the rug and carpet of a cozy parlor, and glittered on the sides of the tea-cups and well brightened tea-pot, as Senator Burr was drawing off his boots, preparatory to inserting his feet in a pair of new handsome slippers, which his wife had been working for him while away on his Senatorial tour. Mrs. Burr, looking the very picture of delight, was superintending the arrangements of the table, ever and anon mingling admonitory remarks to a number of frolicksome juveniles, who were effervescing in all those modes of untold gambol and mischief that have astonished mothers ever since the Flood.

"Tom, let the door knob alone, there's a man! Mary! Mary! don't pull the cat's tail poor pussy! Jim, you mustn't climb on that table no, no! You don't know, my dear, what a surprise it is to us all, to see you here to-night!" said she, at last, when she found a space to say something to her husband.

"Yes, yes, I thought I'd just make a run down, spend the night, and have a little comfort at home." . . .

"Well," said his wife, after the business of the tea-table was getting rather slack, "and what have they been doing in the Senate?"

Now, it was a very unusual thing for gentle little Mrs. Burr ever to trouble her head with what was going on in the House of the State, very wisely considering that she had enough to do to mind her own. Mr. Burr therefore opened his eyes in surprise, and said,

"Not very much of importance."

"Well, but is it true that they have been passing a law forbidding people to give meat and drink to those poor colored folks that come along? I heard they were talking of some such law, but I didn't think any Christian Legislature would pass it."

"Why, Mary, you are getting to be a politician all at once."

"No. nonsense! I wouldn't give a fip for all your politics, generally, but I think this is something downright cruel and unchristian. I hope, my dear, no such law has been passed."

"There has been a law passed forbidding people to help off the slaves that come over from Kentucky; my dear, so much of that thing has been done by these reckless Abolitionists, that our brethren in Kentucky are very strongly excited, and it seems necessary, and no more than Christian, and kind, that something should be done by our State to quiet the excitement."

"And what is the law? It don't forbid us to shelter these poor creatures a night, does it, and to give 'em something comfortable to eat, and a few old clothes, and send 'em quietly about their business!"

"Why, yes, my dear that would be aiding and abetting, you know."

Mrs. Burr was a timid, blushing, little woman, of about four feet in height, . . . as for courage, a moderate-sized cock turkey had been known to put her to rout at the very first gobble. . . . Her husband and children were her entire world, and in these she ruled more by entreaty and persuasion than by command or argument. There was only one thing that was capable of arousing her, and that provocation came in on the side of her unusually gentle and sympathetic nature anything in the shape of cruelty would throw her into a passion, which was the more alarming and inexplicable in proportion to the general softness of her nature. Generally the most indulgent and easy to be entreated of all mothers, still her boys had a very reverent remembrance of a most vehement chastisement she once bestowed on them because she found them leagued with several graceless boys of the neighborhood, stoning a defenceless kitten. . . .

On the present occasion, Mrs. Burr rose quickly, with very red cheeks, which quite improved her general appearance, and walked up to her husband with quite a resolute air, and said, in a determined tone,

"Now, John, I want to know if you think such a law as that is right and Christian?"

"You won't shoot me, now, Mary, if I say I do!"

"I never could have thought it of you, John; you didn't vote for it?"

"Even so, my fair politician."

"You ought to be ashamed, John! Poor, homeless, houseless creatures! It's a shameful, wicked, abominable law, and I break it for one the first time I get a chance; and I hope I *shall* have a chance I do. Things have got to a pretty pass, if a woman can't give a warm supper and a bed to poor, starving creatures, just because they are slaves, and have been abused and oppressed all their lives, poor things."

"But, Mary, just listen to me. Your feelings are all quite right, dear and interesting and I love you for them; but, then, dear, we mustn't suffer our feelings to run away with our judgment. [Y]ou must consider it's not a matter of private feeling[;] there are great public interests involved[, and] there is such a state of public agitation rising, that we must put aside our private feelings."

"Now, John, I don't know anything about politics, but I can read my Bible; and there I see that I must feed the hungry, clothe the naked, and comfort the desolate and that Bible I mean to follow."

"But in cases where your doing so would involve a great public evil."

"Obeying God never brings on public evils. I know it can't. It's always safest all round to *do as He* bids us."

"Now, listen to me, Mary, and I can state to you a very clear argument to show."

"Oh, nonsense, John; you can talk all night but you wouldn't do it. I put it to you, John would *you* now turn away a poor, shivering, hungry creature from your door, because he was a runaway? *Would* you, now?"

Now, if the truth must be told, our Senator had the misfortune to be a man who had a particularly humane and accessible nature, and turning away anybody that was in trouble never had been his forte; and what was worse for him in this particular pinch of the argument was, that his wife knew it, and of course was making an assault on rather an indefensible point.—. . .

"I should like to see you doing that, John—I really should. Turning a woman out of doors in a snow storm, for instance; or may be you'd take her up and put her in jail, wouldn't you? You would make a grand hand at that."

"Of course it would be a very painful duty," began Mr. Burr, in a moderate tone.

"Duty! John! don't use that word. You know it isn't a duty—it can't be a duty. If folks want to keep their slaves from running away, let 'em treat 'em well—that's my doctrine. If I had slaves, (as I hope I never shall have,) I'd risk their wanting to run away from me or you either, John. I tell you folks don't run away when they're happy; and when they do run, poor creatures, they suffer enough with cold and hunger and fear without everybody's turning against them; and law or no law, I never will, so help me God."

"Mary! Mary! My dear, let me reason with you."

"I hate reasoning, John; especially reasoning on such subjects. There's a way you political folks have of coming round and round a plain right thing— and you don't believe in it yourselves, when it comes to practice. I know *you* well enough, John; you don't believe it's right, any more than I do, and you wouldn't do it any sooner than I."

At this critical juncture, old Cudjoe, the black man of all works, put his head into the door and wished "Missis would come into the kitchen;" and our Senator, tolerably relieved, looked after his little wife with a whimsical mixture of amusement and vexation, and, seating himself in the arm-chair, began to read the papers.

After a moment, his wife's voice was heard at the door, in a quick, earnest tone, "John! John! I do wish you'd come here a moment."

He laid down his paper, and went into the kitchen, and started, quite amazed at the sight that presented itself. A young and slender woman, with garments torn and frozen, with one shoe gone, and the stocking torn away from the cut and bleeding foot, was laid back in a deadly swoon upon two chairs. There was the impress of the despised race on her face, yet none could help feeling its mournful and pathetic beauty—while its stony sharpness, its cold, fixed, deathly aspect, struck a solemn chill over him. He drew his breath short, and stood in silence. His wife and their only colored domestic, old Aunt Dinah; were busily engaged in restorative measures; while old Cudjoe had got the boy on his knee, and was busy pulling off his shoes and stockings, and chafing his little cold feet.

"Sure, now, if she aint a sight to behold," said old Dinah, compassionately; "'pears like 'twas the heat that made her faint. She was tol'able peart when she cum in, and asked if she couldn't warm herself here a spell; and I was just a asking her where she come from, and she fainted right down. Never done much hard work, guess, by the looks of her hands."

"Poor creature!" said Mrs. Burr, compassionately, as the woman slowly unclosed her large, dark eyes, and looked vacantly at her. Suddenly an expression of agony crossed her face, and she sprung up, saying, "Oh, my Harry! Have they got him?"

The boy, at this, jumped from Cudjoe's knee, and, running to her side, put up his arms—"Oh, he's here! he's here!"

"Oh, ma'am," said she, mildly, to Mrs. Burr, "do protect us; don't let them get him?"

"Nobody shall hurt you here, poor woman," said Mrs. Burr, encouragingly. "You are safe; don't be afraid."

"God bless you!" said the woman, covering her face, and sobbing; while the little boy, seeing her crying, tried to get into her lap.

With many gentle and womanly offices, . . . the poor woman was, in time, rendered more calm. A temporary bed was provided for her on the settle, near the fire, and, after a short time, she fell into a heavy slumber, with the child, who seemed no less weary, soundly sleeping on her arm—for the mother resisted with nervous anxiety the kindest attempts to take him from her; and even in sleep her arm encircled him with an unrelaxing clasp, as if she could not even then be beguiled of her vigilant hold.

Mr. and Mrs. Burr had gone back to the parlor, where, strange as it may appear, no reference was made on either side to the preceding conversation. . . .

"I wonder who and what she is?" said Mr. Burr, at last. . . .

"When she wakes up, and feels a little rested, we will see," said Mrs. Burr.

"I say, wife!" said Mr. Burr, . . . "She couldn't wear one of your gowns, could she, by any letting down or such matter? . . ."

A quite scarce perceptible smile glimmered in Mrs. Burr's face, as she answered, "We'll see."

Another pause, and Mr. Burr again broke out—

"I say, wife!"

"Well, what now?"

"Why, there's that old bombazine cloak that you keep on purpose to put over me when I take my afternoon's nap—you might as well give her that—she needs clothes."

At this moment, Dinah looked in to say that the woman was awake, and wanted to see missis.

The woman was now sitting up on the settle, by the fire. She was looking steadily into the blaze, with a calm, heart-broken expression, very different from her former agitated wildness.

"Did you want me?" said Mrs. Burr, in gentle tones. "I hope you feel better now, poor woman."

A long-drawn, shivering sigh was the only answer; but she lifted her dark eyes, and fixed them on her with such a forlorn and imploring expression, that the tears came into the little woman's eyes.

"You needn't be afraid of anything; we are friends here, poor woman; tell me where you came from and what you want," said she.

"I came from Kentucky," said the woman.

"When?" said Mr. Burr, taking up the interrogatory.

"To-night."

"How did you come?"

"I crossed on the ice. . . . I did. God helping me, I crossed on the ice; for they were behind me—right behind—and there was no other way. . . . The Lord helped me; nobody knows how much the Lord can help 'em, till they try." . . .

"Were you a slave?" said Mr. Burr.

"Yes, sir; I belonged to a man in Kentucky."

"Was he unkind to you?"

"No, sir; he was a good master."

"And was your mistress unkind to you?"

"No, sir—no; my mistress was always good to me."

"What could induce you to leave a good home, then, and run away, and go through such dangers?"

The woman looked up at Mrs. Burr with a keen, scrutinizing glance, and it did not escape her that she was dressed in deep mourning.

"Ma'am," she said, suddenly, "have you ever lost a child"?

The question was unexpected, and it was a thrust on a new wound; for it was only a month since a darling child of the family had been laid in the grave.

Mr. Burr turned around and walked to the window, and Mrs. Burr burst into tears; but, recovering her voice, she said—

"Why do you ask that? I have lost a little one."

"Then you will feel for me. I have lost two, one after another—left 'em buried there when I came away; and I had only this one left. I never slept without him; he was all I had; he was my comfort and pride, day and night; and, ma'am, they were going to take him away from me—to *sell* him—sell him down South, ma'am, to go all alone—a baby that had never been away from his mother in his life. I couldn't stand it, ma'am; I knew I should never be good for anything if they did; and when I knew the papers were signed, and he was sold; I took him and came off in the night; and they chased me—the man that bought him, and some of mass'r's folks—and they were coming down right behind me, and I heard 'em; I jumped right on to the ice, and how I got across I don't know; but first I knew, a man was helping me up the bank."

The woman did not sob nor weep—she had gone to a place where tears are dry; but every one around her was, in some way characteristic of themselves, showing signs of hearty sympathy.

. . . Mrs. Burr had her face fairly hidden in her pocket-handkerchief; and old Dinah, with tears streaming down her black, honest face, was ejaculating, "Lord have mercy on us!" with all the fervor of a camp meeting; while old Cudjoe, rubbing his eyes very hard with his cuffs, and making a most uncommon variety of wry faces, occasionally responded in the same key with great fervor. Our Senator was a statesman, and of course could not be expected to cry like other mortals—and so he turned his back to the company, and looked out of the window, and seemed particularly busy in clearing his throat and wiping his spectacle glasses, occasionally blowing his nose in a manner that was calculated to excite suspicion, had any one been in a state to observe critically.

"How came you to tell me you had a kind master?" he suddenly exclaimed. . . .

"Because he *was* a kind master—I'll say that of him any way; and my mistress was kind; but they couldn't help themselves—they were owing money—and there was some way, I can't tell how, that the man had hold on them, and they were obliged to give him his will. . . . I knew 'twas no use of my trying to live if they did it; for't 'pears like this child is all I have."

"Have you no husband?"

"Yes, but he belongs to another man; his master is real hard to him, and won't let him come to see me, hardly ever; and he has grown harder and harder upon us, and he threatens to sell him down South; it's like I'll never see *him* again!" . . .

"And where do you mean to go, my poor woman?" asked Mrs. Burr.

"To Canada, if I only knew where that was. Is it very far off, is Canada?" said she, looking up, with a simple, confiding air, to Mrs. Burr's face.

"Poor thing!" said Mrs. Burr, involuntarily.

"Is't a very great way, think?" said the woman, earnestly.

"Much farther than you think, poor child," said Mrs. Burr; "but we will try to think what can be done for you. Here, Dinah, make her up a bed in your own room, close by the kitchen, and I'll think what to do for her in the morning. Meanwhile, never fear, poor woman; put your trust in God; he will protect you."

Mrs. Burr and her husband re-entered the parlor. . . . Mr. Burr strode up and down the room, grumbling to himself "Pish! Pshaw! Confounded awkward business!" . . .

"I say, wife, she'll have to get away from here this very night. That fellow will be down on the scent bright and early to-morrow morning; if 'twas only the woman, she could lie quiet till it was over; but that chap can't be kept still by a troop of horse and foot. . . . A pretty kettle of fish it would be for me, too! to be caught with them both here, just now! . . ."

"To-night! How is it possible—where to?"

"Well, I know pretty well where to," said the Senator, beginning to put on his boots with a reflective air; . . . "It's a confounded awkward, ugly business, . . . and that's a fact! . . . It will have to be done, though, for aught I see; hang it all!" . . .

"You see," he said, "there's my old client, Van Trompe, has come over from Kentucky, and set all his slaves free, and he has bought a place seven miles up the creek, here, back in the woods, where nobody goes, unless they go on purpose; and it's a place that isn't found in a hurry. There she'd be safe enough; but the plague of the thing is, nobody could drive a carriage there to-night, but *me*. . . . Cudjoe must put in the horses as quietly as may be about twelve o'clock, and I'll take her over; and then, to give color to the matter, he must carry me on to the next tavern, to take the stage for Columbus, that comes by about three or four and so it will look as if I had the carriage only for that. I shall get into business bright and early in the morning. But I'm thinking I shall feel rather cheap there, after all that's been said and done; but hang it, I can't help it."

"Your heart is better than your head in this case, John," said the wife, laying her little white hand on his. "Could I ever have loved you, had I not known you better than you know yourself!" . . . At the door . . . he stopped a moment, and then coming back, he said, with some hesitation,

"Mary, I don't know how you'd feel about it, but there's that drawer full of things of poor little Henry's!" So saying, he turned quickly on his heel, and shut the door after him.

His wife opened the little bedroom door adjoining her room, and, taking the candle, set it down on the top of a bureau there; then from a small recess she took a key, and put it thoughtfully in the lock of a drawer, and made a sudden pause. . . . And oh! mother that reads this, has there never been in your house a drawer, or a closet, the opening of which has been to you like the opening again of a little grave? Ah! happy mother that you are, if it has not been so!

Mrs. Burr slowly opened the drawer; there were little coats of many a form and pattern, piles of aprons, and rows of small stockings; and even a pair of little shoes, worn and rubbed at the toes, were peeping from the folds of a paper. There was a toy horse and wagon, a top, a ball—memorials gathered with many a tear, and many a heartbreak! She sat down by the drawer, and leaning her head on her hands over it, wept till the tears fell through her fingers into the drawer; then suddenly raising her head, she began, with nervous haste, selecting the plainest and most substantial articles, and gathering them into a bundle.

. . . "If our own dear, loving little Henry looks down from Heaven, he would be glad to have us do this. I could not find it in my heart to give them away to any common persons to anybody that was happy; but I give them to a mother more heart-broken and sorrowful than I am; and I hope God will send his blessing with them!"

There are in this world blessed souls, whose sorrows all spring up into joys for others whose earthly hopes laid in the grave with many tears, are the seed from which spring healing flowers and balm for the desolate and the distressed. Among such was the delicate woman who sits there by the lamp, dropping slow tears, while she prepares the memorials of her own lost one for the outcast wanderer.

After a while, Mrs. Burr opened a wardrobe, and taking from thence a plain serviceable dress or two, she sat down busily to her work-table, and, with needle, scissors, and thimble, at hand, quietly commenced the "letting down" process which her husband had recommended, and continued busily at it till the old clock in the corner struck twelve, and she heard the low rattling of wheels at the door.

"Mary," said her husband, coming in, with his overcoat in his hand, "you must wake her up now we must be off."

Mrs. Burr hastily deposited the various articles she had collected in a small plain trunk and locking it, desired her husband to see it in the carriage, and then proceeded to call the woman. Soon arrayed in a cloak, bonnet, and shawl, that had belonged to her benefactress, she appeared at the door with her child in her arms. Mr. Burr hurried into the carriage steps. Eliza leaned out of the carriage, and put out her hand—a hand as soft and beautiful as was given in return. She fixed her large, dark eyes, full of earnest meaning, on Mrs. Burr's face, and seemed going to speak. Her lips moved—she tried once or twice, but there was no sound and pointing upward, with a look never to be forgotten, she fell back in the seat, and covered her face. The door was shut, and the carriage drove on.

What a situation now for a patriotic Senator, that had been all the week before spurring up the Legislature of his native State to pass more stringent resolutions against escaping fugitives, their haborers and abettors! Our good Senator in his native State had not been exceeded by any of his brethren at Washington, in the sort of eloquence which has won for them immortal renown! How sublimely he had sat with his hands in his pockets, and scouted all sentimental weakness of those who would put the welfare of a few miserable fugitives before great State interests! He was as bold as a lion about it, and "mightily convinced" not only himself, but everybody that heard him; but then his idea of a fugitive was only an idea of the letters that spell the word—or at the most, the image of a little newspaper picture of a man with stick and bundle, with "Ran away from the subscriber" under it. The magic of the real presence of distress, the imploring human eye, the frail, trembling human hand, the despairing appeal of helpless agony—these he had never tried; he had never thought that a fugitive might be a hapless mother, a defenceless child—like that one which was now wearing his lost boy's little well known cap; and so, as our poor Senator was not stone or steel—as he was a man, and a downright noble-hearted one, too—he was, as everybody must see, in a sad case for his patriotism. And you need not exult over him, good brother of the Southern States, for we have some inklings that many of you, under similar circumstances, would not do much better. We have reason to know, in Kentucky, as in Mississippi, are noble and generous hearts, to whom never was tale of suffering told in vain. Ah! good brother! it is fair for you to expect of us services which your own brave, honorable heart would not allow you to render, were you in our place? . . .

It was full late in the night when the carriage emerged, dripping and bespattered, out of the creek, and stood at the door of a large farmhouse. . . .

Honest old John Van Trompe was once quite a considerable landholder and slave-owner in the state of Kentucky. Having "nothing of the bear about him but the skin," and being gifted by Nature with a great, honest, just heart, quite equal to his gigantic frame, he had been for some years witnessing with repressed uneasiness the workings of a system equally bad for oppressor and oppressed. At last, one day, John's great heart had swelled altogether too big to wear his bonds any longer; so he just took his pocket-book out of his desk, and went over into Ohio, and bought a quarter of a township of good, rich land, made out free papers for all his people—men, women, and children— packed them up in wagons, and sent them off to settle down; and then honest John turned his face up the creek, and sat quietly down on a snug, retired farm, to enjoy his conscience and his reflections.

"Are you the man that will shelter a poor woman and child from slave-catchers?" said the Senator, explicitly.

"I rather think I am," said honest John, with some considerable emphasis. . . .

"If there's anybody comes," said the good man, stretching his tall, muscular form upward, "why here I'm ready for him; and I've got seven sons, each six foot high, and they'll be ready for 'em. . . ."

Weary, jaded, and spiritless, Eliza dragged herself up to the door, with her child lying in a heavy sleep on her arm. The great, rough man held the candle to her face, and uttering a kind of compassionate grunt, opened the door of a small bed-room adjoining to the large kitchen where they were standing, and motioned her to go in. . . .

"Now I say, gal, you needn't be a bit afeard, let who will come here. I'm up to all that sort o' thing, said he, pointing to two or three goodly rifles over the mantel-piece. . . . So *now* you jist go to sleep now, as quiet as if yer mother was a rockin ye," said he, as he shut the door. . . .

The Senator in a few words briefly explained Eliza's history.

"Oh! ou! aw! now, I want to know," said the good man pitifully, "sho! now sho! That's natur now! poor crittur! Hunted down now like a deer! hunted down! jest for havin natural feelins, and doin what no kind o' mother could help a-doin! . . ."

"Thank you, my good friend," said the Senator, "I must be along, to take the night stage for Columbus."

"Ah! well, then, if you must. I'll go a piece with you, and show you a cross road that will take you there better than the road you came on. That road's mighty bad."

John equipped himself, and with a lantern in hand was soon seen guiding the Senator's carriage towards a road that ran down in a hollow back of his dwelling. When they parted, the Senator put into his hand a ten dollar bill.

"It's for her," he said, briefly.

"Aye, aye," said John, with equal conciseness.

They shook hands and parted.

Source: Harriet Beecher Stowe, excerpts from *Uncle Tom's Cabin*, *National Era*, July 24 and 31, 1851.

25. Sojourner Truth's "Aren't I a Woman?" Speech, as Reported in 1851 and 1863

New York abolitionist and woman's rights activist Sojourner Truth (1797–1883) attended the Ohio Woman's Rights Convention in Akron, in May 1851, and gave a speech that would later become famous when published by Frances Dana Gage in 1863. While Gage's rendition is the most quoted version of the speech, another description was published immediately following the convention in the *Anti-Slavery Bugle* and was probably more accurate. The Gage version employed the dialect of southern slaves and included the compelling refrain, "and a'n't I a woman?" while the *Bugle* depiction was written in standard English and included no repetitive phrases. Truth, who grew up in a Dutch community in New York, did not learn English until her late childhood, making the southern slave dialect unlikely. Both speeches are printed below.

*   *   *

Anti-Slavery Bugle Report on Sojourner Truth's Speech, 1851

One of the most unique and interesting speeches of the convention was made by Sojourner Truth, an emancipated slave. It is impossible to transfer it to paper, or convey any adequate idea of the effect it produced upon the audience. Those only can appreciate it who saw her powerful form, her whole-souled, earnest gesture, and listened to her strong and truthful tones. She came forward to the platform and addressing the President said with great simplicity:

May I say a few words? Receiving an affirmative answer, she proceeded; I want to say a few words about this matter. I am a woman's rights [sic]. I have as much muscle as any man, and can do as much work as any man. I have plowed and reaped and husked and chopped and mowed, and can any man do more than that? I have heard much about the sexes being equal; I can carry as much as any man, and can eat as much too, if I can get it. I am strong as any man that is now.

As for intellect, all I can say is, if woman have a pint and man a quart—why can't she have her little pint full? You need not be afraid to give us our rights for fear we will take too much—for we won't take more than our pint'll hold.

The poor men seem to be all in confusion and don't know what to do. Why children, if you have woman's rights give it to her and you will feel better. You will have your own rights, and they won't be so much trouble.

I can't read, but I can hear. I have heard the Bible and have learned that Eve caused man to sin. Well if woman upset the world, do give her a chance to set it right side up again. The lady has spoken about Jesus, how he never spurned woman from him, and she was right. When Lazarus died, Mary and Martha came to him with faith and love and besought him to raise their brother. And Jesus wept—and Lazarus came forth. And how came Jesus into the world? Through God who created him and woman who bore him. Man, where is your part?

But the women are coming up blessed be God and a few of the men are coming up with them. But man is in a tight place, the poor slave is on him, woman is coming on him, and he is surely between a hawk and a buzzard.

Source: Sojourner Truth, "Aren't I a Woman?" speech, *Anti-Slavery Bugle*, June 21, 1851.

*   *   *

1863 Version Reported by Frances Dana Gage

"Wall, chilern, whar dar is so much racket dar must be somethin' out o' kilter. I tink dat 'twixt de niggers of de Souf and de womin at de Norf, all talkin' 'bout rights, de white men will be in a fix pretty soon. But what's all dis here talkin' 'bout?

"Dat man ober dar say dat womin needs to be helped into carriages, and lifted ober ditches, and to hab de best place everywhar. Nobody eber helps me into carriages, or ober mud-puddles, or gibs me any best place!" And raising herself to her full height, and her voice to a pitch like rolling thunder, she asked. "And a'n't I a woman? Look at me! Look at my arm! (and she bared her right arm to the shoulder, showing her tremendous muscular power). I have ploughed, and planted, and gathered into barns, and no man could head me! And a'n't I a woman? I could work as much and eat as much as a man—when I could get it—and bear de lash as well! And a'n't I a woman? I have borne thirteen chilern, and seen 'em mos' all sold off to slavery, and when I cried out with my mother's grief, none but Jesus heard me! And a'n't I a woman?

"Den dey talks 'bout dis ting in de head; what dis dey call it?" ("Intellect," whispered some one near.) "Dat's it, honey. What's dat got to do wid womin's rights or nigger's rights? If my cup won't hold but a pint, and yourn holds a quart, wouldn't ye be mean not to let me have my little half-measure full?" And she pointed her significant finger, and sent a keen glance at the minister who had made the argument. The cheering was long and loud.

"Den dat little man in black dar, he say women can't have as much rights as men, 'cause Christ wan't a woman! Whar did your Christ come from?" Rolling thunder couldn't have stilled that crowd, as did those deep, wonderful tones, as she stood there with outstretched arms and eyes of fire. Raising her voice still louder, she repeated, "Whar did your Christ come from? From God and a woman! Man had nothin' to do wid Him." Oh, what a rebuke that was to that little man.

Turning again to another objector, she took up the defense of Mother Eve. I can not follow her through it all. It was pointed, and witty, and solemn; eliciting at almost every sentence deafening applause; and she ended by asserting: "If de fust woman God ever made was strong enough to turn de world upside down all alone, dese women togedder (and she glanced her eye over the platform) ought to be able to turn it back, and get it right side up again! And now dey is asking to do it, de men better let 'em." Long-continued cheering greeted this. "'Bleeged to ye for hearin' on me, and now ole Sojourner han't got nothin' more to say."

Amid roars of applause, she returned to her corner, leaving more than one of us with streaming eyes, and hearts beating with gratitude. She had taken us up in her strong arms and carried us safely over the slough of difficulty turning the whole tide in our favor. I have never in my life seen anything like the magical influence that subdued the mobbish spirit of the day, and turned the sneers and jeers of an excited crowd into notes of respect and admiration. Hundreds rushed up to shake hands with her, and congratulate the glorious old mother, and bid her God-speed on her mission of "testifyin' agin concerning the wickedness of this 'ere people."

Source: Elizabeth C. Stanton, S. B. Anthony, and Matilda J. Gage, *History of Woman Suffrage*, vol. 1 (Rochester, N.Y.: Charles Mann, 1887), 116.

26. Frances Ellen Watkins Harper on Free Labor, 1854

Frances Ellen Watkins Harper (1825–1911) was a writer and reformer who became well known for her antislavery lectures and poetry. She grew up in Baltimore, raised mostly by her aunt and uncle who ran a school for free blacks. She moved to Ohio and then Pennsylvania and spent most of her adult life writing and lecturing about her reform concerns, one of which was the Free Produce movement (also known as Free Labor). This movement discouraged abolitionists from purchasing the products of slavery, including sugar, cotton, and tobacco. It was popular among Quakers, but it never became a successful part of abolitionism.

*   *   *

Free Labor
I wear an easy garment,
O'er it no toiling slave
Wept tears of hopeless anguish,
In his passage to the grave.

And from its ample folds
Shall rise no cry to God,
Upon its warp and woof shall be
No stain of tears and blood.

Oh, lightly shall it press my form
Unladened with a sigh,
I shall not 'mid its rustling hear,
Some sad despairing cry.

This fabric is too light to bear
The weight of bondsmen's tears,
I shall not in its texture trace
The agony of years.

Too light to bear a smother'd sigh,
From some lorn woman's heart,
Whose only wreath of household love
Is rudely torn apart.

> Then lightly shall it press my form
>   Unburden'd by a sigh;
> And from its seams and folds shall rise,
>   No voice to pierce the sky,
>
> And witness at the throne of God
>   In language deep and strong
> That I have nerv'd Oppression's hand,
>   For deeds of guilt and wrong.

Source: Frances Ellen Watkins Harper, *Poems on Miscellaneous Subjects* (Boston: J. B. Yerrinton & Son, printers, 1854; Philadelphia: Merrihew & Thompson, 1857), 35. A microfilm version of the 1857 edition was used for this document.

27. Jessie Frémont Song, 1856

Jessie Frémont (1824–1902) grew up the daughter of powerful Missouri senator Thomas Hart Benton. She received an excellent education and became fascinated with politics at an early age. Over her father's objections, she eloped in 1841 with Lieutenant John C. Frémont. In 1856, John Frémont was nominated as the Republican Party's first presidential candidate. This afforded Jessie the opportunity to employ her extensive political knowledge to help run her husband's campaign. She also became a very popular and adored figure among northern audiences, as the song below reveals.

*   *   *

Jessie Fremont
Air—Jessie the Flower of Dumblane
The sun-burst has dawned over all the glad mountains,
While freedom and glory rise up hand in hand
To met our young chieftain from liberty's fountains,
With Jessie, sweet Jessie, the flower o' the land!
How blithe is the summons o'er all the wide nation,
How swells the bold music that marshals our band!
He comes like a hero to fill the proud station—
With Jessie, sweet Jessie, the flower o' the land!

She's wise and she's prudent; she's good as she's bonnie;
For virtue and valor she takes a brave stand;
For the Chieftain's White Mansion she's better than onie,
So give her "God speed!" there, the flower o' the land.

Let honest hearts greet her, and victory meet her,
You'll never [repent?] it—so join hand in hand,
Till firm with our leader in [rapier?] we seat her—
Our noble young Jessie, the flower o' the land.

Source: "Jessie Frémont," *New York Herald*, July 14, 1856.

Jessie B. Frémont, lithograph, circa 1856. A beautiful and beloved public figure, she was the brains behind her husband John C. Frémont's Republican presidential campaign in 1856. (Source: Courtesy of the American Antiquarian Society)

28. Lydia Maria Child's Letter
to Governor Wise Regarding John Brown, 1859

After John Brown's failed raid on Harpers Ferry, then in the state of Virginia, and his subsequent capture and incarceration, many antislavery advocates in the North rallied to his cause. Lydia Maria Child (1802–1880), by then a well-known author, famous for her abolitionism, requested permission from Governor Henry Wise of Virginia to visit and "nurse" Brown. The governor replied to Child's request and, unbeknownst to her, shared their correspondence with the press. Child responded with the letter below, sent to the *New York Tribune*. In it, she offered an abolitionist history of the rise of "Slave Power" and charged the South with trampling on the Constitution. Child's letter led to a scathing public response by Margaretta Mason, wife of a Virginia senator, to which Child again responded in kind. In 1860, the American Anti-Slavery Society published all of the correspondence, and it became a best seller.

*   *   *

To Governor Wise:

In your civil but very diplomatic reply to my letter, you inform me that I have a constitutional right to visit Virginia, for peaceful purposes, in common with every citizen of the United States. I was perfectly well aware that such was the theory of constitutional obligation in the Slave States; but I was also aware of what you omit to mention, viz.: that the Constitution has, in reality, been completely and systematically nullified, whenever it suited the convenience or the policy of the Slave Power. Your constitutional obligation, for which you profess so much respect, has never proved any protection to citizens of the Free States, who happened to have a black, brown, or yellow complexion; nor to any white citizen whom you even suspected of entertaining opinions opposite to your own, on a question of vast importance to the temporal welfare and moral example of our common country. This total disregard of constitutional obligation has been manifested not merely by the Lynch Law of mobs in the Slave States, but by the deliberate action of magistrates and legislators. . . . Mr. Hedrick, Professor of Political Economy in the University of North Carolina, had a constitutional right to reside in that State. What regard was paid to that right, when he was driven from his home, merely for declaring that he considered Slavery an impolitic system, injurious to the prosperity of States? What respect for constitutional rights was manifested by Alabama, when a bookseller in Mobile was compelled to flee for his life, because he had, at the special request of some of the citizens, imported a few copies of a novel that every body was curious to read? . . . With these, and a multitude of other examples before your eyes, it would seem as if the less that was said about respect for constitutional obligations at the South, the better. Slavery is, in fact, an infringement of all law, and adheres to no law, save for its own purposes of oppression.

You accuse Captain John Brown of "whetting knives of butchery for the mothers, sisters, daughters and babes" of Virginia; and you inform me of the well-known fact that he is "arraigned for the crimes of murder, robbery and treason." I will not here stop to explain why I believe that old hero to be no criminal, but a martyr to righteous principles which he sought to advance by methods sanctioned by his own religious views, though not by mine. Allowing that Capt. Brown did attempt a scheme in which murder, robbery and treason were, to his own consciousness, involved, I do not see how Gov. Wise can consistently arraign him for crimes he has himself commended. You have threatened to trample on the Constitution, and break the Union, if a majority of the legal voters in these Confederated States dared to elect a President unfavorable to the extension of Slavery. Is not such a declaration proof of premeditated treason? In the Spring of 1842, you made a speech in Congress, from which I copy the following:—

> Once set before the people of the Great Valley the conquest of the rich Mexican Provinces, and you might as well attempt to stop the wind. This Government might send its troops, but they would run over them like a herd of buffalo. . . . Give me five millions of dollars, and I would undertake to do it myself. Although I do not know how to set a single squadron in the field, I could find men to do it. Slavery should pour itself abroad, without restraint, and find no limit but the Southern Ocean. The Camanches should no longer hold the richest mines of Mexico. Every golden image which had received the profanation of a false worship, should soon be melted down into good American eagles. I would cause as much gold to cross the Rio del Norte as the mules of Mexico could carry; aye, and I would make better use of it, too, than any lazy, bigoted priesthood under heaven.

When you thus boasted that you and your "booted loafers" would overrun the troops of the United States "like a herd of buffalo," if the Government sent them to arrest your invasion of a neighboring nation, at peace with the United States, did you not pledge yourself to commit treason? Was it not by robbery, even of churches, that you proposed to load the mules of Mexico with gold for the United States? Was it not by the murder of unoffending Mexicans that you expected to advance those schemes of avarice and ambition? What humanity had you for Mexican "mothers and babes," whom you proposed to make childless and fatherless? And for what purpose was this wholesale massacre to take place? Not to right the wrongs of any oppressed class; not to sustain any great principles of justice, or of freedom; but merely to enable "Slavery to pour itself forth without restraint." . . .

If Captain Brown intended, as you say, to commit treason, robbery and murder, I think I have shown that he could find ample authority for such proceedings in the public declarations of Gov. Wise. And if, as he himself declares, he merely intended to free the oppressed, where could he read a more forcible lesson than is furnished by the State Seal of Virginia? I looked at it thoughtfully before I opened your letter; and though it had always appeared to me very suggestive, it never seemed to me so much so as it now did in connection with Captain John Brown. A liberty-loving hero stands with his foot upon a prostrate despot; under his strong arm, manacles and chains lie broken; and the motto is, "Sic Semper Tyrannis": "Thus be it ever done to Tyrants." And this is the blazon of a State whose most profitable business is the Internal Slave-Trade!—in whose highways coffles of human chattels, chained and manacled, are frequently seen! And the Seal and the Coffles are both looked upon by other chattels, constantly exposed to the same fate! What if some Vezey, or Nat Turner, should be growing up among those apparently quiet spectators? It is in no spirit of taunt or of exultation that I ask this question. I never think of it but with anxiety, sadness, and sympathy. I know that a slave-holding community necessarily lives in the midst of gunpowder; and, in this age, sparks of free thought are flying in every direction. You cannot quench the fires of free thought and human sympathy by any process of cunning or force; but there is a method by which you can effectually wet the gunpowder. England has already tried it, with safety and success. Would that you could be persuaded to set aside the prejudices of education, and candidly examine the actual working of that experiment! Virginia is so richly endowed by nature that Free Institutions alone are wanting to render her the most prosperous and powerful of the States.

In your letter, you suggest that such a scheme as Captain Brown's is the natural result of the opinions with which I sympathize. Even if I thought this to be a correct statement, though I should deeply regret it, I could not draw the conclusion that humanity ought to be stifled, and truth struck dumb, for fear that long-successful despotism might be endangered by their utterance. But the fact is, you mistake the source of that strange outbreak. No abolition arguments or denunciations, however earnestly, loudly, or harshly proclaimed, would have produced that result. It was the legitimate consequence of the continual and constantly increasing aggressions of the Slave Power.

The Slave States, in their desperate efforts to sustain a bad and dangerous institution, have encroached more and more upon the liberties of the Free States. Our inherent love of law and order, and our superstitious attachment to the Union, you have mistaken for cowardice; and rarely have you let slip any opportunity to add insult to aggression.

The manifested opposition to Slavery began with the lectures and pamphlets of a few disinterested men and women, who based their movements upon purely moral and religious grounds; but their expostulations were met with a storm of rage, with tar and feathers, brickbats, demolished houses, and other applications of Lynch Law. When the dust of the conflict began to subside a little, their numbers were found to be greatly increased by the efforts to exterminate them. They had become an influence in the State too important to be overlooked by shrewd calculators. Political economists began to look at the subject from a lower point of view. They used their abilities to demonstrate that slavery was a wasteful system, and that the Free States were taxed, to an enormous extent, to sustain an institution which, at heart, two-thirds of them abhorred. . . . At last, politicians were compelled to take some action on the subject. It soon became known to all the people that the Slave States had always managed to hold in their hands the political power of the Union, and that while they constituted only one-third of the white population of these States, they held more than two-thirds of all the lucrative, and once honorable offices; an indignity to which none but a subjugated people had ever submitted. The knowledge also became generally diffused, that while the Southern States owned their Democracy at home, and voted for them, they also systematically bribed the nominally Democratic party, at the North, with the offices adroitly kept at their disposal.

Through these, and other instrumentalities, the sentiments of the original Garrisonian Abolitionist became very widely extended, in forms more or less diluted. But by far the most efficient co-labors we have ever had have been the Slave States themselves. By denying us the sacred Right of Petition, they roused the free spirit of the North, as it never could have been roused by the loud trumpet of Garrison, or the soul-animating bugle of Phillips. They bought the great slave, Daniel, and according to their established usage, paid him no wages for his labor. By his cooperation, they forced the Fugitive Slave Law upon us, in violation of all our humane instincts and all our principles of justice. And what did they procure for the Abolitionists by that despotic process? A deeper and wider detestation of Slavery throughout the Free States, and the publication of *Uncle Tom's Cabin*, an eloquent outburst of moral indignation, whose echoes wakened the world to look upon their shame.

By filibustering and fraud, they dismembered Mexico, and having thus obtained the soil of Texas, they tried to introduce it as a Slave State into the Union. Failing to effect their purpose by constitutional means, they accomplished it by a most open and palpable violation of the Constitution, and by obtaining the votes of Senators on the false pretences. . . .

Soon afterward, a Southern Slave Administration ceded to the powerful monarchy of Great Britain several hundred thousands of square miles, that must have been made into Free States, to which that same Administration had declared that the United States had "an unquestionable right"; and then they turned upon the weak Republic of Mexico, and, in order to make more Slave States, wrested from her twice as many hundred thousands of square miles, to which we had not a shadow of right.

Notwithstanding all these extra efforts, they saw symptoms that the political power so long held with a firm grasp was in danger of slipping from their hands, by reason of the extension of Abolition sentiments, and the greater prosperity of Free States. Emboldened by continual success in aggression, they made use of the pretence of "Squatter Sovereignty" to break the league into which they had formerly cajoled the servile representatives of our blinded people, by which all the territory of the United States south of 36° 30' was guaranteed to Slavery, and all north of it to Freedom. Thus Kansas became the battle-ground of the antagonistic elements in our Government. Ruffians hired by the Slave Power were sent thither temporarily, to do the voting, and drive from the polls the legal voters, who were often murdered in the process. . . . This was their exemplification of Squatter Sovereignty. A Massachusetts Senator, distinguished for candor, courtesy, and stainless integrity, was half murdered by slaveholders, merely for having the manliness to state these facts to the assembled Congress of the nation. Peaceful emigrants from the North, who went to Kansas for no other purpose than to till the soil, erect mills, and establish manufactories, schools, and churches, were robbed, outraged, and murdered. For many months, a war more ferocious than the warfare of wild Indians was carried on against a people almost unresisting, because they relied upon the Central Government for aid. And all this while, the power of the United States, wielded by the Slave Oligarchy, was on the side of the aggressors. They literally tied the stones, and let loose the mad dogs. This was the state of things when the hero of Osawatomie and his brave sons went to the rescue. It was he who first turned the tide of Border-Ruffian triumph, by showing them that blows were to be taken as well as given.

You may believe it or not, Gov. Wise, but it is certainly the truth that, because slaveholders so recklessly sowed the wind in Kansas, they reaped a whirlwind at Harper's Ferry.

The people of the North had a very strong attachment to the Union; but, by your desperate measures, you have weakened it beyond all power of restoration. They are not your enemies, as you suppose, but they cannot consent to be your tools for any ignoble task you may choose to propose. . . . A majority of them would rejoice to have the Slave States fulfil their oft-repeated threat of withdrawal from the Union. It has ceased to be a bugbear, for we begin to despair of being able, by any other process, to give the world the example of a real republic. The moral sense of these States is outraged by being accomplices in sustaining an institution vicious in all its aspects; and it is now generally understood that we purchase our disgrace at great pecuniary expense. If you would only make the offer of a separation in serious earnest, you would here [sic] the hearty response of millions, "Go, gentlemen, and

'Stand not upon the order of your going,

But go at once!'"

Yours, with all due respect,

L. MARIA CHILD.

Source: Anti-Slavery Tracts No. 1, New Series, in *Correspondence of Lydia Maria Child, Gov. Wise and Mrs. Mason, of Virginia* (New York: American Anti-Slavery Society, 1860).

29. Susan B. Anthony Letter Describing a "Wide Awake" Republican Serenade, 1860

The Wide Awakes were military-like marching clubs of young Republican men that emerged in response to the nomination of Illinois congressmen Abraham Lincoln. Elizabeth Cady Stanton and a group of Republican women presented the local Wide Awakes with a banner. Stanton also offered the young men an encouraging speech. In response, the group serenaded Stanton and her family, as Susan B. Anthony describes below in a letter to two of Stanton's sons.

* * *

Susan B. Anthony to Henry B. Stanton Jr. and Gerrit S. Stanton
Seneca Falls, Sept. 27, 1860
My Dear Kitt & Gatt,
Has any body told of the grand affair that came off here at your Castle last Monday evening?

In the first place Theodore, your Cousin Nellie Eaton,—the most beauti-ful & lovely of young women,—and myself, walked over to Union Hall to a

"Wide Awake" meeting—expecting to hear a grand speech from the Hon. H.B. Stanton—but lo, it was only a "Wide awake drill"—& Miss Eaton & I shortly left them, and returned home—presently the Hon HBS came—with Tribune, and letters for Susan B. Gatt—We were all reading & talking, when the sound of martial music struck our ears.—Soon it was decided that the "Wide Awakes" were coming down upon us—what was to be done for their reception—the House & Grounds should be illuminated, the person in whose honor the torch light visit was, should be prepared to give them a speech of welcome, and all should give them a most cordial greeting.

Your Mother produced the two wide awake lamps from the garrett—lamps & candles were set in all the windows—your Mother & Miss Eaton,—each with wide awake torch in hand,—took their stand on the circle mound, between the two front gates—& the Hon. H. B. and S. B. stood guard to them—

Down marched the Wide awakes with steady tramp, & strait into the gate in single file they came—until our Quartette were completely encircled with the caped, capped, torch lighted host—then range their Captain's cry— "halt"—and then a silence, for the space of a half minute—when the Hon. H. B. doffing his hat, & bowing most gracefully, said, "Gentlemen Wide awakes— we welcome you to our home—You are here in honor of Mrs. Stanton, and she no doubt is ready to extend to you a hearty greeting—I have the pleasure of introducing you to Mrs. Stanton"—Then Mrs. Stanton said, "Gentlemen Wide Awakes, I give you welcome, but being unable to make an impromptu speech I delegate Mr. Stanton the pleasant duty"—Then the Hon. H. B. again said, "Gentlemen Wide Awakes, we welcome you here—& something about their lamps being kept trimmed & burning &c &c," and soon came to the final pause—Then, their Captain Failing made a speech to your Mother, Mrs. Stanton—told how sorry he was that he was absent when she presented the banner and speech to the Wide awakes—then he called three cheers for Mrs. Stanton—and "hip-hip" and away went the ringing hurrahs—Some one then halloed, three cheers for Mr. Stanton—"hip, hip" and away they went—and yet again another voice—"three cheers for the little Stantons,"—Some one said how many of them—the cry was seven—The Hon. H.B. cried "for mercy sake take them all in a lump"—and so they cheered again—Then Susan B. Anthone [sic] was called on for a speech. She briefly told them she hoped they'd not only keep Wide awake to inaugurate Abram Lincoln—but also to go to the aid of the Slaves, in case of an insurrection, or another John Brown invasion in Virginia—Then spoke the Hon. H.B. again, most eloquently of Old Abe—then followed three cheers for Miss Anthony—three cheers for Miss Easton—the daughter of Major Eaton of the United States Army—&

lastly three cheers for <u>Old Abe</u>—Then they marched around the house to the tap of the drum, & passed down the Canal way to Mr. Murrays—then to the Congressional nominee's, Mr. Chamberlain—

We had but fairly got settled, when a second torch light invasion occurred—Soon the sound of music discovered it to be a <u>serenade</u>—again we lighted up the windows—Your Mother & Miss Eaton Waltzed & Polkaed on the piazza while they played—then the Glee Club was invited into the parlor & regaled with pears and melons—When all were gone & silence again reigned—lo, where was Theodore—gone with the Wide awakes—Near Eleven Oclock—he came—escorted by Abe Leary & his Mother—thus ended the Grand Gala in honor of your <u>Mothers splendid banner speech</u> to the Seneca Falls Wide Awakes.

Source: Ann D. Gordon, ed., *The Selected Papers of Elizabeth Cady Stanton and Susan B. Anthony: Volume 1: In the School of Anti-Slavery, 1840–1866* (New Brunswick, N.J.: Rutgers University Press, 1997), 441–43.

30. Anna Dickinson's Letter in Support of the Reelection of Lincoln, 1864

Anna Dickinson (1842–1932) became a wildly famous lecturer during the Civil War, supporting Republican candidates and pushing for abolition. In the letter below, written to Theodore Tilton, the editor of the New York paper the *Independent*, she displays a firm grasp of electoral politics and the upcoming 1864 presidential contest. Instead of joining a breakaway group of Republicans who created a splinter party and nominated John C. Frémont for president, Dickinson chose to use her considerable influence to support the reelection of Lincoln.

*   *   *

You ask me . . . how I feel in regard to the Presidential campaign, now fairly inaugurated. From all parts of the country I receive letters containing the same inquiries— . . . letters of warning, entreaty, advice, denunciation, abuse, upbraiding, for having deserted a good cause. . . .

These letters were first an annoyance, then a trouble, finally an absolute persecution.

Therefore, without in the least supposing myself to be a person whose word and work in the world are of special worth or import, may I beg a space

Anna Dickinson, between 1855 and 1865. Dickinson became one of the most famous Republican Party lecturers during the Civil War. (Source: Library of Congress)

in your columns for a public answer, and a little talk that will set at rest all these disagreeable matters? I wish to say:

That my love for the dear cause is as great as ever (greater it could not be), my devotion to it as intense as three years or six months ago, and desertion of it impossible; though some so-called loyal men and papers have done their best to drive me from it, by misrepresentations and calumny:

That I have no "party," save that which strives with sword and pen, with blood and treasure, and precious lives, to save this country—a home for the oppressed—and to rebuild the old waste places made desolate by slavery and a traitor's war:

That, as it has been the honor and the privilege of my life to have done what I could with this party in the past, so it would be my everlasting dishonor and shame to refuse now to work with it, whatever work may be proffered or found:

That I wish all people (who care to know) to understand that, when I conclude to desert my post, I shall travel straight to Richmond, and not stop to any half-way station. . . .

Last winter, believing there were men in the country who would make better presidents than the one we now have, I strove to build up a public sentiment that would demand and support one of these "better men."

I believed, further, that, by postponing the Convention from the 7th of June to the 1st of September, we had much to gain—the nomination of the Copperhead Democracy of the North, the announcement of its platform, the principles (or want of principle) on which it intended to work, its plans for the future; in a word, compelling it to show its hand before the loyalists played a card, and knowing with just what they were to meet and contend.

This was something. Beyond this the Summer Campaigns might not close as they began, and, as on this ending, not this beginning, depended, to a certain extent, the popularity and consequent success of whatever loyal representative might be placed before the people, I thought that no such representative should be nominated till these things should be decided—as a too-early decision might end in a late indecision, if not open rupture in the party.

Whatever words I then spoke, I believed to be in the best interests of the country. Personally, I had everything to lose, and nothing to gain by the course pursued. I was laughed at, ridiculed, ostracized by people who up to that time had given me naught save most generous help, and over-liberal praise. I found

"Hard indeed the stranger's scoff
Hard the old friends failing off,"

And used sometimes to think, tugging away at my cars, how easy it would be slipping down stream—how weary pulling against the current; yet I felt then that I was in the right and did not hesitate; I feel now that I was in the right, and do not regret.

That has all passed. Others felt as I. What remains?

Naught save the heartfelt union the most earnest, persevering work—the most determined support of the party represented by Abraham Lincoln, from this moment till election morning!

Either this party must succeed, or the grand cause will fail.

Either this party must triumph, or the country will be led into an ignoble and deceitful peace, ending by a Union rent asunder.

Either this party must conquer, or all that has been gained for humanity to-day, for the ages yet to be, will be flung under foot and trampled to death by a man-hailing aristocracy, a God-defying slave power!

Either this party must win, or the hope of the world will be destroyed, and "governments of the people, by the people, for the people, perish from the earth."

Either this party must control, or Heaven will weep, and Hell laugh aloud, as Liberty, Truth, and Justice are swept from the land by men who know only the will of their master, the Evil One, to do his work.

"But," said an earnest Abolitionist to me, a few days since, "I thought thee would not support Abraham Lincoln; I am surprised at thy readiness to work for him."

"My friend," I answered, "this is no personal contest. I shall not work for Abraham Lincoln; I shall work for the salvation of my country's life, that stands at stake—for the defeat of this disloyal peace party, that will bring ruin and death if it come into power."

"But why not work for some other man in whom thou hast perfect confidence?"

"Because all such work does but divide the friends of the Union, and so plays into the hands of its enemies. . . ."

"Well, I feel as thee felt before the nomination; I am opposed to Abraham Lincoln; I think it would be wrong for me to do anything to secure his re-election; and I am not willing to do evil that good may come."

"Does thee approve of war?" I asked.

"No. Decidedly not! Not in the main, but of this war I do very heartily approve."

"Thee does?"

"Certainly I do."

"And yet," I said, "we are in it, everyday, doing evil that good may come—maiming noble specimens of men, spilling precious blood, offering thousands of dear lives, desolating homes, causing mourning and wailing, broken hearts, and darkened hearthstones all over the land, that liberty and free government may be saved, and that this country may remain a heritage to our children, a refuge for the wronged, the down-trodden, the oppressed of all the earth."

"That is very true, very true. I had not taken that into consideration; I will think of that."

My friends, let us all think of that.

First save the life of the nation; then we can carry our leader to a higher plane, a broader and nobler work than any he has yet accomplished.

The coming election-day will strike a final blow, will lay out cold and dead a struggling rebellion; or it will pour fresh life and vigor into all its veings, and will send it on its way a giant, conquering and to conquer.

Who, then, can pause or hesitate?

> One last great battle for the right—
> One short, sharp struggle to be free
> To do is to succeed—our fight
> Is waged in Heaven's approving sight—
> The smile of God is victory!

Source: "The Duty of the Hour: A Letter from Anna E. Dickinson," *Independent,* September 8, 1864.

Index

University of Iowa, 34
"uplift," 36–37, 38, 128
utopian communities, 48

Van Broekhoven, Deborah B., 43
Varon, Elizabeth, 42, 57, 60
Veblen, Thorstein, 16
Vermont, 14, 66
Virginia, 7, 13, 41–42, 198–203
"virtue," 8–9, 29, 34–35
voting rights, 2–3, 7–8, 58, 59; and
    1850 "Declaration of Sentiments,"
    47, 173, 174, 175

Ward, Nancy, 98, 100
Warren, Mercy Otis, 58
Watkins, Francis Ellen. *See* Harper,
    Frances Ellen Watkins
weaving, 16–17
Webster, Daniel, 61
Weld, Theodore Dwight, 143
Wellman, Judith, 47

Western Female Institute, 33
West Indies, 13
Wheatley, Phillis, 3
Whig Party, xvii, xix, 60–62, 65, 67
Wickersham, Huldah, 63
"Wide Awake" groups, 72
Wilberforce College, 34
Willard, Emma Hart, 32
Wise, Henry, 71, 198–203
Wollstonecraft, Mary, xv, *xvi*, 47, 48
woman's rights movement, 46–52
women of color. *See* African American
    women
"women's sphere." *See* "separate
    spheres" ideology
Worcester convention (1850), 48–51
Wright, Fanny, 48
Wright, Martha Coffin, 47

Zagarri, Rosemarie, 58, 59
Zboray, Mary, 57
Zboray, Ronald, 57

About the Authors

Carol Lasser is professor of history at Oberlin College. Her publications include: *Educating Men and Women Together: Coeducation in a Changing World*; *Friends and Sisters: Letters between Lucy Stone and Antoinette Brown Blackwell, 1846–1893* (coeditor, with Marlene D. Merrill); and articles on women, race, and abolitionism. With Gary Kornblith, she edited the *Textbooks and Teaching* section of the *Journal of American History*; a selection of articles from this endeavor is appearing as *Teaching American History: Essays Adapted from the* Journal of American History, *2001–2007*. Also with Gary Kornblith, she is completing a book tentatively titled *Elusive Utopia: A History of Race in Oberlin, Ohio*.

Stacey Robertson is the Oglesby Professor of American Heritage, Chair of the History Department, and Director of the Women's Studies Program at Bradley University, where she has been teaching since 1994. She is the author of *Parker Pillsbury: Radical Abolitionist, Male Feminist* and *Hearts Beating for Liberty: Women Abolitionists in the Old Northwest*. She is the recipient of several teaching awards and has lectured extensively for the Illinois Humanities Council Road Scholars program and presented papers on her research at many conferences.